D0504644

The Court of
RICHARD II

Also by Gervase Mathew
BYZANTINE AESTHETICS

Richard II.
Detail from the Wilton Diptych in the
National Gallery, London.

The Court of
RICHARD II

Gervase Mathew

JOHN MURRAY

© Gervase Mathew 1968

Printed in Great Britain for
John Murray, Albemarle Street, London
by The Camelot Press Ltd, London
and Southampton

TO

Nevill Coghill

AND TO THE MEMORY OF

Sir Maurice Powicke

Contents

Plates

[See Notes on the Plates, p. 199.]

Plates

[ix]

Foreword

In its original form this book was first suggested to me by Professor F. M. Powicke, who proposed that I should write on late fourteenth-century England and combine political history with an analysis of social ideals. But many years of lecturing for the Oxford English Faculty led me to place an equal emphasis on the sudden developments in late fourteenth-century poetry and fiction. Again, some detailed work on paintings and on carvings led me to attempt to determine the changes in art forms between about 1380 and 1425. I believe that these four strands can be interwoven: political history, changes in social structure and social ideals, developments in literature and altering art forms should not be isolated from each other. Much of this work came to centre in a study of the court of Richard II, the creative phase in a period of English court culture which ended after 1422 in the long minority of Henry VI.

This book has been shaped by the conditions of life at Oxford. Thus, while being based partly on manuscript sources a quite undue proportion of the MSS. consulted is in the Bodleian. It incorporates the conclusions of several lecture courses that I have given in Balliol Hall, and has been influenced by Oxford discussions. Like all students of the history of this period I owe much to the work of K. B. McFarlane. Minor problems have been discussed with Peter Dronke, Elaine Griffiths, Walter Oakeshott, C. A. Robson, G. V. Smithers and J. R. R. Tolkien. I can recognize more pervasive influences from my friends C. A. J. Armstrong, Nevill Coghill, C. S. Lewis, Maurice Keen and W. A. Pantin.

Outside of Oxford my friend John Beckwith has helped me greatly in my work on art history, and Mrs Katharine West has made some very useful suggestions in the preparation of the manuscript. I am grateful for the patience of my friend Kenelm Foster. And, as in all I do, my debt to my brother David is inestimable.   G. M.

The International Court Culture

Court life was a factor in the society of western Europe from the late fourteenth until the early twentieth century. It died during the 1914 war but it was already sickening; the last court in England was that of Edward VII. Throughout its history it possessed a number of characteristics that differentiated it from the *Curia Regis* of the early medieval kings. There was the presence of women of influence and standing. There was a strict ceremonial that merged into an elaborate etiquette. There was an intricate system of patronage often exercised in the disposal of quite minor sinecures. There was the tendency for courtiers to form distinct groupings and this in turn could lead to a web of court intrigues. There were at least elements of luxury. And perhaps most significant of all there was the conception of fashion. Fashion was shown both in clothes and in food and in drink. It could also affect manners. It brought with it a new form of values in which contemporaneity was prized. It is likely that in 1390 in several English magnates' households, old fashions in dress, food, drink and manners were valued because they were old-fashioned. At the court to be old-fashioned was simply to be unfashionable. Changing fashions reflected the tastes of the King. It was perhaps the mark of the new courts that they centred not so much on the power as on the preferences of the monarch.

Aspects of this vanished court culture have been described by two writers of genius, St Simon and Stendhal. There were to be differing nuances in different periods and at times it would develop a Baroque façade, but its essential structure remained unaltered and it derived from the international court culture of the late fourteenth and early fifteenth century.

This can be traced first in Naples during the reign of King

Robert of Anjou from 1309 to 1343. His Neapolitan dynasty was a younger branch of the royal house of France and still intermarried with it. There was always to be a North French element in their court. This is apparent in the delight in tournaments—there were six tourneys held at Naples between January and May 1331—and in their predilection for the Gothic, so marked in architecture and latent in the work of court painters like Simone Martini. A Provençal element was also strong and was being perpetually reinforced from the wide lands that the Angevins held along the Rhone, and all this was set in an essentially south Italian milieu; there were great Court families like the San Severini who had held high office under the Emperor Frederick II and the relatively elaborate civil service was ultimately derived from the half Byzantine half Arabic administration of the Norman Kings of Sicily. It forms a clear example of cross fertilization.

There was also an external factor; the Angevin dynasty was oriented to the Byzantine sphere. The founder, Charles of Anjou, had planned the conquest of the Eastern empire. Their possession of the Duchy of Durazzo in Albania kept open the road to Constantinople. There were close contacts of intimate enmity with the Imperial house of the Palaeologoi. It would be a mistake to emphasize Byzantine influences on the creation of the western court culture. There was never to be a western equivalent to the stiff décor of the Byzantine court, its distaste for novelty and the rhythms of its court ceremonial conceived as a liturgy of an imperial sovereignty. Yet in the western courts there were always to be some Byzantine echoes, however transmuted and remote, and it seems likely that these had passed through Naples.

But the immediate and moulding cause of Neapolitan court culture were the tastes and personality of Robert of Anjou. He was a great 'clerk', a learned man, and this gave his court its civilian character and led to his patronage of 'good letters', even in the vernacular. He was patron both to Petrarch and to the young Boccaccio—and it is significant that Chaucer's *Knightes Tale* and his *Troilus and Criseyde* had their origins in Angevin Naples and that at the end of the century court painters like

[2]

Stefano da Verona still clearly derive from Simone Martini. The characteristics of the court cultures of 1400 were all apparent under Robert of Anjou: the presence of the sovereign and the possibility of close personal contact with him; the use of sinecures and high honorary office as a reward; the presence of luxury and the possibility of credit, both perhaps feasible because of the neighbourhood of a great city—Naples or Paris or London. The presence of women and their easy relationship with men led inevitably to the cultivation of sensibility.

There was also the new fashion for good letters. This was to have a transforming effect on the vernacular literature of Europe; it brought a new social prestige to the poet, but while he wrote in the vernacular for his court public, fashion demanded that he should show a close knowledge of the classics and be prized primarily as a rhetorician. Chaucer is characteristic when he writes 'and kis the steppes wher-as thou seest pace/Virgil Ovyde Omer Lucan and Stace'.[1] Fashion demanded that the vernacular should be used in two styles, in a 'curial' mode fertile with literary allusions, or frivolously in what would be judged amusingly commonplace language. This was Boccaccio's distinction between writings in the 'volgare illustre' and in the 'Fiorentino di mercato vecchio'. Chaucer was to be a master of both. His use of an English variant of the 'Fiorentino di mercato vecchio' is sufficiently well known from the *Canterbury Tales,* but he could also compose the Ballade which he presented to Queen Anne at Court, possibly about 1390.

> Hyd Absolon thy gilte tresses clere
> Ester ley thou thy mekenesse al a doun
> Hyd Jonathas all thy frendly manere
> Penalopee and Marcia Catoun
> Mak of your wyfhed no comparisoun
> Hyde ye your beautes Isoude and Eleyne
> My lady cometh that al this may disteyne
> Thy faire body lat hit not appere
> Lavyne and thou Lucresse of Rome toun
> And Polixene that boghten love so dere
> And Cleopatre with all thy passioun

Hyde ye your trouthe of love and your renoun
And thou Tisbe that hath of love swich peyne
My lady cometh that al this may disteyne. [2]

Boccaccio was to write the *Decameron*, yet he describes how he first met his court patroness and his inspiration, the Countess of Aquino, on Holy Saturday, March the 30th, 1336, in the church of San Lorenzo at Naples—'a gracious and fair temple named after him who to become a god suffered himself to be burnt upon a grill'. 'Renaissance' is the most overworked term in cultural history, but at least some of the roots of the Italian Renaissance lay in the Gothic international court culture that immediately preceded it.

The effect of Boccaccio on Chaucer was to be as profound as it was unacknowledged; his influence on the Paris court was exercised through the circle of Gontier Col and through the translations of his works by Laurence Premierfait; Boccaccio is obviously a source for the later Italian Renaissance. But he was formed by the Angevin Court of Naples: he had come there first when he was aged fifteen, he had centred there till he was thirty-seven, he was always to maintain his contacts with it. His contemporary significance has been obscured by the nineteenth-century emphasis on his *Decameron*. By his contemporaries he was most prized for his *De Genealogia deorum gentilium* dedicated to Hugh de Lusignan. With this would be classed his *De Claris Mulieribus* dedicated to the Countess of Altavilla, and his stories of illustrious men dedicated to the Seneschal of Naples. It was his early court romances, the *Filocolo,* the *Teseide* and the *Filostrato* that had most influence in the north. He had proved that the new courts could provide a career open to talent. Born in Paris in 1313, probably of a French woman, he had owed his entrée to the Angevin court to the fact that he was the natural son of the Florentine agent of the firm of Bardi, who were then helping to subsidize King Robert. He was buried in 1375 at Certaldo beneath the inscription:

Under this stone lies the ashes and bones of John. His soul rests with God. His life was adorned by the merits of his labour. His study was Poetry his beloved.

[4]   ERRATUM: Caption to Plate 1
For f.473v. *read* f.470v.

remierement fu de par le roy
ordene que les gens de la ville
pour ce quilz estoient en trop
grande quantite demourac
sent aus champs sans entrer
en la ville iusques a ce ste
tant le Royer toutes leurs gens feussent
entrez et puis fu fait. et
auoit le Roy fait crier le iour deuant
que nul ne feust si hardi de ocupir le chemin
de la grant rue en venant au palais de gris
ne de chanoy ne ne se bougassent des places
ou il estoient ung pou pour lempereur le
roy et le roy des rommains passer

te leur furent mis s gens
pour garder aus bouz des
rues qui viennent sur le
chemin de la grant rue qui
gardoient ce deffendoient le
peuple de passer. Et lors
descendirent a pie vincte des sergens darmes
ce prindrent le trauers de la rue alans deuant
les escuiers du corps du Roy leurs maces
en leurs poins. leurs espees garnies du gref
en escherpe. Et pour ce que lempereur auoit
fait sauoir au Roy des ce que il vintra .g.
deuans que a son vint apres il ne vouloit
auoir euls de ses gens pres de lui. mais

1   The entry of Charles of Luxembourg into Paris.
   Bibliothèque Nationale MS. Français 2813, f.473v.

rennement fust laucucucfch   des romams · Er auoit autant de dista
de Rems Capies scoit   du Roy au Roy des romams côme d
lempirim Apres scoit   Roy alempireur· Er auoient lempr
le Roy ainerome ou milieu   le Roy et le Roy des romams chascu
du front de la sale Apies   parement ou nel de drap dor borde de tr
le Roy de frame scoit le roy au aus armes de frame· et par dessus

2   A banquet at Paris.
    Bibliothèque Nationale MS. Français 2813, f.473.

And Coluccio Salutati was to write: 'There is no age that will be silent of you.' He had always had a zest for honour: 'We are all actuated by the desire of praise, glory is the peculiar incentive to every excellence'—and perhaps this led him to develop his conception of the poet that he had first learned from Petrarch his 'father and master'.

According to the seventh section of the fourteenth book of his *Genealogy of the Gods* the poet is essentially a learned man. He is not only possessed of a strong and abundant vocabulary but he has mastered the principles of all the liberal arts, holds in his memory the history of nations and is familiar with all seas, rivers and mountains. This is precisely the kind of knowledge that was displayed so publicly by Geoffrey Chaucer and John Gower.[3] With this there went a new and aristocratic ideal of the poet in contrast to an earlier medieval conception of the versifying minstrel. Petrarch had written to Tommaso Calogero: 'Poetry is for delight, not for necessity like cobbling and baking and the vile mechanic arts.' He had written to Francesco Nelli: 'Poetry, that Divine Gift, belongs by necessity to the few; to write verse does not make a poet.' For Boccaccio in the *Genealogy of the Gods*, poets are 'the rarest of men'.

Yet Boccaccio, unlike Petrarch but like Machault and Deschamps, Chaucer and Gower, was a professional entertainer. This perhaps partly resulted from the exigencies of court life with its perpetual need for evening entertainment. It led him to develop a theory of realist story-telling as part of the function of a poet. For this he claimed the authority of classical comedy: 'Plautus and Terence describe the manners and words of different sorts of men and if these things have not actually taken place they could have taken place.' 'I admit that poets are the apes of nature.' In fact this classical source had probably been reinforced by the North French *fableau* and by a number of bawdy anecdotes which had not yet reached literary form, but the result was to be the realist European novel.

The romantic novel in western Europe had descended from the Hellenistic romances of the third century A.D.[4] They had a limited cast; the heroine and the hero and at times a shadowy villain and an occasional confidant. They had a limited plot; mounting improbable trials that were the test of constancy in love, or the tension between conflicting loyalties. Their public demanded a happy ending and a moral lesson. It is likely that their appeal lay in the self-identification by members of their audience with hero or with heroine. This is a tradition that has never died, but in the second half of the fourteenth century it was supplemented. The *Canterbury Tales* and the *novelle* of the *Decameron* not only developed a fresh cast and a realist comedy of manners: they frequently denied the happy ending; they were usually amoral. It is this that distinguishes them so sharply from the great mass of medieval didactic literature. In their final form their public must have been found as much among the *haute bourgeoisie* as at the courts, but it is tenable that their techniques first developed in the evening story-tellings in the new international court circle.

In contrast to Boccaccio, Petrarch had only a sporadic effect on the literary movements that were to be associated with the new court culture. Yet the effect was lasting; at least from 1340 until his death in 1374, his reputation had been international ('I have written to my friends in Britain, in Gaul, in the Spains'); King Robert of Naples, the Emperor Charles IV, the Visconti and the Carrara had been among his patrons. Later ideals of the courtier are foreshadowed by his panegyric on Giacomo Colonna, 'the most polished of men *(ad unguem factus homo)*'. He had accepted and reinforced the attitude to good letters that marked the court of Naples: 'Among earthly delights there are none more noble than good letters, none more gentle, more lasting, more faithful.' He was the first to formulate an attitude to scholasticism which will explain the deep lack of interest in it at the courts of Paris and London: 'What is more loathsome than an old logician?'—'some British Cyclops vomiting a malformed syllogism'. Petrarchan conceptions of love and friendship can be traced as late as the sixteenth-century English court circles, in Wyatt, in Surrey, in Sidney. In the fourteenth century his influence pervaded not only through his writings but through his friendships. He was quiveringly sensitive, he had great charm, much sophistication and a certain naïveté. The cultivation of sensibility in court literature was to be deeply affected by some of his *rime* and by his echoes from Arnaut Daniel. The only two temporal things that he had desired were love and fame, both of which he had known under many forms: 'The mind is not inflated by praise but raised by it to greater excellence; I speak from some experience.' Giovanni Boccaccio had accorded him '*auctoritas*'[5] by classing him and Dante with 'the illustrious ancients'. To Chaucer he is 'my maister Petrak' and 'Fraunceys Petrak the lauriat poete'.

But Petrarch did not bequeath to the new court cultures his desire for the eternal. A completely assured religious sense was perhaps the deepest of his instincts. It was very personal to him—'Iscariot injured Christ more by his despair than by his treachery'—and yet dominated by his study of St Augustine. Augustine would mean nothing to Chaucer[6] except some reminiscence of his Rule: 'let Austin have his swink to him reserved'.

There was never to be anything Petrarchan about the religion of the English court. Richard II would seem to have had a rather febrile piety,[7] the obverse of his worldly elegance. Some of his courtiers like the third Earl of Salisbury and Sir Lewis Clifford had Wycliffite tendencies which were perhaps primarily anti-clerical. But for most the Catholic faith was probably as enclosing and as distant as the sky. It is possible to reconstruct Geoffrey Chaucer's approach to religion. It would seem that he accepted without question the framework of medieval Catholicism, and like Richard II he had a strong personal devotion to the Mother of God. Yet the Goddess Fortune meant more to him than any saint and his conviction that so much was predetermined was linked with a strong interest in the stars. All this was shot through by a certain scepticism:

> His spirit chaunged hous and wente ther
> As I cam never I can not tellen wher.[8]

and again—

> A thousand tymes have I herd men telle
> That ther is joye in heven and peyne in helle

[7]

And I acorde wel that hit is so
But natheles yit wot I wel also
That ther nis noon dwelling in this contree
That either hath in heven or helle y be.[9]

This was a scepticism that went with a sense of self irony and with the capacity of not passing moral judgements, qualities that Boccaccio possessed, not Petrarch.

Just as Petrarch's essentially religious conception of Sapientia had little effect in the new court culture, so I have found no trace of his central conception of *'virtus'*. *Virtus* is the quality by which man returns to his primeval nobility (*'primaeva nobilitas'*) and reaches his full stature in realizing the possibilities of his own nature.[10] I would suggest that it is this concept that makes the humanist. If so, there was no humanism in the international court culture of the late fourteenth and early fifteenth centuries, where the ideals of hero and of heroine derived unbroken from late twelfth-century conventions. It was not until the sixteenth century that the Petrarchan *'virtus'* had its full effect in evolving the character of the courtier (*il cortegiano*).

The association between a highly organized court life and new literary movements was vital for the whole development of European literature. In England it was to last until the dethronement of Charles I and in France until the accession to power of the Regent Orleans. It was always to be affected by the literary preferences of the ruler and of his favourites and it began with the learned preferences of King Robert of Anjou.

It was natural that the influence of Neapolitan court culture should gradually have permeated Italy; it is first apparent at the Visconti court at Milan and at the Carrara court at Padua. But it is odd that it should have passed so soon to the north; possibly the papal court at Avignon acted as a 'carrier'. It is likely that contacts through Avignon helped to develop the court life at Prague under Charles IV of Luxemburg. Certainly Avignon stimulated the development of the court at Paris. This is first apparent under Charles V; perhaps it began early in the 1370s. It stayed fully developed throughout the reign of Charles VI from 1380 to 1422 and was so strongly rooted that it could survive the intermittent insanity of the King.

At Paris, as at Naples and later at London, the court came to centre in a group of distinct palaces, some in the capital, some well out in the environs. Besides the Castel Nuovo in Naples there had been La Carbonosa and the palace out at Baia. At Paris, besides the new Louvre and the hôtel St Paul there were St Germain and the Castle of Beauty at the edge of the wood of Vincennes.[11] In England, besides the royal residences at Westminster and at the Tower there were to be Sheen and Eltham and Langley, and later Windsor Manor. The cadre of the court followed the King's person:

> and whan this book is maad yive hit the Quene
> on my behalfe at Eltham or at Shene.[12]

The Paris Court developed its own elaborate system of sinecures and honorary offices, its hierarchy of patronesses and patrons and its own literary movements. Guillaume Machault was its link with an earlier France; he had been in the households of John of Luxemburg, of Charles of Navarre, and of Pierre de Lusignan before King Charles V became his patron. He died in 1377 but his influence was constant until the end of the century, perhaps precisely because he linked two worlds. Much in his work derives from the thirteenth century and from the first half of the *Roman de la Rose* written by Guillaume de Loris: his ideal knight is 'dous', 'humble', 'cortois', and goes on forays and seeks adventure to win his lady's favour. He was himself a minstrel and composed the music to his songs. But he was modern in his display of classical learning and in his cultivation and analysis of sensibility, and like Chaucer he was especially prized as a rhetorician ('*Mort Machaud le noble rhetorique*'). Chaucer was to translate his *Dit dou Lyon* and his *Fontaine Amoureuse* is a source for the *Book of the Duchesse*.

But Chaucer's French counterpart was Eustache Deschamps. Like Chaucer he was a clerk and a poet, a diplomat and a courtier. He was born at Vertus in Champagne about 1342 and had entered the service of the Valois through the University of Orleans. He had been employed on the King's business with the Luxemburgs at Prague, at Buda, and in Italy, and had been rewarded with pensions and offices: he had been appointed Bailli of Valois and Senlis and a Master of the Treasury. He died about 1406, yet during these years he had written nearly fifteen hundred poems and the *Art de Dictier*. This prose treatise acclimatized in the northern courts the new Italian conception of the poet, as opposed to the minstrel; in it he distinguishes between the natural music which is the gift of poetry and the artificial music which can be produced by any mechanic by voice or instrument. There is much of Boccaccio in the realism of his comedy of manners and his quick appreciation of the absurd. But he had other roots besides those in Italy; he also derived from the thirteenth-century Paris Averroists in the Faculty of Arts and from Jean de Meun who had written the second part of the *Roman de la Rose*. Cynical as to motive, his contempt for human stupidity and his sense of human filth was tempered by a strong self-irony.

In spite of his long court experience there was much of the bourgeois in Deschamps. This is not so with Sir Othon de Granson, whom Chaucer reckoned the 'flour of hem that make in France'; nor, more oddly, with the group of learned writers[13] who made their living at the Valois court as Orators or as Secretaries. Often enough these were of bourgeois origins but their learning had made them free of a new world in which they could compare each other naturally to Socrates and Plato, Cicero and Quintilian; a quality much prized was '*elegantia*'.

The most powerful of this grouping were Gontier and Pierre Col in the Chancellery and the Signet Office. Jacques de Nouvion, 'both Socrates and Plato and Augustine',[14] was secretary to the Duke of Orleans. Nicholas de Clamanges was a much used diplomat. The Duke of Berri employed Jean de Montreuil as his secretary and Laurence Premierfait as his Orator.

The most admired among them was Christine de Pisan.[15] She had been born in 1364 and was the daughter of Tommaso Pisano the royal physician and astrologer. Her husband Etienne de Castel had died when she was twenty-five. From 1389 to 1418 she possessed an influence in court circles quite incommensurate to her position as Chamberwoman to Queen Isabeau. Among her patrons were the Duke of Orleans and of Berri, the Countess of Montpellier and the Earl of Salisbury. Her prestige was partly due to her elaborately cultivated sensibility. She developed the theme of mingled joy and anguish.

De triste cuer chanter joyeusement.[16]

She described an ideal court manhood that was perpetually adolescent and perhaps slightly epicene.

Car il est jeune et joliz
Doulx et Courtois de hault prise
Le plus bel des Fleurs de Liz.[17]

But she was admired most for her omniscience; Ovid and Virgil, Dante, Petrarch and Boccaccio were among her sources. The art of war was among her subjects. Eustache Deschamps begins by comparing her with Boethius; she is termed a 'Cicero in eloquence', a 'Cato in wisdom', 'a Rose'.

The elaborate structure of the Paris Court had developed from the relatively simple organization of the *Curia Regis* of Philip the Fair at the time of his death in 1314. There was the sacrosanct position of the King as an anointed 'fils de Saint Louis' emphasized by his miraculous power of healing and there was the strong bureaucratic element already in the 'Conseil', in the 'Chambre aux deniers' and among the 'Maitres des requêtes de l'Hôtel'. These elements, which enabled the monarchy to survive the growing power of the great magnates as they constructed their subordinate states, had lasted through the sporadic chaos from 1322 to 1359 and were still present in 1390. In France as in England, the late fourteenth-century court was built round the skeleton of the late thirteenth-century *Curia Regis*.

The English Court

The *Curia Regis* of Edward I had clearly not been a court in the sense that has been discussed; it had primarily been the centre of the royal administration, and secondarily had possessed the qualities of a great magnate's household. But there was at least a court with Edward III at Windsor and with his eldest son at Bordeaux. It is perhaps not altogether irrelevant that Queen Philippa of Hainault was closely related to the Angevins at Naples.

In the first place there was the influence of women of position like the Countess of Salisbury, the Countess of Kent and the number of *domicellae*, maids of honour and ladies-in-waiting who were maintained by Queen Philippa. The presence of *meretrices* brought up from the country for the great feasts of the Church can only have emphasized the masculinity of the earlier *Curia Regis*. The King's mistress, Alice Perrers, Lady Windsor, was accorded a quite different standing: while she was still a *domicella* of the queen she had received £375 worth of jewels;[1] and at the Smithfield jousts of 1375 she presided as the Lady of the Sun.

Besides this there was the clear emergence of a court art characterized by delicacy of treatment, a delight in combined colours and by the cost of its materials. The painting of the Palace Chapel at Westminster, St Stephen's, was begun in the spring of 1350 and practically completed in the autumn of 1361.[2] It was to be destroyed by James Wyatt in 1800, but from the detailed descriptions, the unsatisfying copies and the few fragments that remain, it had the marks of a delicate novel luxury. John Topham describes it[3] as 'one universal blaze of splendour and magnificence' and writes of 'the profusion of gilding and minute tracery and diaper' and of the colours glazed over gold and silver leaf. Edward and Philippa were represented with nine of their children, forty 'servers' described as youths and thirty-six 'knights'. The figure work sounds rather effeminately graceful; the angels were feathered like peacocks and there were experiments in perspective. The Master Painter, Hugh of St Albans, used vermilion from Montpellier and it seems likely that he had Italian contacts through Avignon.[4] Apparently his style continued to be admired; about 1395 Richard II was to have the gold grounding deepened and to heighten the crown of the youngest of the Magi.[5]

The names are known of over thirty painters who worked at Edward III's expense[6] and it is clear that they were employed as much for secular art as for religious: there was a Painted Chamber at Windsor, and there is a list of colours purchased by the painter William Burdon when he decorated the tower at Windsor called La Rose in 1365 and 1366. He used 67 lb. of white lead, 12 lb. of verdigris, 18 lb. of red lead, 8 lb. of vermilion and 7 lb. of blue and 1,400 leaves of gold.[7]

In all this court art, as in the literature associated with it, there was an obvious delight in bright primary colours. It reflected a 'Froissart' culture that was essentially heraldic, and some of the most successful court artists like Gilbert Prince were also painters of armorial bearings. The life of the circumscribed court circle seems almost over-consciously gay with its fine feasts and joustings.

It was in this court circle that Geoffrey Chaucer reached maturity. He had had family contacts with the earlier *Curia Regis* through his mother Agnes de Copton. He is first referred to at Christmas 1357 when he was page to the Countess of Ulster, Edward III's daughter-in-law; he was then perhaps about twelve. It seems likely that he later became one of the King's pages.[8] In 1367, the year of Richard II's birth, he was granted an annuity of twenty marks as one of the royal *valetti*. In 1368 he was a royal *escuyer*, a title perhaps best translated as equerry. He had already married Philippa, a *domicella* of the queen.[9] About 1370 he wrote the *Book of the Duchesse*, his first court poem that can be dated; it seems likely that by then he had composed ballades and virelays and his translation of the

Romaunt of the Rose. His talent was to develop like a spiral; his *Parlement of Foules*, and his *Legend of Good Women* are perhaps the most characteristic court poems of the circle of Richard II.

If Chaucer was to come to represent the literary fashions of Richard's court, it was Froissart who best reflects those at the court of Edward III. Jean Froissart was born in Hainault in 1338 and when he was eighteen came to England to enter the service of Queen Philippa and to compose virelays and ballades for her and for her ladies. He was to stay in her service until she died and his first travels were at her expense. He was at Avignon in 1360 but he came back to Windsor in 1361. He heard of her death in Italy where he had gone in the retinue of Lionel of Clarence, and in the poem, that he wrote then, he commemorates the largesse that he had received from her and the fact that she had made him her equerry. He was to visit Richard II about 1394, bringing a copy of his love poems, but he was never to belong to the new court culture either at Paris or London. He was to find his patrons in the lesser princely households—the Duke of Brabant at Coudenberg, the Count of Foix at Orthez, the Count at Blois. When he died in about 1410 almost unnoticed he had outlived his generation; the difference between his *Chroniques* and the *Canterbury Tales* is some measure of the gulf between the courts of Edward III and Richard II.

For the difference between King Richard's court and that of his grandfather was not merely in degree but in kind. It was not only that by the 1390s the court was clearly much larger, but it had acquired a certain civilian character, a zest for fashion notable in its dress, and above all a formal and elaborate ceremonial which had earlier been lacking.

The court that the Black Prince had maintained at Bordeaux seems to have been larger than any of his father's but it had been permanently geared for war. Probably this had always been true of those of King Edward; it is the impression conveyed by the earliest of the court poems, the *Vow of the Heron*, and by Adam de Murimuth's account of the festivities at Windsor, where a variety of dishes and an abundance of wine were preceded by jousting. The status of the courtiers seems to have been determined by their reputation for prowess. There was also an emphasis on informality. The quality of 'franchyse'[10] was considered to be the mark of good breeding and to show itself through a spontaneous ease of manner. Thus the Chandos Herald records that when the Black Prince returned in triumph to Bordeaux after his Spanish campaign he dismounted and entered the city holding hands with his wife and son and that he was always accustomed to thank his servants 'moult humblement.' Like his father Edward he jousted at Windsor against all comers for franchyse was inextricably linked with the quality of fellowship.[11] There is a description[12] of Richard II in 1398 sitting crowned on his throne in silence from dinner until vespers and when 'he looked at any one that man had to bow the knee'. This is very different from Edward III dancing at the Christmas feast at Guildford and bearing his motto

> Hey hey the whyte swan
> By Gode' soul I am thy man.

The continuity of English court life was broken by the early years of Richard's minority when his small household probably had its centre at his mother's manor at Kennington. Richard had been born at Bordeaux on the feast of the Epiphany in 1367. His elder brother Edward died in 1371 and when Richard was six he was appointed the nominal regent of the realm. His father, Edward of Woodstock, the Black Prince, died in the summer of 1376 and his grandfather Edward III a year later. Richard was crowned when he was ten with a new elaborate ceremonial which is likely to have influenced him all his life. He was perhaps the more conscious of his sacred kingship because for long he was so powerless; he did not assume full power until he was twenty-two.

His protracted minority was broken by two episodes whose after effects stayed with him always; his part in the Peasant Rising and his marriage. His role in the rising of 1381 has been romanticized by nineteenth-century illustrators. It is certain that he never conceived himself as 'Captain of the Commons' or showed any sympathy for the common people; indeed, it is likely that he afterwards remembered the revolted peasants and city proletariat with the horror with which a French lord would have remembered the Jacquerie. But he can never have forgotten that at Smithfield on the late afternoon of June the 15th, 1381, he saved his life and his regality by his own quick wit and physical courage and through the protection of the saints and of the Mother of God. Perhaps he half-remembered that he had shown his quick wit through trickery. Here was a complete formula on which he was to rely in many crises.

Richard's marriage to Anne of Luxemburg on the 14th of January, 1382, also had its interlocking consequences. It had first been proposed that he should wed Caterina Visconti, the daughter of Barnabo of Milan. Such a wedding might have affected the culture of the English court circle; and it certainly would have strengthened the ties with Italy that were to mean so much to Chaucer's poetry. The Visconti had sought the marriage alliance offering as dowry 'an unestimable quantity of gold'. The Luxemburg marriage was sought from England and prompted by the Papacy. It brought no dowry—instead Anne's brother had to be offered a loan of £15,000—but it afforded the opportunity of detaching the House of Luxemburg from its old alliance with the House of Valois and brought with it an international social prestige, since Anne was the daughter of the Holy Roman Emperor Charles IV, King of Bohemia.

It is probably a mistake to conceive of Anne as a German or a Bohemian. Queen Anne was cosmopolitan and it is characteristic of the period that the international culture that formed her background had strong North French inflections. Her sisters Katherine and Elizabeth had married into the House of Austria and her eldest sister Margaretha was the wife of Louis of Anjou, King of Hungary and of Poland. But her aunt Bona had been Queen of France; her father's first wife had been Blanche of Valois; her niece was the Duchess of Bourbon; and she was cousin to the Dampierres and the Beaumont Avesnes.[13] Her family had the literary associations quite lacking to the Plantagenets. Her uncle Wenzel of Luxemburg, Duke of Brabant, was a poet and a patron of poets; a predecessor of Charles of Orleans. His court at Coudenberg was a centre for French literary movements and he was a primary patron of Eustache Deschamps. Her father had been a patron of Petrarch; her grandfather a patron of Guillaume Machault; her great-grandfather was the rather negligent patron of Dante.

Her marriage had been the result of elaborate negotiations between the two courts. The first Luxemburg envoy came to London as early as 1380.[14] In March 1381 the Imperial Proctors were in residence at the English Court—the Duke of Teschen, the Chamberlain, and the Seneschal of the Household. That December Anne reached England with a great retinue. The formative years of her childhood seem to have been spent in her father's palace on the Hradschin at Prague. It is at least a likely possibility that some of the ceremonies of Richard's court were derived from the Imperial ceremonial of the Luxemburgs, and it is tenable that he modelled himself on what he had heard of his father-in-law, Charles IV, not on what he had heard of his own grandfather, Edward III.

In itself the marriage was clearly a success, perhaps all the more because it was childless. It is evident that Richard conceived it in terms of romantic and impassioned love: he was to destroy Sheen Palace because Anne had died there and to strike down the Earl of Arundel to the floor of Westminster Abbey because of an imagined insult to the Queen. Possibly all that he associated with her had some glamour for him.

As Richard grew older he conceived himself increasingly as an emperor rather than as a King; in 1397 he claimed to be *'entier emperour de son roiaulme'*.[15] The idea that he should himself become Holy Roman Emperor had a strong appeal, and between 1394 and 1397 his negotiations to become King of the Romans seem serious enough: he established close relations with Cologne; he sent the Earls of Nottingham and Rutland to be his agents in the Rhineland; he granted annual pensions of £1000 to two of the Electors.[16] The term 'foreign policy' must always be used with caution in a medieval context, but at least Richard developed his own horizons. When he was a boy the magnates of his council had been divided between two rival policies, the 'Way of Flanders' and the 'Way of Spain', but whether war was to be waged in the Netherlands or beyond the Pyrenees its purpose was the overthrow of France or of French influence. Richard was to aim at peace with France, partly perhaps because his policies had a wider setting. After Queen Anne's death in the early summer of 1394 he was contemplating a second marriage with the heiress of the throne of Aragon;[17] a close relation was maintained with the republic of Genoa; and in 1396 and 1397 he was planning to send an expedition against Gian Galeazzo Visconti. He corresponded intimately with the Emperor Manuel Palaeologos. A diplomatic service developed with the court culture; Geoffrey Chaucer had his part in both.

The Peasant Rising and the Luxemburg marriage had been perhaps the two most formative experiences in the minority of the young king; his early attempts to rid himself of the tutelage of his uncles and of the magnates had all the characteristics of a Fronde. By the spring of 1384 there was already very clearly a court, and a court party with its programme. Richard and his wife Anne were both seventeen. His mother Joan of Kent, the Princess of Wales, was aged forty-six. Froissart had described her as '*la plus belle de tout la roiaulme d'Engleterre et la plus amoureuse*'. The obviously crucial importance of Sir Simon Burley in the court circle is most easily explained if he was her friend and possibly in some sense her lover. He was Vice Chamberlain as well as Castellan of Windsor and had organized the Chamber Knights and squires into an efficient royal bodyguard;[18] in this he was helped by his nephew Sir Baldwin Raddington, the Keeper of the Wardrobe. Closely linked with this grouping were the King's secretary John Bacon, Keeper of the Jewels and of the Signet, and the Clerk of the King's Chapel, Richard Medford.

In this still small court Richard seems to have had two close friends: Thomas Mowbray, then aged eighteen,[19] and Robert de Vere, aged twenty-two. By the male line Mowbray only belonged to an old baronial family but his grandmother, Margaret of Brotherton, had brought him a strain of royal blood and would leave him the Bigod inheritance that made him rank among the greater magnates. He was to be Duke of Norfolk when he died in 1399. In the crisis of 1387 he deserted the King for the opposition perhaps through jealousy of de Vere. But they were reconciled in 1389. His career suggests that he possessed courage, enterprise and considerable subtlety. There is no sign of subtlety in Robert de Vere but he showed courage and enterprise and love of magnificence; his bed with its blue hangings embroidered in gold with fleur-de-lys and with owls was valued at over £68.[20] He was not technically a 'favourite' and certainly not a 'mignon' for he was a magnate in his own right, ninth Earl of Oxford and Chamberlain of England and husband of the King's first cousin, Philippa de Coucy. It is likely that Richard conceived of the relationship as a passionate and equal friendship. When the embalmed body was brought back from exile to be buried at Kings Colne, Richard had the coffin opened that he might touch de Vere's hand and again see his face. Another influence at the court was Agnes Launcecrona, apparently a Bohemian, one of Queen Anne's ladies and perhaps her confidante; she had accepted Robert de Vere as her lover and then they had planned to marry if his first marriage could be annulled.

The policy of the court party was to assert and to extend the royal prerogative but they did not yet possess the means to do so. They could count on the cautious and sober support of the Chancellor, William de la Pole, on that of Sir Robert Tresilian, Chief Justice of the Kings Bench, and on a group among the London victualling guilds led by Nicholas Brembre. But neither their wealth nor their manpower was adequate to over-awe hostile magnates.

There were months of uneasy equilibrium; both factions led a joint expedition against Scotland. Then there were counter manœuvres. It was Richard's intention to gain control of the Irish Pale and the north Welsh marches, an obvious catchment area for the raising of armed levies; this was possibly suggested by Robert de Vere. On the 1st of December, 1385, de Vere was created Marquis of Dublin, on the 13th of October, 1386, he was created Duke of Ireland, on the 8th of September, 1387, he was appointed Justice of Chester; that summer Richard made his first progress through North Wales and in August he induced five of the Justices to give judgement in favour of the Royal prerogative. Meanwhile, the opposition had controlled the parliament that met on the 1st of October, 1386, and had removed William de la Pole from the Chancellorship and impeached and imprisoned him; they had appointed a committee of eleven magnates to reform the Royal Household. In November the King's uncle, Thomas of Woodstock, Duke of Gloucester, and Thomas Beauchamp, Earl of Warwick, marched on London. Near Highgate they were joined by Richard Fitzalan, Earl of Arundel and they gained temporary control of the city. After they had fallen back on Huntingdon they were joined by two younger men, Henry of Bolingbroke, son of the King's uncle John of Gaunt, and Thomas Mowbray who had become Fitzalan's son-in-law. The five were to be known as the Lords Appellant.

Some military action was inevitable. Robert de Vere had raised a small army in north Wales and Cheshire and in December struck south-east to join the King at London. The appellants intercepted him in Oxfordshire and on the 20th of December, 1387, he was routed at Radcot Bridge.[21] Six days later the appellants entered London and on the 27th of December they gained possession of the Tower and of the King. De Vere had escaped to exile but Burley, Tresilian and Brembre were executed.

All through 1388 the appellants remained in control of the Kingdom. But they had no principle of cohesion. It seems likely that the King was able to divide them. On the 3rd of May, 1389, he re-assumed the royal power at a meeting of the Council at Westminster.

3 The white hart from the Wilton Diptych.
   National Gallery, London.

4 The Court of Heaven.
Detail from the Wilton Diptych, National Gallery, London.

III

Life at the Court

There were clearly four main factors then in the development of Richard's court. There were the traditions derived from the court of Edward III, since part of the personnel was the same. There were constant influences from the contemporary court at Paris; these were probably increasingly strong during the 1390s. They will explain part of the new literary movement, the increasing use of badges and of livery collars, the proliferation of new titles as a mark of the hierarchic grading of the court, and the new cult of Edward the Confessor as the Royal Ancestor and as the dynastic counterpart of St Louis. Then there must have been the personal tastes of the King, which explain the zest for elegance and fashion, the invention of the handkerchief, the emphasis on hot baths. Finally there is the influence of his first wife, Queen Anne of Luxemburg and of her retinue.

By 1385 an elaborate court was fully functioning and life within it was conditioned by the preferences of the King. It is possible to know Richard II more intimately than any other medieval English Sovereign. He was tall; when his skeleton was examined in 1871 it was found to be nearly six feet high. His thick dark yellow hair fell heavily to his shoulders. He had a pale white skin which probably flushed easily. He remained clean-shaven later than was customary,[1] perhaps to prolong his look of adolescence. Later in the 1390s he was elaborately barbered, with tufts of beard on either side of his chin and a slight moustache at the extremities of his lips,[2] but even then at times he returned to being fully shaved.[3] The zest with which he had himself portrayed suggests that he was convinced of his own beauty. He was physically brave. He showed a rash courage on several occasions: at Smithfield in 1381, and when he rode into Bolingbroke's camp at Flint in 1399, and perhaps in 1397 when

c

he went in person to arrest his uncle Thomas at Pleshey. Three times he led his army in the field. But unlike his father and his grandfather he never jousted. This is curious, for he had an interest in horseflesh, and sent four envoys to Prague to improve his stud from the Luxemburg stables.[4] Perhaps unlike his father and his grandfather he would have found it insufferable to be unhorsed. It may have been part of his conception of the royal dignity that as King he could preside at tournaments but not take part in them. He was passionate in his friendships but perhaps fickle in them.[5] He had a long memory for injuries.[6] He was given to sudden gusts of violent anger,[7] but it is likely that when he wished he had considerable charm which he expressed demonstratively.[8] He delighted in giving great grants of land, new offices and titles: he invented the rank of Marquess for Robert de Vere and later created the Marquessate of Dorset; and he made five new Dukes in 1397.

A prodigal generosity ('largesse') and the quality of being physically rash ('outrageus') were both highly prized among the upper class of his time.[9] But Richard had two traits which must have caused mistrust: it is certain that he was recklessly careless of his pledged word, and probable that he usually planned several moves ahead. The easiest explanation of his reign is that, like John of Gaunt but unlike the Black Prince, he played life as if it were chess, not draughts. He was defeated not because he was a bad chess-player but because he had taken too many calculated risks.

Three of his tastes affected the whole character of his court; he cared for books; he was devoted to fine and exotic cooking; and he was passionately interested in dress.

It is exceedingly improbable that Richard ever knew any of the classics but it is likely that they formed part of his conception of good letters. In 1395 he commissioned a Latin epitaph for his tomb in Westminster Abbey and in it he had himself compared to Homer ('*Omerus*'). He may well have savoured the list of names in Chaucer's poems: Virgil and Ovid and Lucan, Statius and Claudian. His two vernaculars were French and English. When he was thirteen he bought a *Romance of the Rose* and romances of Gawain and of Perceval and a Bible in French. Since he paid £28 for them[10] they must have been manuscripts de luxe. Later he was to keep books in his private closet and this suggests that he could read as well as listen. Nineteen of these were rebound between 1386 and 1388:[11] their covers were of red satin or of blue and white satin; their markers and their fastening strings were of blue silk; some had gold clasps. It is possible that his taste had been influenced by that of his tutor Sir Simon Burley, who owned ten romances in 1387, nine in French and one in English.[12] But he also had a desire for novelties. We know from the dedication of the *Confessio Amantis* that he had commissioned John Gower to write him 'some newe thing'. In this he may have been affected by the literary fashions of the Valois court; his friend John de Montacute, Earl of Salisbury, wrote French poems which were admired in the circle of Christine de Pisan. The association between the court and the new literary movements was made possible by Richard's liking for books.

The nature of the court feasts was determined by his interest in fine cooking and the zest for new combinations of contrasting flavours. His court cookery book *The Forme of Cury* has been preserved: the manuscript came into the possession of the Staffords, was presented by Edmund Stafford to Queen Elizabeth and later was part of the Harleian Collection; it was printed for the Society of Antiquaries in the reign of George III.[13] It is stated in its prologue that Richard is accounted 'the best and ryallest vyander[14] of all Christian Kings' and that the book is compiled by his master cook with the 'assent and avysement of maisters of phisik and of philosophie' that dwelt in his court. It consists of 196 recipes, and throughout there is an emphasis on the exotic; the recipe for cooking oysters in Greek wine seems characteristic.[15] A considerable luxury trade is presupposed: spices are in common use; there is much pepper, sometimes whole,[16] sometimes powdered,[17] and much ginger; there are frequent references to cinnamon, cardamom, nutmeg and saffron and in one case to spikenard; sugar of Cyprus seems specially prized,[18] but there is also white sugar[19] and sugar clarified with wine.[20] During these years there were close trade contacts between Genoa and Southampton, and it is likely that the far-eastern spices were brought by Genoese ships from Trebizond and from Caffa in the Crimea. Although there is an obvious delight in the use of costly ingredients, *The Forme of Cury* does not suggest the excess of Georgian banquets. The recipes fall naturally into three courses: there are 'potages', main dishes, and 'sotiltees' which are either sweets or savouries. A characteristic potage is venison broth; a typical sotiltee is the 'moree', mulberries cooked with honey. The 'mawmenee' may be chosen to represent the main courses:[21] it had a basis of minced flesh of pheasant, to which Greek wine, cinnamon, cloves and ginger were added and then two pounds of sugar. Sugar and spice are combined frequently. In another main dish[22] the basis is provided by shelled oysters; these were cooked in wine together with rice, ginger, sugar and mace.

There is no reference to the haunches of venison, the loins of beef, the mutton or the roasted ox which might be expected at a medieval feast and which probably featured often enough at the dinner of a country magnate. At Richard's court, meat does not seem to have been served whole at table:[23] there are directions as to how it should be 'teysed' or 'morterysed' before being cooked, and the main course must often have resembled a gigantic pâté. Hare's flesh was a common basis of such pâtés, but one of them was constructed from deers' livers cooked in wine. All this suggests that in the court circle men and women eat with spoons, not with their hands. It would seem that the sotiltees at the end of the meal were intended to appeal also to the eye. At times they were carefully shaped and directions are given as to their colouring; saffron, or red, or 'jaulnas' which is orange-tawny.

Remote Italian influences seem to have been fashionable. In *The Forme of Cury* 'Lumbard Mustard' is a favoured condiment and olive oil is often used in place of butter. Rhenish wine was drunk and wine from La Rochelle, but there are frequent references to Vernage, a strong white wine from Northern Italy. Perhaps zabaglione is the only surviving dish that Richard would have savoured. A novel interest in the intricacies of the art of cooking was a mark of the international court culture of the late fourteenth and early fifteenth centuries and was to be a legacy to Europe.

Possibly Richard valued the recipes of his Master Cook for their elaborate and modern elegance. He may have had a similar reaction to the creations of his Master Tailor, Walter Raufe. It would seem inconceivable that Richard ever considered himself to be vain, but possible that he thought of himself as proud. In the 1390s vanity in dress was recognized as the expression of '*superbia*'. On the south wall of the nave of the church of Brooke in Norfolk there is a painting of Superbia as a young man with waved hair and crowned with roses; he is elaborately dressed and girdled, and is gazing at a looking-glass which he holds in his right hand while in his left hand he holds a double comb. On the north side of the nave at Hoxne in Suffolk, Superbia is a richly dressed young man with bell-mouthed sleeves, holding in one hand a sceptre and in the other a looking-glass. Both wall-paintings have been dated between 1390 and 1400.

It seems clear that it was Richard's intense interest in his own dress that was responsible for the extravagant and quickly changing fashions of his court. In the new court milieu tailoring at last developed into an art. This is a point first made by the author of *Richard the Redeless*,[24] who records the reactions of the town middle class in the autumn of 1399.[25]

> But now ther is a gyse: the queyntest of alle
> A wondir coriouse crafte: come now of late
> That men clepith kerving.[26]

He asserts that a tailor might now charge twenty times the cost of his material. He describes the courtier who carried his whole fortune on his body and who in order to win a Duke's praise feared no debt and begged and borrowed from the town burgesses:

> And douteth no dette: so dukes hem preise
> And begith and borwith: of burgeis in tounes.[27]

A whole section of his poem has as one of its texts '*qui mollibus vestiuntur in domibus regum sunt*'.[28]

Court dress seems first to have become magnificent in the early years of Richard's personal rule. In 1388 Sir Simon Burley owned[29] a tabard of cloth-of-gold embroidered with roses and lined with green tartarine, a scarlet tabard embroidered with the sun and with golden letters, a white leather coat embroidered with the Burley badge of the Stakes and ornamented with 54 gold buttons, an ermine cape and a cloak of pure minever. Such display was financially possible since rich dress was portable capital and money could be raised in its security. In 1387 and 1388 Simon Burley had raised money from six London citizens on the security of his clothes and of his beds.[30]

There were rapid developments in dress. Harley MS. 536 contains a poem on 'The Times' written partly in Latin and partly in English which can be dated with some certainty to 1389 since it refers to the flight of Jack Noble—apparently Robert de Vere. It complains of the new fashions of skin-tight hose and of long pointed shoes, of padded shoulders and high collars. Perhaps the most noticeable changes were the replacement of the cloak by a long-sleeved gown or 'houpelande', the replacement of the hat by a loose hood often shaped like a turban, and a profusion of jewellery that went with a delight in vivid colours.

It is possible to reconstruct in some detail the costume of a successful courtier about the year 1394. He would have worn a shirt and short drawers ('braies') made of fine linen. Household accounts suggest that linen from Paris and Rheims and Dinant was specially prized, but linen from Brabant was also used. He would then put on close-fitting hose covering the feet, legs and thighs, including a cod-piece—perhaps for the first time. Then there was the under doublet, the 'gipon', worn presumably for warmth, ending at the hips and fastened to the hose, and ornate leather shoes with pointed toes. The art of the tailor was shown in the cote hardie and the houpelande. The cote hardie was the upper doublet and by now the custom was to embroider it with heraldry or badges; it had close-fitting sleeves to the wrist and was worn with a tight girdle, metal-clasped and increasingly jewelled. The houpelande was a long high-necked gown with wide sleeves that fell to the knees and at times almost to the ankles. It was noted in *Richard the Redeless*: 'the slevis slide on the erthe'.[31] The purpose of the tailor's art was to emphasise the four points most prized in men: long arms and legs, broad shoulders and a slender waist.[32] The last was especially valued: 'in the medill als a mayden menskfully schapen'.[33] (Plate 13)

The cote hardies and houpelandes were of many different colours. In about 1411 Thomas Hoccleve describes a meeting with an elderly man who looked back on the days when he held an 'office lucratyffe' and possessed gowns of scarlet, of sangwyn murrey,[34] of dark and light blue, of green and of the faire vyolet.[35] The illuminations of Harleian MS. 1319 show blue houpelandes embroidered with different patterns in gold and silver,[36] and Hoccleve describes a scarlet houpelande edged with fur which cost more than £20.

Both the hems of the cote hardie and the sleeves and collar of the houpelande could be set with precious and semi-precious stones. Richard is stated to have owned a dress valued at more than a £1,000; if so, it was perhaps not too dissimilar from that worn by Youth in the *Parlement of Thre Ages*, which was of green patterned in gold thread:

> Embroddirde alle with besants and beralles full riche
> His colere with calsydoynnes clustrede full thike
> With many dymande full dere dight one his sleves
> The semys with saphirs sett were full many
> With emeraudes and amatistes appon iche syde
> With full riche rubyes raylede by the hemmes.[37]

The use of the white hart badge and of the royal collar may be studied as part of the jewellery of dress. As worn by a magnate the white hart could be a jewel: John Holland, Duke of Exeter, possessed a 'livery of the Hart' set with three rubies and two sapphires.[38] Richard had used it as personal ornament before he distributed it as a badge; three brooches of the white hart set with rubies were among the King's jewels in September 1380.[39] It seems likely that he chose it to be his badge because it was already a favourite personal ornament, and that it was a favourite ornament because a white hind had been the emblem of his mother, Joan of Kent. When worn as a badge the white hart would be sewn on the left breast; it was of white silk, and since the royal crown round the neck and the chain attached to it are described as of gold they must have been worked in gold thread. (Plate 4)

In contrast to the white hart there is no evidence that the collar was ever distributed as a badge by the King. In the Wilton Diptych there are wreaths of broom around the harts. The white hart, the broom, and the rising sun are the three emblems on Richard's effigy. Two broomscod collars are known to have belonged to the King; one was ornamented with four rubies, three sapphires and twenty-seven pearls and the other with twenty-three pearls and a ruby.[40] (Frontispiece)

There is evidence that the use of jewellery was common among the greater magnates, and so too, was the use of cloth-of-gold,[41] but it is likely that the intricacies of fashion were only followed within the court circles. Thomas Hoccleve records of John of Gaunt that 'his garnements were not fulle wide'.[42] The invention of the linen handkerchief was for the King's personal use and failed to establish itself in late medieval England. It is described in detail in the wardrobe accounts: '*parvis peciis factus ad liberandum domino regi ad portandum in manu suo pro naso suo tergendo et mundando*'.[43]

For women, fashion was more conservative than it was for men, presumably since it was not affected by the changing dresses of the King. Yet the presence of great numbers of court ladies was a distinctive mark of the Household of Richard II. The fourth clause of Thomas Haxey's Petition on the 1st of February, 1397, complained of the excessive cost to the realm due to the presence at the court of so many ladies with their retinues. It should be possible to reconstruct a list of women with court influence: Lady Luttrel and Lady de Mohun and probably Lady Burghersh; Lady Swynford, for over twenty years the mistress and for three years the wife of John of Gaunt; her young daughter, Lady Ferrers, who was afterwards Countess of Westmorland; probably the Duchesses of York and of Albemarle; certainly the Duchess of Exeter. Each would be attended by demoiselles. This can be paralleled at the Court of Paris; a mark of the new international court culture was the presence of many women and the elaborate dances that this made possible. In 1392 Eustache Deschamps described the Visconti Court at Pavia:

> Il fait tresbeau demourer
> En doulz Chastel de Pavie
> Ou l'en seult dames trouver
> Qui mainent joieuse vie
> Car c'est noble compaignie
> Et qui dance volontiers.

Such dances led to a fresh demand for songs. For the women and men either sang as they danced ('caroled'), or danced to a song (a 'conduit'), or joined in the refrain of the song they danced to (a 'virelay'). Even the ballade, though it established itself as a separate literary form, can be considered as a dance-song.

Yet besides this demand for lyrics there was a court public for narrative poems. There was now a large sophisticated audience of women as well as of men who needed to be entertained by stories. Convention determined that these stories should be in verse and fashion would have suggested that they should be new. Often such stories would be recited serially. In *Le dit dou Florin* Froissart states that he read his romance *Meliador* for the first time at the court of Foix in the winter of 1388/9. He read it aloud nightly and it lasted for ten weeks; since there are nearly 31,000 lines in *Meliador*, perhaps he read about 480 lines a night. The lines would obviously have been read slowly. *Palamon and Arcite* is clearly a court story, incorporated later in the *Canterbury Tales*; it reaches its appropriate ending 'and God save al this faire company' in 2,249 lines, but it is divided into three parts. *Troilus and Criseyde* and *The Legend of Good Women* are easily serialized. But *The Parlement of Foules* is a poem for Valentine's day which must always have been recited as a unit, and it is in 699 lines. If the *Canterbury Tales* were read, then each, with the exception of the Knight's, must have been recounted without a break.

Perhaps during the winter months there was need for longer

indoor entertainment. Dinner seems to have begun between eleven and twelve. The time between dinner and vespers was set aside for the Royal Audience.[44] The dancing and the story telling would have taken place between vespers (perhaps about three) and the supper of wine and spiced cakes[45] that closed the day.

There were still minstrels—Robert de Vere had four in his household in 1388—but they were becoming outmoded, and in the new court culture they had been supplemented by authors who declaimed their own verse. These had a prestige the minstrel lacked; in Naples, Paris and London they were often courtiers of established rank like Eustache Deschamps and Geoffrey Chaucer. Deschamps noted in his *Art de Dictier*[46] in 1391 that the artificial music of the minstrels could be learnt by '*le plus rude homme du mond*' but that '*musique naturele*' was primarily inspired by a loving will to give praise to ladies '*volunte amoureuse a la louenge des dames*'.[47]

It is also probable that at times poems and stories would be read aloud by equerries or by demoiselles. In a bi-lingual court such readings would take place both in French and English. In 1390 the most prominent courtiers who were also poets were Sir John de Montacute and Sir John Clanvowe. John de Montacute who was later to become Earl of Salisbury and a knight of the Garter composed his rondeaus and ballades in French. The *Cinkante Balades* of John Gower were also intended for a court audience ('*Por desporter vo noble Court roial*').[48] I would consider it possible that there were also lost French ballades and virelais by Chaucer. Owing to the fifteenth century transmission of texts it would be natural that much more of the French court literature should be lost than of the English.

But Sir John Clanvowe, who was one of Richard's Chamber Knights, wrote his *Book of Cupid* in English. This is more commonly known as *The Cuckoo and the Nightingale*.[49] It contains an echo from the *Knight's Tale*, and influenced Hoccleve. It is clearly a court poem.

> Under a maple that is fayr and grene
> Before the chambre window of the Quene.[50]

It is probable that English was becoming increasingly predominant as a court language and that this affected the whole course of
English poetry and prose.

But though poetry had become fashionable it would be easy to
overestimate its small share in the ordinary life of the court.

> The minstralcye, the service at the feste
> The grete yiftes to the moste and leste
> The rich array of Theseus paleys
> Ne who sat first ne last upon the deys
> What ladies fairest been or best daunsinge
> Or which of hem can dauncen best and singe
> Ne who most felingly speketh of love
> What haukes sitten on the perche above
> What houndes liggen on the floor adoun
> Of al this make I now no mencioun.[51]

IV

The Royal Palaces

An attempt to analyse the life at the Court during the 1390s should include a reconstruction of its physical setting in the country palaces at Eltham, Langley, Sheen, and later, Windsor Manor; and in that warren, the palaces at Westminster.

Partly through excavation and partly through the study of the royal accounts[1] it has recently become possible to reconstruct Eltham palace with some exactness. Eltham had been a manor house of the De Vesci and had passed to the Crown in 1311. Edward III had made it a palace and had spent £2,237 on its building between 1350 and 1359. It was surrounded by a wide moat and entered by the Great Bridge. There were groups of large timber-framed buildings on stone foundations: there was the King's Great Chamber and the Queen's Great Chamber and a covered way between them; there was the Great Hall and the small hall and the garden with its vineyard; a bath-house and a wardrobe were added in 1367. Beyond the moat there stretched a park. Richard II enlarged and modernized Eltham between 1384 and 1388. He began by adding a new bath-house, a 'painted wall' and a painted chamber, a Dancing Chamber ('Camera Tripudiancium'), new stained glass and a new turf garden 'for the pleasure of the King and Queen'. He rebuilt the Royal Lodgings and added special accommodation for favoured courtiers. This was divided between chambers and apartments. The apartments were probably free-standing buildings: John of Gaunt had his own apartments at Eltham, and so had Thomas Mowbray and Robert de Vere and Lady Luttrell, who was perhaps in the Tudor court phrase 'the Mother of the Maids'. The chambers seem to have been allotted with court office, as with 'The Chamber of the Controller of the Household'. Richard also built a spicery, a saucery and a Private Saucery;

evidence for a new emphasis on the complexities of cooking. Eltham continued to expand and in 1396 a Lower or Outer Court was laid out beyond the moat. It was to become the favourite palace of Henry IV; he added a study in which he could keep his books; it had seven great windows and forty-two square feet of glass painted with birds and monsters ('babwyns').

The palace at Kings Langley in Hertfordshire was on a smaller scale than Eltham. The King only came there on occasion, perhaps for the hunting or to keep Lent in the large Dominican priory which was divided from it merely by a wicket. It is characteristic that de Vere and Mowbray had their own chambers at Langley in contrast to their own apartments in the greater palace. It had been a hunting lodge of King Edward,[2] with a bath-house ('*Les Stues*') which he had built in 1368–9. Richard began in 1384 by enlarging and embellishing the bath-house; it was shaped like a small hall with ten glazed windows and was paved with stone from the Eglemont quarries; beneath it was a great oven. About the winter of 1386 he built new royal apartments and chambers for de Vere and Mowbray and laid out the queen's garden. Between the summers of 1388 and 1389 he added two new timbered houses, a chamber for the Earl of Stafford and a covered cloister.[3] It all played a very small part in his life but after he had been murdered at Pontefract his body was taken to be buried there.

In contrast, Sheen (with its annexe of royal lodgings called La Neyt) was larger than Eltham and perhaps in the early 1390s was more important. It had been part of the royal manor of Kingston in Surrey. Edward III had spent £2,000 on converting it into a palace and had died there on the 21st of June, 1377. Free-standing timber-framed buildings were arranged round two large courts; the postern of the Down Court opened on to the Thames and the royal barges moored there. Close to it there was an island called La Neyt, where Richard had a Royal Lodging built between 1384 and 1388; he thus secured a privacy that had been unknown to any previous King. The Lodging was fragile and luxurious: 2,000 painted tiles were commissioned for 'the chamber assigned to the King's Bath'. This suggests that the walls as well as the floors of the room were tiled; it probably centred in the '*cuva ad Balneam*', a bath with large bronze taps for hot and cold water.[4] Across the river the palace continued to grow and all Richard's additions to it were marked by two novelties: personal latrines, which were most probably conceived as a part of elegance; and fireplaces in small rooms, which perhaps like hot baths had become an essential part of comfort. He built three more Great Houses for his courtiers: the first consisted of nine chambers, each with its latrine; the other two were of four chambers with four latrines and four fireplaces. Later he added a set of chambers with eight fireplaces.

Queen Anne died in the Royal Lodging at La Neyt in the summer of 1394. By writ under the Privy Seal on the 9th of April, 1395, Richard ordered John Gedney, Clerk of the Works, to demolish to the ground not only La Neyt but all the buildings at Sheen.[5] Possibly the associations of Sheen had become unbearable.

During the winter after Queen Anne died Richard began building, slightly feverishly, a new palace at Windsor Manor, on the site of a hunting lodge of King Edward's in the park five miles south of Windsor Castle. By the end of 1396 Richard had already spent £1,164 on it.[6] A King's House had been built with five painted chambers and with a chapel 70 ft. long decorated with white harts with gilded horns. Had it been completed it is probable that Windsor would have been more elegant and more gay than Sheen: the court artist Thomas Prince was employed in frescoing its walls and there was a considerable outlay in wainscoting. When Richard went to Ireland in the late spring of 1399 he left the child Queen Isabelle at Windsor. He was never to return there and under Henry IV it was eclipsed by Eltham.

There were also three royal manors that Richard gave to Queen Anne apparently in 1384—Havering in Essex, Woodstock in Oxfordshire and Leeds Castle in Kent[7]—but though they were kept in repair I have found no evidence that the Queen visited them. Shortly before she died, she gave Leeds Castle to Joan de Mohun. King Richard confirmed the grant. He was brought there from the Tower as a prisoner at the end of October 1399.

The Palace at Westminster was always present as a background to the life in the country palaces; unlike them it was the centre of administration. The Exchequer was there, in its two-storey building, and the Court of Common Pleas and the King's Bench. Richard II moved the Court of Chancery into the White Hall of the palace in 1393. It is hard to visualize the palace complex as it was in the 1390s. There were the Great Palace, the Privy Palace, and the Prince's Palace; all distinct buildings, each apparently stone built, each probably two storeys high. Huddled among them were probably lath-and-plaster tenements for the courtiers' lodging, with an occasional high timbered building like the White Hall.[8] Though it must have lacked grandeur, it did not lack colour or, necessarily, comfort. *The Book of the Duchesse* describes a courtier's ideal lodging:[9]

> and sooth to seyn my chambre was
> Full well depeynted and with glas
> Were all the windows well y glased
>
> . . .
>
> and alle the walles with colour fyne
> were peynted bothe text and glose
> of al the Romaunce of the Rose.

In such a room the chief comfort would be the bed. The ideal bed is described in the same poem:

> I wil yive him a fether bed
> Rayed with golde and right wel cled
> In fyn blak satin doutremere
> and many a pilow.[10]

It would probably have been the colour within the palace complex which would have most impressed a visitor. There is a traveller's account of 1322: 'near the abbey stands that celebrated palace of the Kings of England . . . on whose walls all the warlike scenes of the Bible are painted with marvellous skill'.[11] This refers primarily to the elaborately Painted Chamber of Henry III.[12] But the fourteenth-century Westminster accounts in British

[35]

Museum Additional MS. 30263 show that the Great Hall, the Little Hall, the Marculph Chamber and a number of the small houses were also covered with paintings.[13] That these would be constantly renovated and replaced, primarily for decoration and without a fixed iconographic scheme, may be illustrated from the fragments in the Great Chapter House, into which the court overflowed and where Parliament had formerly been held: under Edward III it had been painted with the Majesty of God surrounded by Angels and Virtues; under Richard II it was decorated by green scrolls bearing white roses on a vermilion ground, by running dogs and by scenes from the Apocalypse.

Westminster had taken its shape as a palace during the transient thirteenth-century court culture of Henry III; Edward II had spent £2,000 on embellishing it; Edward III had given it the great bell, 'Edward of Westminster', the decorations of its private chapel, St Stephen's, and new council rooms like the 'Chambre des Etoiles', the Star Chamber. It seems to have been Richard II's intention to give it the grandeur that it had previously lacked.

As early as 1385 Richard commissioned thirteen stone statues of kings for the palace, representing Edward the Confessor and his twelve successors. The use of such secular statuary was French in origin, and the conception that it was the Confessor and not the Conqueror who was the founder of the royal line was perhaps a novelty; it was the prelude to his adoption of St Edward's arms as his own. Later he ordered two large statues of kings, most probably of the Confessor and of himself. He built a new Great Gateway to the Palace, and a campanile and ordered marble pillars. On the 3rd of November, 1393, he began the re-building of the Great Hall, employing Henry Yevele and Hugh Herland.[14] The Hall remains a monument to Richard's court architecture:[15] it was decorated with carvings of white harts, and was intended to be used for court feasts and court ceremonials. In all Richard spent £12,304 on Westminster during his last years.[16]

There is some evidence that during the 1390s he was decorating the Tower as a royal residence. Perhaps it was intended to

5   Richard II in Westminster Abbey.

6   The Great Hall at Westminster.

have the same relation to Westminster Palace as Windsor Castle to Windsor Manor. He spent £200 there on ornament in 1398 and ordered 105 square feet of painted glass, worked with fleurs-de-lys and bordered by the royal arms.[17] A series of discoveries were made there in the Byward Tower in 1953,[18] including floor tiles bearing leopards and the white hart, decorative wall paintings in gold and vermilion, popinjays and fleurs-de-lys.

V

Court Art and Aesthetics

The years between 1389 and 1399 form a watershed in English art. They include the creation of a new school in manuscript illumination as well as the final development of perpendicular architecture. They provide evidence of a passion for jewellery in the court circles as well as for experiments in panel-painting. The Apocalypse series in the Westminster Chapter House, like some of the cycles in the village churches, reflects new tastes in wall-painting. An increasing demand for free-standing sculpture and relief was being met by the development of the alabaster workshops: alabasters are first recorded as being exported in 1382; by 1400 the trade was fully organized and alabasters had spread through England from the centres of manufacture at Burton and Nottingham and perhaps at York and Lincoln; they were painted and gilded and set in wooden frames. These developments in art continue uninterrupted until about 1429. The real break in English court culture was caused by the minority of Henry VI, not by the deposition of Richard II.

But though royal patronage stimulated movements in architecture and sculpture, as at Westminster Hall and with the giant statues of the kings at Westminster and Canterbury, it was only paramount in the creation of *objets de luxe*: jewellery and the class of illuminated manuscripts which came to be associated with the work of Herman Scheere. Possibly this was due to the personal taste of King Richard. It seems clear from the inventory of his treasure compiled in 1399[1] that he delighted in the minute and costly; there were his clasp showing a demoiselle carrying a parrot; his golden child seated on a leopard; his silver statue of a demoiselle; and his silver-gilt ship with its eight men-at-arms. Much of this must have had the appeal of Fabergé work, though it was probably more sophisticated. He had much silver-gilt and goblets of painted and enamelled glass, covered silver basins and silver ewers with inscriptions both in English and French 'Wyth Goddes Help'; 'a bonn estreyn'—jewelled chaplets and girdles and isolated jewels like his sapphire set with four diamonds. The real value of his treasure must have lain in the quantity of his gems; rubies, diamonds and sapphires. There are 338 items in the inventory, but they do not include the goods Richard had left at Haverford[2] or the royal crown valued at £4,000.

It is likely that as in other matters Richard's personal taste for jewels set a fashion at his court. An inventory of the jewels of Thomas Percy Earl of Worcester[3] states that he possessed a gold circlet garnished with emeralds, pearls, sapphires and rubies with a diamond in its centre; a jewel that consisted of one emerald, three rubies and three sapphires; and also three gold clasps and a girdle, all set with gems. Jewellery was of course portable capital, but this inventory also suggests the display that was demanded from a prominent courtier.

A court fashion in *objets de luxe* may best explain some of the new developments in book production and illustration. It is possible that Anne of Luxemburg had brought with her from Prague a taste for illustrated books as well as for good letters; there is no evidence that either had appealed to Richard's father or mother. Charles IV of Luxemburg was one of the chief patrons of international Gothic painting; he maintained close links with the papal court at Avignon; Italian, French, German and Flemish influences mingled in the ateliers of Prague. Yet there were also tendencies that seem specifically Luxemburg:[4] the use of modelling by light rather than by line; the attempt to convey the volume of a body in three dimensions; the consequent effort to portray depth in space.

The illuminations in the *Liber Regalis*, the Westminster manuscript on the coronation rites, were probably painted in 1382 or 1383. It has been suggested that they were the work of a Bohemian in the queen's service;[5] certainly they reflect Luxemburg standards of taste and have no English precedent. They seem intended to appeal primarily to a delight in colour: gold backgrounds are enriched with an over-painting in gilt; the blue is deep ultramarine; the figure-work is often opalescent, for white is painted above green and then tinted with pink.

The Great Missal of Westminster painted in 1383 and 1384, perhaps by Thomas Preston, also suggests a demand for novelty. There is North Italian influence in its crowded crucifixion scene against a deep gold background and there seems to be an odd experiment in breaking the composition in two halves. In the margins traditional East Anglian motifs—the oak, the ivy, the marigold, the daisy—mingle with golden balls hanging from slender sprays. The missal was commissioned by Abbot Lytlington but its use in the royal abbey may imply some association with the court.

Four of Richard's personal manuscripts seem to have been preserved. The most illuminating of them is a Book of Divinations, *Libellus Geomancie*, which is now Bodley MS. 581. It is stated to have been prepared for the solace of King Richard by the least of his servants in March 1391, and probably reflects the deepest private interests of the King. It begins with the adage, 'A wise man will grow wiser by listening', and with some aphorisms on Kingship. This is followed by a treatise on physiognomy and on what may be learnt from the study of man's features. Then there is a Philosophy of Dreams (*Philosophia Visionis*) which deals with their causes, effects and interpretation. Then after a short section on divinations the book culminates on fol. 87ʳ with King Richard's Rosary, the *Rosarium Regis Ricardi*. This is a list of questions which when asked under the appropriate conjunction of planets and with the use of diagrams, which are carefully figured in the text, would enable the king to receive answers on such problems as the strength of chastity, the welfare of the King and kingdom and the fidelity of friends. The volume is pervaded by trust in the power of the planets: a study of planetary conjunctions might provide a clue to several of Richard's actions in the political crises of his reign.

Since this seems to be a unique manuscript commissioned by Richard for his own use, its format illustrates his taste in book production. It is in clear and beautiful script and there are ninety sheets, 10¼ in. high by 7⅜ in. wide. The capitals are always illuminated, often seven of them to the page, but sometimes as many as thirty-two. All the borders are illuminated, often with the spray motifs that descended from East Anglia. There are seventeen illustrations: sixteen of these show single figures, each of them standing abruptly against a chequer background of gold and pink, black and light blue and grey; the first is a miniature portrait of the King, still shown as a beardless adolescent although he was already twenty-four. The recurrent colours of the manuscript are gold, two reds and two blues—one of these perhaps made from lapis lazuli; the predominant colour is deep gold. The effect is that of jewels upon embroidery.

Three other illuminated manuscripts have been identified as coming from Richard's library, though it is unlikely that they were so much used by him. There is *The Book against the twelve errors and heresies of the Lollards* by the Court Dominican Roger Dymoke, with its royal portrait, heraldry and badges, its grotesques and its elaborate foliage. It is now Trinity Hall MS. 17. Then there are two books of Statutes, one now at Cambridge (St John's College MS. A.7) and one in the British Museum (MS. Cotton Nero D.VI). Perhaps all came from the same court workshop as the illuminated charter that Richard granted to Croyland in 1393.

Their style has been termed Italianate-English; more exactly they seem to be a blend between North Italian and East Anglian elements. They form a variant in international court art linked closely with the illuminations in the de Bohun manuscripts and perhaps ultimately with the wall-paintings in St Stephen's Chapel in Westminster Palace, but during the 1390s they became an old-fashioned variant. There were to be completely novel attempts to convey the sense of space and to create individual portraits through new experiments in facial modelling; there was a new realization of the human body and a fresh, wider range of colours. All this must have either satisfied or created fresh aesthetic standards at the court, and it was to culminate in the intensely sensitive painting of the school of Herman Scheere; but much of it was first apparent in the great Carmelite missal which was probably completed by 1393. The ostriches in the margin of the great Carmelite Missal make it likely that Queen Anne was one of its donors since her badge was an ostrich crowned and chained.[6]

Only the miniatures in the missal have survived but it is clear from them that it was of considerable size and was a manuscript de luxe given to the London Whitefriars. At least three Masters were employed in illustrating it[7] and all were of the first rank. One of them seems certainly English; his work is related to that in the Westminster Missal. The second had techniques very similar to the artist of the *Liber Regalis*: he achieves the same opal tints; there are the same white highlights and soft red shading; there are tiled patterns in the foreground and gilt arabesques. It is a tenable hypothesis that the second Master of the Carmelite Missal was a painter from the Bohemian court who had come to England with Queen Anne, had illustrated the *Liber Regalis*, and who since then had acquired some English mannerisms.

The third Master is the most significant: he is not only an innovator among English miniaturists, he is also the founder of a tradition. He is essentially a painter of bodies; he concentrates on their solidity, on their placing in space and on their relationship to each other. All this seems an echo from the court painters of the Luxemburgs, but there is no sign that he was a Bohemian; Prague had been a diffusion centre for a generation. He was oddly and completely un-Gothic. He was never geometric and his figures were modelled by the light. He was an accomplished colourist who had increased the range of his colour schemes by experiments in over-paintings, but he had little zest for the dramatic or the sumptuous; his Virgin was born in a bed with a grey coverlet and a dark green canopy, the walls of the house were in two shades of terracotta and the tiles on the roof were grey blue. It seems clear that the Third Master was neither North French nor English and though influenced from North Italy he was not Italian; perhaps his most likely provenance is from the Duke of Gueldres' court at Arnhem in the Netherlands.[8]

The close court contacts between Richard and his ally the Duke of Gueldres may also give a clue to the immediate background of Herman Scheere, the most sophisticated and the most talented of the court miniaturists. There is a group of illuminated manuscripts which are linked together by the use of the same courtly mottoes—an illustrated book of French and Latin prayers now in the British Museum[9] is perhaps the earliest among them. On folio 37 there is a signature 'Hermannus Scheere me fecit'; on folio 67 there are the mottoes *'Omnia leuia sunt amanti'*; *'Tout dus en une'*; *'Quit bien ayme tart oblie'* ('All things are light to the lover'; 'Both in one'; 'Who loves well forgets slowly'). *'Omnia leuia sunt amanti'* appears again as a signature motto in the full page Annunciation in the Beaufort Book of Hours.[10] A husband and wife kneel on either side of the Virgin's house as Gabriel gives her his message. There are decorative motifs in gold but the house itself is white shaded with grey; the hangings within it are patterns in green and gold; a green cloth covers the Virgin's prie-dieu. The floor is gold, tinted with red, and so is Gabriel's hair; the dress of the Virgin is a dark deep blue and that of Gabriel pale red. Another motto is added in the Annunciation scene: *'Si quis amat non laborat Dedaer'*. 'He who loves does not labour' is a natural sequel to the fact that all things are light to a lover. *'Dedaer'* seems unintelligible. In what is known as the Chichele Breviary[11] the motto runs: *'Si quis amat non laborat quod herman'*. (Plate 9)

The words *'Omnia leuia sunt amanti'* are written in the Great Bible of Richard II[12] and some of the many miniatures within it are in Herman Scheere's style. Few medieval bibles were so completely illustrated as that ascribed to Richard's use; besides the conventional initials, pictures were set in its text as if it were a romance. I still think it possible that Richard commissioned it in the last years of his reign, but the weight of modern opinion places it about 1410. Herman Scheere was employed on secular subjects as well as religious; it was a period in which the two genres merged easily. It has now been established that he illustrated the manuscript of Gower's *Confessio Amantis* which is in the Bodleian. On the other hand it is certain that he did not paint the portraits of Thomas Hoccleve and Prince Henry in Arundel MS 38, but it is almost certain that they came from his workshop. The more talented portrait of Chaucer in Harleian MS. 4866 is possibly a copy of a portrait by Scheere which was once in Arundel MS. 38. Hoccleve could never have paid for this Arundel manuscript of his *De Regimine* but it is likely that it was commissioned by Prince Henry, to whom the poem had been dedicated. It would have been natural if it had been ordered in 1413 from the Scheere workshop, which seems to have been dependent on the patronage of the court circle. There is no evidence that Herman Scheere ever had an ecclesiastical patron. On the most likely hypothesis he began as a court painter for King Richard, perhaps passed through the service of the Beauforts to that of the House of Lancaster and ended in the household of John, Duke of Bedford, Henry IV's younger son; for there are two inscriptions in the Bedford Book of Hours: 'Herman your meke seruant' and 'I am Herman your own seruant'. Yet there is evidence that at one time after Richard's death he served a patron who was opposed to the Lancastrians. There is a Book of Hours in the Bodleian[13] which is indisputably his[14] and this contains a miniature of the beheading of Archbishop Scrope of York[15] as a frontispiece to his office as a saint.[16] Archbishop Scrope was executed in 1405 because of his opposition to Henry IV.

It is easier to establish Herman's associations than his provenance. He is presumably the Herman Lymnour who was a witness to the will of Peter of Cologne in London in 1407. But there is nothing in his art that suggests the Rhineland. His painting seems to have been affected by the English and North French influences that would have been inevitable in the milieu in which he worked, but basically his style suggests the Netherlands. It would be a very tenable hypothesis that he had also come to the court of England from the court of Gueldres.

In contrast the painter John Siferwas seems very English. In the fourteenth century the Siferwases were a knightly family in Herefordshire and also had associations with the diocese of Salisbury. John Siferwas may have been born about 1360, for on the 19th of May, 1380, he was ordained an acolyte at Farnham by the Bishop of Winchester, and was then a Dominican at the

Guildford priory. He was still living on the 4th of September, 1421, when he was left a bequest in a London will. He is wearing a Dominican habit in his self-portrait in the Lovell Lectionary[17] and he was perhaps one of King Richard's court Dominicans. It seems certain that he was head of a considerable and fashionable atelier. Among his patrons were Richard Medford,[18] Bishop of Salisbury from 1395 to 1407, Robert Bruynyng, Abbot of Sherborne from 1385 to 1415, and John Lord Lovell who died in 1408: he painted portraits of all three. But his human portraiture, although accomplished, is dead; only his portraits of birds are intensely individual and alive. (Plate 10)

This may give a clue to the provenance of the sketchbook preserved in the Pepysian Collection at Magdalene College, Cambridge.[19] It is a pattern-book used at some artist's atelier in late fourteenth-century England; now that I have worked on it slowly and in detail I am hesitantly convinced that at least the birds in it were drawn by John Siferwas. Their identity with birds in the Sherborne Missal signed by him seems too obvious to result from a coincidence. If this is so the Pepysian MS. may be the pattern-book of the Siferwas workshop. It is in several hands, of which only one shows marked talent. It was perhaps compiled over two generations, ending about 1430, and was intended to provide figures not only for manuscript illumination but for embroidery, stained glass and wall painting. It would have been used both for secular and religious art. Besides the many different birds and the cat washing herself, there are the grotesques, the 'babwyns' that Henry IV favoured, the Virgin, Saints, a knight in armour and, in the Master's hand, the taut bent body of a naked woman. (Plates 11, 12)

It is clear that John Siferwas had at least two assistants and probable that he produced work in quite different genres. Two manuscripts are signed by him: the Sherborne Missal and the Lovell Lectionary. The Sherborne Missal[20] must have been among the largest of medieval manuscripts—even now when its margins have been trimmed it measures 21 inches by 15. It was perhaps painted about 1396. The great Crucifixion scene, with its margins tinted to resemble wood, suggests a panel painting. It is an experiment in dramatic tensions. The composition centres in the far corner where the Good Thief seems to spring triumphant from his cross under the nailed right hand of Christ, in the foreground to the right Mary swoons among the Holy Women. But on Christ's left, fashionably dressed courtiers are talking as they ride by, the unrepentant thief hangs disconsolately and in the far distance there are the small white towers of Jerusalem. Perspective is a term that should be used hesitantly but at least Siferwas is attempting to convey a sense of distance by an abruptly diminishing scale of figures. His works lack the sensitiveness of those of Herman Scheere but he combined a zest for the minute with mastery of line, a sense of altering proportions and broken rhythms and an utter sympathy with animal life. All this is apparent along the margins of the Sherborne Missal and in the decoration of the Lectionary that Lord Lovell commissioned from him as a gift to Salisbury Cathedral.[21]

There is a reference to his scribe, John Was, and it is probable that his workshop produced manuscripts as well as illustrating them. It is likely that they also provided sketches for wall-paintings: there are heads in the Last Judgement scene in the Chapter House at Westminster which though quite uninspired are obviously related to the Siferwas style in figure-work. This is most easily explicable if they are the work of a journeyman painter using designs from a Siferwas pattern book. If this was so it would suggest that he may have had an established reputation by about 1390. He had an obvious influence on the style of a Book of Hours at Trinity College, Cambridge, which is possibly late fourteenth-century, and on the illustrations of the *Livres du Graunt Caam*, the text of Marco Polo in the Bodleian[22] which has been dated about 1400.

The picture of Venice (folio 218) in the *Livres du Graunt Caam*, with its high white Gothic houses; the two statued columns by the Doge's palace; the men and women on its balconies; the skiffs and galleys on the Grand Canal; seems to reflect a court taste for delicately minute, crowded and realistic detail. It has its parallel in Chaucer. (Plate 16)

As a luxury trade, miniature painting had some similarity

with the new fashion in detailed court embroidery. Richard had a white satin doublet embroidered with golden orange-trees bearing a hundred silver-gilt oranges; the white satin sleeves were hung with fifteen silver cockles and thirty mussels and whelks in silver-gilt;[23] this was very different from the essential sobriety of the early fourteenth-century embroidery known as Opus Anglicanum. The inventory of the King's Treasure suggests that he delighted in the improbable combination of costly materials: he owned an ivory looking-glass in a golden frame set with enamelled and jewelled roses, with a queen in enamel on its back; another of his ivories had a cover enamelled with a mermaid; one of his silver ewers was enamelled with birds; and he had a triptych in enamelled silver-gilt with 'diverses ymageries'.

The Wilton Diptych[24] may best be considered in relation to this class of small and precious objects. It is $14\frac{1}{2}$ by 21 inches, and thus too small for the altar of a church, but it might have been used for the King's portable altar. The paintings on the back of the diptych suggest that it was Richard's personal possession, for they show his coat of arms—the Cornish choughs and the cross fleury of the Confessor impaled with the French lilies and the English leopards and surmounted by a helm bearing the royal lion—and this is balanced by his badge of the white hart. Two different masters would seem to have been employed upon this cover. The coat of arms is accomplished late fourteenth-century heraldry, and it was the primary duty of the King's Painter to provide heraldic banners and devices. Gilbert Prince of Litlington in Sussex was the King's Painter until he died in Cripplegate in 1393. He was succeeded by Thomas Prince, who was perhaps his son, and who was still holding the office in 1402; it would have been natural for Thomas Prince to paint the arms on the back of a royal diptych. The white hart is among the greatest of English paintings and must be by a different hand; not only the draughtsmanship but the emphasis on intrinsic life suggests that it may be the work of John Siferwas. (Plate 3)

But neither Siferwas nor Prince can be associated with the

painting on the front of the diptych. The two panels form one composition. In the first, Richard has been ushered into the Court of Heaven by his patron St John the Baptist and his two predecessors King Edmund the Martyr and King Edward the Confessor. He kneels gazing up at the Child Christ, and has raised his hands to receive from Him the standard of St George. In the Court of Heaven the Child Christ leans out towards the King from his Mother's arm, one hand raised in blessing, the other stretching out to hand him the standard which is held by an attending angel as a squire. But the Child Christ is also Christ Crucified; His halo is stippled with the Crown of Thorns and contains the three nails of His passion. Round His Mother eleven angels are grouped like young courtiers: one has his arm thrown over another's shoulders in friendship; nine show the white hart badge embroidered above their hearts; three are pointing toward the King. They wear chaplets; perhaps it is 'the new guise of Bohemia' of which John Gower wrote in the *Confessio Amantis*. Both panels have a background of patterned gold leaf. The Court of Heaven is dominated by three tones of blue relieved by white and gold and green; the green of the meadow grass in the foreground; the cloth of gold round the Child Christ contrasted with the yellow gold of the angels' hair; and three whites—that of the flesh tints, that of the standard, that of the flowers among the grass. The angels' wings as they curve upward are shaded from white to grey and then to black. It is likely that the Master of the Wilton Diptych was valued by his contemporaries for a colourist as much as for a draughtsman. He responded to the fashion for miniatures by applying a miniaturist's technique to a panel-painting. (Frontispiece; Plate 4)

After so much controversy it may be possible to place the Wilton Diptych with some exactness. The subject would seem to be Richard's coronation; there may be eleven angels round the Virgin because this happened in his eleventh year. We know that it was painted after 1390 because of the use of the white hart badge and probably after 1394 because of the use of the Arms of the Confessor. It was painted before 1400 since, in spite of a counter theory, it seems inconceivable to me that anyone except

Richard would have commissioned such an *objet de luxe*. Perhaps 1395 after Anne's death is the most likely date, since had there been a queen her device might have been painted on the reverse. The coronation had taken place on the 16th of July, 1377, but probably for Richard it was always a present fact; looking at the panel he would have been reminded that he had received the standard from the hands of Christ, that in every crisis he was under His protection and that of His mother and that his patron saints were with him always. Such reflections may have formed part of the intimate overconfidence of the King.

The Wilton Diptych has never suffered restoration; the full-length portrait of Richard II which now hangs in the nave of Westminster Abbey was grossly restored in 1866. It may have been painted about 1390 for a room in Westminster Palace. Even now there are signs that it is the work of a master—the modelling of the face, the texture of the ermine lining to the cloak, the delicacy of the small crowned Rs that decorate the gown—but there is no sign that he was English. The Diptych and the Westminster Panel are discussed in detail in the notes upon the plates. (Plate 5)

Dr Evans has ascribed[25] an English origin to a diptych in the Museo Nazionale in Florence which has been dated about 1390. This seems to me likely enough. If so it also illustrates the fashion for treating a panel like a miniature. On the leaf that shows the Adoration of the Magi[26] the movements of the nine figures seem to interlock, there is a delicate rendering of each textile, each hair seems painted separately. Such paintings may have been common in the Court circle; in 1397 Thomas of Woodstock had in his house at Pleshey three triptychs painted with images.

The development of secular wall-painting as a fine art had been checked by the new fashion for the use of tapestries both among the magnates and at the court. The Black Prince had left a set of arras but the vogue seems to have developed in the 1380s and '90s. In 1397 among the goods of Thomas of Woodstock, Duke of Gloucester, were tapestries representing the Siege of the Castle of Love, the History of Love, Lancelot in battle, the

Siege Perilous, the stories of Godfrey de Bouillon and of Charlemagne and what was apparently a *roman courtois*. Such secular tapestries would have provided entertainment as well as decoration—they would have satisfied the growing zest for fiction—but the Duke's religious tapestries primarily represented single scenes: he owned a Nativity, a Purification, a Presentation of Christ in the temple, a laying of Christ in the tomb; perhaps they were intended to serve not only for decoration but as the subjects of devout meditation.

On occasion the two genres mingled: in 1393 John of Gaunt owned arras representing Moses and Pharaoh, King Clovis, and the Life of the Lover and the Beloved. At times tapestries were purely decorative: in 1392 Richard Fitzalan, Earl of Arundel, possessed blue hangings made in London and woven with red roses and coats of arms. It is clear that tapestries from Arras were specially prized and were sometimes gifts from the Duke of Burgundy. In 1394 the Duke gave Richard an arras of Virtues and Vices followed by Kings and Emperors, a Calvary and a Life of St Ursin.

There is a fairly complete list of the royal tapestries in the time of Henry V. Many of them may have been commissioned by him or by his father but it is likely that they include the tapestries of Richard II. There were the stories of Bevis of Hamton, of St Edward the Confessor, of Sir Perceval, of Charlemagne, of Octavian of Rome, of Pharamond and of Antenor. There was a tournament, the Life of Love, the Tree of Youth, a lady in a tent. There were many courtly scenes referred to by their titles, like '*Dame cest chapelet me donez*'. There are religious scenes like the Annunciation, the Five Joys of Our Lady and the Three Kings of Cologne. A taste for elaborate tapestry work was one of the marks of the continuous English court culture between 1389 and 1429.[27]

When the walls were hung with such tapestries there was no need for the secular paintings in which Henry III had delighted. There are references to 'painted chambers' in Richard's fragile country palaces at Eltham and Windsor Manor. But these may have been decorated with devices like that of the young Queen

Isabelle—the white falcon and a spray of rosemary—or by light-hearted paintings like that on a chest, now at Queens' College, Cambridge, where a girl holds her heart out to a man while he holds out a ring.

The only surviving wall-paintings that can be associated with Richard's court are those in the room in the Byward Tower at the Tower of London. There is no evidence that the room was a chapel—it was more probably an office—but apart from heraldic devices the subjects painted were religious. There was the King's patron John the Baptist with his lamb, a Virgin, an almost obliterated figure and then, dominating the scheme, St Michael with his weighing scales and the sweep of outstretched wings. All the figures are rendered monumentally; all seem to be by one master; and although they have only survived in fragments the difference between them and the contemporary wall-paintings in the Chapter-House at Westminster is one of kind not of degree.

The paintings in the Chapter-House of Westminster differ in style and period but the Last Judgement was perhaps completed about 1392 and the illustrations of the Apocalypse added before 1400. At times they have charm but they seem to be the work of journeymen and to be based on drawings from the pattern-book of some London atelier.

The sketches that are presupposed in the Apocalypse series on the other hand were probably first designed for manuscript illustration. There would seem to have been originally 96 scenes each approximately 19 in. square; the composition of those that survive is overcrowded. The Apocalypse scenes reflect the late fourteenth-century zest for realistically detailed and continuous narrative: ermine tippets are used to indicate rank—the officials who preside over St John's banishment to Patmos wear long furred gowns with hanging sleeves, while the pink tunics of the executioners only reach their hips; Patmos is a small rocky island; the story begins with St John in the presence of the Emperor Domitian. The pigments used were expensive —there is gold and silver as well as vermilion, green and blue.

While much is known of the poetry of the last years of Richard II the painting can only be judged from its fragments. Yet it is clear how much they had in common. Perhaps this was inevitable; they were being provided for identical publics moulded by the social and economic changes of the late fourteenth century, and being influenced within the circle of the court by the personal taste of the King for a delicate sophistication and for bright clear colours. History and literature and painting should never be studied in complete isolation.

7   The Studley Royal Bowl.
Victoria and Albert Museum, London.

8   The Rokewode Mazer.
Victoria and Albert Museum, London.

VI

Thomas Usk and Thomas Hoccleve

In the late fourteenth century, England possessed the greatest vernacular literature in Europe—which was not to happen again until the reign of James I. It was marked by a creative dynamism which led to the development of completely new forms of verse, of prose, and of the novel. It was dominated by writers of supreme and recognized talent such as Geoffrey Chaucer and the authors of the *Vision of Piers Plowman*, of *Gawain and the Grene Knight*, and of *Pearl*; and also by others whose real talents are often underestimated—John Gower, Thomas Usk, Thomas Hoccleve, and the authors of *Degrevant* and of the *Parlement of Thre Ages*. Yet it is clear that this literature could not have come into existence without the demands of new publics, whose nature may be determined partly from intrinsic evidence and partly from a study of manuscript transmission. The most influential of these publics were the Court and the *haute bourgeoisie* of London.

It was a mark of the international court culture to be closely linked with a capital city and in some fashion dependent on it. Boileau's advice[1] to a dramatist, '*Etudiez la cour et connoissez la ville*', is a key to the understanding of both Chaucer and Gower. Richard's court was close linked with the rich men of the city; they were an obvious source of supply to counterbalance its mounting extravagance. Quite apart from the forced loans towards the end of the reign there is the odd episode of September 1392 when the King announced that he would pardon the city at the intercession of the Queen and accept a fine of £3,000 and a gift of £10,000 more.[2] Courtiers such as Simon Burley raised loans from lesser citizens[3] and found some of their pleasure among them. Thomas Hoccleve writes that he drank in the taverns by Westminster Gate and went as far as St Paul's to buy sweet wine and wafers for 'Venus femele lusty children deer'. While for the London *haute bourgeoisie*, in the 1390s often of three or four generations standing, the court provided access not only to the person of the sovereign but to the fashions of the upper class.[4]

Both the life and writing of Thomas Usk were conditioned by the fact that he lived in the city purlieus of the court. From 1381 to 1383 he was secretary to John de Northampton, Mayor of London; in the summer of 1384 he was imprisoned for sedition, but he gained an audience with Richard and procured his own pardon by accusing Northampton of treason. It seems likely that during the next three years he was used as the intermediary between the Court and Richard's faction among the citizens who followed the leadership of Nicholas Brembre; at least this would explain why he was chosen for death by the Lords Appellant. In the autumn of 1387 he was appointed Under Sheriff of London at the request of the King. That winter the opposition lords gained control of the city and Usk was arrested. He was sentenced to death on the 3rd of March, 1388, and hanged the same evening.

It seems probable that Thomas Usk wrote his *Testament of Love*[5] in 1386 or 1387. A complete novelty in literary form, it is in prose, which was unprecedented for an allegory of love; and it is in a new form of rhythmical prose that foreshadows the Elizabethan Euphuists.[6] The style proves that it was written to be declaimed aloud, and probably the public for which it was intended was the Court. This would explain why it survived among the Chaucer manuscripts (it was treated as part of the Chaucer canon until 1860) and why it is so obviously intended to appeal to powerful patrons. The ideal described seems to be that of accomplished courtiers: 'Lyons in the felde and lambes in chambre/egles at assaute and maydens in halle/foxes in counsayle, stille in their dedes.' Usk seems consciously a part of the new literary movement ('In Latin and French hath many soverayne wittes had great delight'), and he knew the group of French court poems upon the Marguerite theme, *Troilus and Criseyde*, the *House of Fame* and Chaucer's translation of *Boethius*.

The *Testament*, though too long, is carefully shaped. The first letters of its thirty-two chapters are *margareteofvirtwha vemercionthinusk*—'Margarete of virtw have merci on thin Usk'. It is precisely because Usk conveys so perfectly his love for Margarete that the *Testament* is such good allegory: the mystical sense of scripture must be founded on a literal sense. He wrote of his love for her:

They wene forsothe that suche accorde may notbe but the rose of may-denhede be plucked. Do way do way they knowe nothing of this. For consent of two hertes alone maketh the fasteninge of the knotte, neither lawe of kynde ne mannes law determineth neither the age ne the qualite of persones but only accord bitwene thilke tway.[7]

The attitude to women is courtly, not bourgeois:

In paradyse for your helpe was this tree graffed out of whiche al linage of man discendeth. If a man be noble frute of noble frute it is sprongen: the blisse of paradyse to mennes sory hertes yet in this tree abydeth.[8]

And again

Blisse of two hertes in ful love knitte may not aright ben imagined.

Love had told him that she had taught her servants 'to make songes of playnte and of blisse and to endyten letters of rhetorike in queynt understandinges and to bethinke hem in what wyse they might best their ladies in good service plese.'[9]

It seems likely that to Usk and his audience the *Testament of Love* was a 'letter of rhetorike in queynt understandinges'. He calls it a 'tretys'. Margarete had been to him like manna in the desert and like the manna she had symbolized truths higher than herself. 'How was it that sightful manna in deserte to children of Israel was spiritual meate. Bodily also it was for mennes bodies it norisseth, yet never the later Christ it signi-fyed.' (Here 'never the later' means nevertheless.) Margarete was not only a woman, she was a pearl; she was 'utter blisse'. She signified God's Grace, God's Wisdom and Holy Church. Into these crowding allegories Usk poured encyclopædic know-ledge.

Thomas Hoccleve was a younger contemporary of Thomas

Usk and of rather similar status; he spent most of his life as a clerk in the Privy Seal's office.[10] If an hypothesis of Professor V. H. Galbraith[11] is correct he cannot have been born later than about 1360. In 1407 he wrote in his autobiographical poem *La Male Regle*:

> But twenty wynter past continuelly
> Excesse at borde hath leyd his knyf with me.[12]

It was his primary boast that he was a personal disciple of Chaucer. It was said to him

> Sonne I have herd or this men speke of thee
> Thow wert acqueynted with Chaucers parde.[13]

He writes of 'my worthy maister Chaucers . . . the first fynder of our faire language'.[14] After the revolution of 1399 he received some patronage from Henry IV and from the Countess of Westmorland, but he never established himself as Lydgate did and his verses convey very vividly the agonies as well as the pleasures of the court proletariat. His annuity was paid for the last time on the 11th of February, 1426; it is likely that he died soon after. He had never known financial security; his salary from the Privy Seal's office was only six marks a year and when his poems brought him an annuity he was already deep in debt. He had been cheated with false promises ('Ye courteours fulle often ye deceyve').[15] He had at first stayed unmarried since he hoped to be rewarded with a benefice if he were ordained.

> I gasyd longe firste and waytid faste
> After some benefice and whan nan came
> By proces I me wedded atte laste.[16]

He had married for love ('only for love I chees hire to my make'),[17] but he regretted his lost liberty. He could use the language of the court:

> Hye and noble prince excellent
> My lorde the prince O my lorde gracious.

but perhaps at times he was impatient of court manners—

So long proces so many a sly cautel
For to deceyve a sely damosele.[18]

He stayed low in the court hierarchy. He writes of his pleasure in being held 'a verray gentil man' in the Westminster cook-shops and in being called 'maister' by the London watermen.[19] He was driven by blind lusts and could not resist the call of 'Bacchus and his lure'.[20]

Yet as these few citations may have suggested his verse was completely novel in English literature. It was novel because it was autobiographical and because the sense of his own weakness was heightened by his consciousness of the filth around him:

My gost is wrappede in an hevy drede.

As early as 1407 he felt close to the putrefaction of the Charnel ('now I am so rype unto my pit').[21] He wrote a poem on his lady with her clay-like cheeks hanging in lumps of dough which is I think unique in medieval literature:

Hir mowthe is nothyn scant with lippes gray
Hir chin unnethe may be seen at al
Hir comly body shape as a foot bal
And shee syngith ful lyke a Papelay.[22]

He could convey his horror of his own death by simile ('the blak faced Ethiopians me envyron'), and he wrote vividly of grossness and lust and treason in the best of his stories, *The Tales of Jonathas and Felicula*, dedicated to the Countess of Westmorland.

Yet he realized this was not what his public would wish from him. He describes how he met an old man in the Strand in 1411 who advised him how to make money:

Sharpe thy pen and write on lustily
Let see my sonne make it fresshe and gay.[23]

The result was the *De Regimine Principum*. If it is possible to judge from the number of manuscripts this was his only work to be popular among his contemporaries. Even this has been judged too harshly. It is accomplished work, with the smooth style prized at the time, the occasional strong line and a cluster of concise classical anecdotes—on 'Camelus', or Regulus, or Scipio Africanus. For it is a learned poem: Hoccleve as much as Usk belongs to the new literary movement of the international court culture. He was in touch with Paris fashion: in 1402 he modelled his *Letter of Cupid* on a poem by Christine de Pisan. He read Eustache Deschamps and, I think, the Latin Boccaccio. He had precisely the kind of classical learning valued at the Valois Court, using as his sources Seneca, Cicero and Quintilian, Ovid and Livy. His was an oddly unsuccessful life and an unmerited oblivion. (Plate 13)

This is the point where it might be worth trying to place John Lydgate, though he was only beginning to write in the 1390s. The practice of referring to him as the Monk of Bury has obscured his real setting; he was a court poet and most of his life was spent in London. His links with his Benedictine abbey seem to have been tenuous; money gifts and court pensions were paid to him in person until November 1441 when he returned to Bury, perhaps to die. There are many parallels to such a life: King Richard's physician, William Tyndeman, was a Cistercian. Lydgate came from a village near Newmarket and was a novice at Bury St Edmunds when he was fifteen. There now seems to be truth in the tradition recorded by Bale that he had studied at Oxford and in France widely, and he boasted 'I have been offte in dyvers londys' while a manuscript note in his *Aesop* states that it was 'made in Oxenford'; certainly he seems to have been about the court in the 1390s. In his Life of Our Lady and in his *Troy Booke* he stated that he had submitted his poems to Chaucer's correction and had relied on his counsel. It was perhaps then that he found his first patroness, the young Countess of Stafford. For two generations he was to make poetry for the Stafford circle, and was to become the favourite court poet of the Lancastrians. The Beauchamps and the Bouchiers, the Countess of Shrewsbury, of Suffolk and of March were among his patrons. Benedict Burgh wrote to him

> Ye be the floure and tresore of poesie
> Garland of Ive and Laure of Victory

and ranked him above Cicero, Homer, Virgil and Horace. It was all a great contrast to Hoccleve. His epitaph described him as the Virgil and the Boccaccio of Britain (the 'Maro'; the 'Bocaceus').

Lydgate was too facile and it was his misfortune that his public was so insatiable; yet the *Reason and Sensuality* and the *Temple of Glas* are major poems and he was always to retain something of the power of the inevitable word:

> And he that made the highe and cristall hevyn
> The firmament and also every spere
> The golden axeltree and the sterres seven

or—

> A world of beaute compassid in her face[24]

or again—

> Redresse of sorrow O Citheria.[25]

In this at least he was Chaucer's heir. For though not a climax he was a culmination in the international court literary movement which had faded in France with Alain Chartier and only survived in one form in the delicate filigree of Charles of Orleans.

He had accepted with appetite the whole canon of good letters that that movement presupposed. It is almost impossible that he should have known Greek, but he praised 'Grete' Homer and Euripides. It is unlikely that he knew Italian, but he praised Dante and Petrarch and Boccaccio; it is clear that he knew Boccaccio well through the French translation of Laurence Premierfaits. It is probable that he had only read Horace and Juvenal from a book of quotations, and suggestive that he believed Cicero to have written 'moral ditties'; but he had studied and used Virgil and Livy and Seneca, Lucan, and Statius. It is especially characteristic that he should write in two languages— the courtly and the common speech. His courtly verse was 'Aureate', gilded with new loans from French and Latin:

> Heavenly eyeghen aungelike in visage
> All that hath nature set in your image.

It has been calculated that he added 800 new words to English.

But he may also have written *London Lickpenny*[26] and perhaps the *Ballet of an Ale Seller* in what an Italian would have called the 'Fiorentino del Mercato Vecchio' style.

Like Chaucer and like Gower he had his links with the city as well as with the court. He was a pageant master as well as a poet, arranging mummings for the court, at Windsor in 1424 and at Eltham in 1427, but also arranging pageants for the city companies, as for the grocers and the mercers in 1429. His verses were inscribed on the cloisters of St Paul's beneath the painting of the Dance of Death.

Lydgate was also linked to the new literary forms by his poignant tenderness for the weak[27] and his 'aureat' vocabulary. The quality of being 'aureat', 'golden', was highly prized. The word was first coined by Lydgate, but he held that it was his 'Maister Chaucer' who had first distilled 'the golde drew-dropes of speche and eloquence into our tunge'.[28] It was associated with the Classics and perhaps especially with the prestige of the Greek that so very few could understand. Lydgate wrote

> 'Wher is Tullius with his sugryd touge
> Or Crisistomus with his golden mouth
> The aureat ditees that be said be red or songe
> Of Omerus in Grece both north and south.'[29]

Possibly the link between Greek and golden had been first suggested by Cicero when he wrote, rather improbably, of the *aureum flumen orationis* of Aristotle. Gold was reckoned the noblest of the 'colours' of rhetoric. Lydgate wrote in the *Fall of Princes* 'refourme the rudeness of my stile with aureate colours of your fresche language'.[30] It was dew distilled from the planet Mercury, 'off Mercurye the aureat influence'[31] and Mercury was the messenger of the gods. It was achieved not by syntax nor by the ordinary rhetorical laws but by the discovery of an unexpected but apparently inevitable adjective or noun; in this it was antithetic to the usual Middle English pleasure in a well-worn epithet.[32] This was a conception that would dominate later poetic experience. It was first applied to English poetry by Geoffrey Chaucer and to English prose by Thomas Usk. With

9   The Annunciation from the 'Beaufort Book of Hours'.
British Museum Roy. MS.2.A.XVIII, f.23v.

10   John, Lord Lovell and John Siferwas.
     British Museum Harl. MS.7026, f.4v.

11   Birds in an artist's sketchbook.
Magdalene College, Cambridge, Pepysian MS.1916, f.13a.

12   Conversation pieces from an artist's sketchbook.
Magdalene College, Cambridge, Pepysian MS.1916, f.4a.

both it is associated with the use of the traditional high style, the *stilus gravis*. There is an odd variant with Thomas Hoccleve, for it was only in his low style, the *stilus humilis*, that he found the unexpected inevitable word.

This *stilus humilis* was regarded as ordinary speech; '*Locutio*' as opposed to '*Eloquentia*'. In the literature associated with the International Court Culture it was considered very entertaining to apply suddenly the highest rhetorical artifice to ordinary speech, but that was precisely because the gulf between '*Locutio*' and '*Eloquentia*' was still universally assumed. Man was distinguished from the other animals by the power of ordinary speech. A cultivated man was distinguished from other men by his eloquence. All poems were forms of eloquence, though verses could be written in ordinary speech, for every poet was inevitably a rhetorician since a poem was created from grammar, rhetoric and music. This was the doctrine that Dante had taught in his *Convivio,* and through Boccaccio and Petrarch the influence of Dante permeated the literary standards of the international court culture. In his prologue to the *Fall of Princes* Lydgate could describe a poem of Chaucer's as a 'Daunt' in English.

VII

Geoffrey Chaucer

Usk, Hoccleve and Lydgate were polarized to Chaucer and seem to have been his personal disciples. His life is much better documented than theirs because of his court employments. When Edward III died in 1377 Chaucer was already established as a courtier and had been rewarded with an annuity of twenty marks, a daily pitcher of wine, two wardships and a controllership in the customs. He continued to prosper in the years of the Minority. He was linked with the household of John of Gaunt; he possessed an annuity of thirty marks from the Duke, twenty for his own services and ten for the services of his wife Philippa as bed-chamber woman to the Duchess. This implies that his wife was in service in the Duke's town house, the Savoy; his sister-in-law was already employed there as mistress to the Duke and governess to his children.

Chaucer was increasingly used in what was beginning to be a diplomatic service. In 1377 he was in Flanders with Sir Thomas Percy, later to be Earl of Worcester. In January 1378 he may have been at the court of Paris with the Earl of Huntingdon; later that year he went to the court of Milan with Sir Edward Berkeley. The fact that his companions were always of much higher rank suggests that he was employed as secretary.

Such employment brought its own forms of protection and of recompense. There was the odd episode in 1380 when Cecilia de Chaumpaigne was induced to stop her action against Chaucer for rape; and on May the 8th, 1382, he was given a rich sinecure—the Controllership of the Petty Customs at London with permission to appoint a deputy. Soon after he seems to have become associated with the new court and may have found a fresh patron in Robert de Vere; on February the 17th, 1385, de Vere signed the permit that both Chaucer's Controllerships should be held as permanent sinecures. One might consider whether this was a reward for *Troilus and Criseyde*. In the parliament of October 1386 he was one of the two knights of the shire for Kent and it is to be presumed that he had been placed there by the King's faction, for when the Opposition carried out the first purge that December he was deprived of both his Controllerships. He was rewarded when the royal party came back into power in May 1389; nine weeks later he was appointed Clerk of the King's Works.

During the 1390s Chaucer's court career is well documented. The Clerkship of the King's Works was a responsible court office, well salaried and with the possibility of many perquisites; it had been the foundation of the fortunes of William Wykeham. Chaucer was in charge of the structure and of the furnishing of Eltham, Sheen and Westminster at a time when Richard was enlarging and modernizing his palaces, but there is nothing in Chaucer's past to suggest that he had the necessary competence. In January 1391 he appointed John Elmhurst to be his deputy at Westminster Palace and in the royal apartments at the Tower; six months later Chaucer was ordered to surrender his office to John Gedney.

It would seem that he had the patronage of the Countess of March; in 1390 he had been appointed a sub-forester in the Mortimer forest of Petherton and she confirmed this in 1398. It must have been primarily a small sinecure for it was to be held by his son Thomas when he was Chief Butler to the King and Constable of Wallingford and the Chilterns. But the basis of Geoffrey Chaucer's life was that Richard continued to be his patron. Payments were made to him in 1393; on February the 28th, 1394, the King arranged that he should be paid £10 every six months; a number of loans were authorized from the Exchequer; he was protected from a suit for debt; he received a royal grant for an annual hogshead of wine, dated December 1397; and on October the 13th, 1398, there was also a gift. Chaucer complained of his empty purse, but this may have been partly a French literary convention.

His son Thomas was one of the more rising of the younger courtiers. He was probably born in about 1368, and about 1394 he made a rich and oddly fashionable marriage with one of the heiresses of Sir John Burghersh; Sir John through his Badlesmere grandmother belonged to an influential cousinage which included the Earls of March and of Oxford. By the spring of 1399 Thomas was the Royal Chief Butler. His career and perhaps his marriage is only explicable if he had the personal favour of the King, but it is probable that he had served in the household of John of Gaunt: in 1399 Richard confirmed for him an annuity of £20 which had been charged on the Lancaster inheritance. He was first cousin to the Beauforts through their mother Katherine Swynford.[1] He joined Henry of Bolingbroke as soon as the revolution had succeeded.

Geoffrey Chaucer must have done the same. On October the 13th, 1399, Henry of Bolingbroke confirmed Richard's grants to him and added another forty marks a year. Chaucer had written to him:

> O Conquerour of Brutes Albioun
> Which that by lyne and free elecioun
> Ben veray King.[2]

Five months later Richard was murdered, most probably by Sir Thomas Swynford, the nephew of Chaucer's wife. Chaucer's annuities were last paid to him in June 1400. It is likely that he died that summer in his house at Westminster.

Chaucer's verses have somehow to be arranged within this framework of his life. There is a rough sequence from extrinsic arguments. The *Compleint to his empty purse* must have been written in the autumn of 1399. One version of the *Legend of Good Women* must have been written before the death of Queen Anne on the 7th of June, 1394.[3] This had been preceded by the *Rose* and by *Creseyde*,[4] by the *House of Fame*, the *Death of Blaunche the Duchesse*, the *Parlement of Foules* and the *Loves of Palamon and Arcite*.[5] *Troilus and Criseyde* was completed before the end of 1387, since it is referred to in the *Testament of Love*. There is a fifteenth-century note on the Shirley MS. of the *Compleynt of Mars*[6] that it was written on the love of John Holland, later Duke of Exeter, for the Duchess of York; this might suggest a date about 1380. The *Book of the Duchesse* must have been written between the death of Blanche of Lancaster in the autumn of 1369 and her husband's re-marriage to Constanza of Castille in the summer of 1371. I make another suggestion more tentatively— that the *Parlement of Foules* is likely to have been written after 1387; I have found no citation from it in the *Testament of Love*, yet if it had been written earlier it should have been an obvious source. Perhaps this is all that we can know from the external evidence for the sequence of Chaucer's poems.

It is patent from intrinsic evidence that Chaucer's work falls into two phases, those of his youth and of his maturity; but it is of course disputed when and why his work became mature. Much has been made of the effect upon him of his second Italian mission in 1378, but the old antithesis between his French and his Italian periods seems untenable; it is more likely that his French period lasted until his death, for he was always open to influences from Paris and in his appreciation of Dante, Petrarch and Boccaccio he was following the fashions of the Valois court. Also it is difficult to determine when his 'Italian' period began. He may have learnt some Italian from London 'Lombards' even before his first mission to Genoa in the winter of 1372; that might indeed explain why he was sent on it. He knew the *Paradiso* and the *Purgatorio* and at least one sonnet of Petrarch's, but the influence from Dante has perhaps been over-estimated,[7] and it was with the young Boccaccio that he was most at home. Of course the Italian influences were there. They underlay the *House of Fame* and *Anelida*, and *Troilus* and five of the *Canterbury Tales*; they can be traced in the *Parlement of Foules* and in the *Legend of Good Women*. But they are not limited to the poems of his maturity.

The *House of Fame* is at times impregnated by Dante; it is probably the 'Daunt' in English ascribed to Chaucer by Lydgate. Yet its eight-syllable couplets do not seem to have the quality of Chaucer's verse in full maturity. In the *House of Fame* he writes

Of Dido quene of that contree
That shortly for to tellen she

> Becam hys love and leet him doo
> That that weddynge longeth too.

This is a contrast to the description of Dido in the *Legend* that ends

> Of Kinges and of Lordes so desyred
> That al the world her beaute hadde yfyred.[8]

The difference seems far deeper than one of metrics.[9] It seems unlikely that Skeat can have been correct in suggesting that only two or three years lay between the *House of Fame* and the *Legend*. If it is granted that the *House of Fame* was a court poem, the court for which it was designed may have been that of Edward III and the Dante manuscript that it presupposes could have been brought back from Florence in November 1373.

It is of course very difficult to discriminate between the rewards that came to Chaucer as an entertainer or as a diplomat, but it seems likely that the pitchers of wine granted to him on April the 23rd, 1374, may have been a return for a contribution to the festivities of St George's day. The *House of Fame* might have been composed for some such occasion and completed in prose. It is probable that by then he had composed not only the *Book of the Duchesse* but the *Book of the Leoun*, the lost *Ceys and Alcioun*, the translation of the *Romaunt of the Rose* which has survived only in a fragment,[10] the *Compleint to his Lady*, the *Compleint unto Pite*, and the *Amorous Compleint* 'Made at Windsor'. That so much of these has been lost suggests that they had a restricted public; their publication may well have meant not the issue of manuscripts from a scrivener but a public reading at the court.

The change from the young to the mature Chaucer seems to be marked by his version of *Boethius* which Dr Skeat dated conjecturally between 1377 and 1381. In Chaucer's own phrase 'the flames of the sun overcome the star light'.[11] The significance of the *Boethius* has often been ignored, partly because it is called a translation, partly because it is in prose; but the modulated rhythms of its prose show a new mastery of English metrics. With the *Boethius* Chaucer thought in a new dimension.

In the first 'prose' of the second book there is a description of Fortune and 'the swiftnesse and the sweigh of hir turninge whele' which is the key to *Troilus*. Fortune's Wheel turns as inevitably as the seasons change ('O thou fool of alle mortal fooles if Fortun bigan to dwelle stable she cesede thanne to ben Fortune'). It is Fortune that makes every form of earthly happiness the theme for a tragedy, since each form of earthly happiness is of its nature transient: 'tragedie' is 'a dittee of a prosperitee for a tyme that endeth in wrecchednesse':[12] the greater the joy, the greater the tragedy of its inevitable eclipse. This is why there is so much stress on the bliss of Troilus.

Yet though ill fortune is as inevitable as winter there need be no autumn; disaster can come unlooked for ('unwar'); as it is written in the *Boethius*, all cryings of tragedies bewail 'the dedes of fortune that with an unwar stroke over torneth realmes of grete nobley.[13] Chaucer was to note the cataclysms of contemporary history: 'grete Barnabo Viscounte', 'God of delyt and scourge of Lumbardy', dying imprisoned by his son-in-law;[14] Pierre de Lusignan murdered in his bed;[15] Pedro of Castille killed by his brother in his tent.[16] He was to witness a cataclysm in England in 1399. It was fatal to put trust in fortune,

> For when men trusteth hir than wol she faille
> And covere hir brighte face with a cloude.[17]

With the *Boethius*, Chaucer for the first time took tragedy and fortune as his themes and would have first been recognized as a philosopher. Perhaps it was about this time that he wrote his *Anelida*; it is an odd unsatisfying poem, as if he had not yet mastered a new technique, and is over-laden with the classical reminiscences that were just becoming fashionable in northern Europe. Yet it contains lines with a new amplitude:

> Singest with vois memorial in the shade
> Under the laurer which that may not fade.[18]

Possibly the *Compleynt of Mars* is also of this period. Between 1377 and 1381 there was in fact no court, and *Anelida* and the *Compleynt of Mars* may have entertained John of Gaunt's great household at the Savoy. But the *Boethius* must have been intended for a different and a wider public; it would have been read by men and women concerned with serious problems, and Chaucer's verses to his scrivener Adam state that one of his duties was to make copies of 'Boece'. This was a public that Chaucer was to share with Gower; it was to be one of the two publics for *Troilus and Criseyde*.

The *Troilus* seems obviously a court poem and the manuscript illumination[19] that shows Chaucer declaiming it to a court public may represent the way in which it was published; it seems addressed to the 'yonge fresshe folk' of Richard's court. I have already suggested that the grant of the sinecures in February 1385 may have been its reward. It is one of the chief masterpieces in medieval European literature, but it can only be considered medieval because it is so didactic.

Like Gower's *Confessio Amantis* it contains 'something of lust, something of lore', but the lore it teaches is on two levels. It is what the fifteenth century termed a 'cortaysie book', and teaches courtly manners, the art of love and the technique of love-making. This will be missed if Pandarus is misconceived as a comic character; he is an experienced English courtier of the late fourteenth century. He is stated to have been a good conversationalist,[20] and though his prolixity and pedantry have been found amusing by some later readers it is likely that in his time they were admired. The speed with which he fetches a cushion for Troilus has been found 'irresistibly comic', but it may only be an example of his care for the minutiae of good manners. He is a man of cultivated sensibility, facilely expressed emotions and quick stratagems—all qualities then prized. He seeks unselfishly the happiness of his friend and of his niece. His lines on constancy in love[21] are among the noblest ever written by Chaucer.

Pandarus teaches by precept, Troilus by example. Love gives Troilus fresh beauty:

ech him lovede that loked on his face.[22]

Love made him a knight second only to Hector[23] and made him have compassion on all in distress,[24] and even to spare the 'smale bestes' when he was hunting.[25] When Chaucer had finished the reading of the third book it must have seemed that he had composed a conventional didactic *roman courtois* with the conventional happy ending:

> And Troilus in luste and in quiete
> Is with Criseyde his owne herte swete.[26]

Yet Troilus had a deeper lesson to teach than 'cortaysie'. The joy in the third book is an essential part of Boethian tragedy: inevitably there is a turn in fortune's wheel. Criseyde is sent to join her father in the Greek camp and because she is separated from Troilus betrays him with Diomed: she is 'with women fewe among the Grekes stronge'.[27]

The plot of *Troilus and Criseyde* is based on the romance of *Il Filostrato* written by the young Boccaccio at the Naples court. But the *Filostrato* was a brutal and flippant story told to illustrate the fickleness of women; Chaucer's Criseyde is not fickle, it is only that she is afraid and in her weakness turns to Diomed to be 'the wall of steel' that Troilus had been to her in Troy. She is always weak and lovable and alive. Chaucer had achieved not only a courtesy book and a Boethian tragedy but the first great novel that has survived in European literature.[28]

The *Troilus* was designed to be either read or sung and the audience for which it was intended was probably far wider than the court; that may have been why it was dedicated to Gower and Strode and not to any noble patron. It treated of courtly manners but the love it dealt with was all earthly love.

The difference between courtly love and all other forms of loving is the subject for *The Parlement of Foules*. This is perhaps later than the *Troilus* and Troilus is referred to in it.[29] It has long been recognized as a court poem for St Valentine's day. There have been attempts to link it with King Richard's betrothal or marriage, but there is no betrothal or marriage in the poem; the heroine, the 'formel eagle', is still left undecided in her choice. It deals with love, not marriage, and though it is quite possible that it is a *roman à clef* there is no reason why the royal eagle should be a king; it would be sufficient if he ranked as of royal blood. He is distinguished from the two other tercel eagles, his rivals, because he is the worthiest knight; because he has practised knighthood longest; because he has most estate and the 'gentilest blode'.[30] These are not phrases that would be applied to the sovereign, but they would be suitable enough for one of the Hollands; especially perhaps for Richard's half-brother John Holland, Earl of Huntingdon and Duke of Exeter, who is stated to have been the hero of the *Compleynt of Mars*; at least he was the most experienced knight among the royal kin.

Venus is described as being in the north-north-west[31] and Dr Manly argued from astronomy that the poem was written in 1374, 1382, or 1390. If the argument is valid, 1390 would seem the more probable: there is an obvious influence from Boccaccio's *Teseide* that makes 1374 seem too early, while in 1382 the new court was only beginning to function.

Perhaps because it is so much a poem for the court, Chaucer seems conventionally class conscious. The 'tercels' and the 'turtel' expound courtly love precisely because they are eagles and a turtle dove.

> Now God forbede a lover shulde chaunge
> The turtel seyde and wex for shame al reed
> Thogh that his lady ever more be straunge
> Yet let him serve hir ever, til he be deed.[32]

The goose and the duck provide the commonsense reaction of the bourgeoisie:

> I seye I rede him though he were my brother
> But she wol love lat him love another[33]

and the reflection that there are more stars in heaven than a pair.[34]

An eagle answers

> Thy kind is of so lowe a wrechednesse
> That what love is thou canst nat see ne gesse.[35]

Perhaps about this time Chaucer was writing *Palamon and Arcite*[36] which survives as the *Knight's Tale*; here too there is dependence on the *Teseide*. But as with the *Filostrato* in the

Troilus, the *Teseide* is medievalized by Chaucer.[37] *Palamon and Arcite* belongs to the literary genre of a metrical romance: it begins with a conflict of loyalties between the claims of friendship and cousinage and those of love,[38] and it is a story of romantic love and adventure with much fighting, a tournament and the happy ending that convention demanded.

> And thus with alle blisse and melodye
> Hath Palamon y wedded Emelye.

It contains some of Chaucer's greatest lines,[39] a vivid description of court life[40] and a number of court allusions:

> She gadereth floures party whyte and rede
> To make a sotil gerland for hir hede[41]

—white and red; King Richard's livery colours. And through all these there is the sound of the turning of fortune's wheel—each man has the destiny that is shaped for him.

It was perhaps soon after this that Chaucer wrote the *Legend of Good Women* with its reference to *Palamon and Arcite*.[42] I would agree with those who hold that text B is clearly the earlier of its two versions and very tentatively I would place this as possibly about 1391.

Such a sequence leaves the ballades and the *Canterbury Tales* unaccounted for. It is likely that Chaucer wrote ballades most of his life and that only a few of them have survived. Some can be placed fairly safely in the last years of Richard II, such as the ballade on Marriage with its reference to the Wife of Bath. The triple roundel on Mercyless Beauty seems an elderly man's poem ('Sin I fro love escaped am so fat'); and so does the Ballade to Rosemounde in which Chaucer compares himself to a pike 'walwed in galauntyne', a large coarse fish in aspic. There is a lament on old age in the *Compleynt of Venus*.[43]

After the autumn of 1391 Chaucer was dependent for patronage on his verse alone. It is likely that the royal gifts of 1394 and 1398 have some relation to particular poems, and it is not impossible that they were connected with the gradual development of the *Canterbury Tales*. The tales seem to belong to quite different periods and often Chaucer was re-using old material in a new framework. Too much ingenuity has been expended in seeking for an over-all pattern. The *Second Nun's Tale,* the life of St Cecyle, seems very early work, perhaps as early as 1370. It seems likely that not only *Palamon and Arcite* but *Dorigen and Arviragus,* the story of Griselda, the prose discussion of the Melibeus and the verse treatise on the turn of fortune's wheel had all been written before the *Canterbury Tales* were planned.[44]

This list could very easily be extended, yet there would still remain enough of the *Canterbury Tales* to mark a revolution in literature. There is the *Prologue* in which the stiff tapestry figures of the long familiar ideal priest and ideal knight, with satirized nuns, friars, and monks, suddenly move and come alive; there is the creation of the Wife of Bath, poignant and comic and unprecedented; there is the first parody in English;[45] the grossness of the fabliau is given its first literary form; while in the *Marchante's Tale* Chaucer reached a height of sophisticated irony that has no parallel in medieval Europe.

Sections of the *Canterbury Tales* may have been read at the court and rewarded, but they can never have been limited to a court public. It is significant that while there are only three manuscripts of the *Book of the Duchess* and fourteen of the *Parlement of Foules,* there are over seventy of the *Tales.* Their popularity in the fifteenth century may suggest that they already had a wide vogue, which would also explain why the manuscripts fall so early into eight variant groups. The first public may have lain as much with the London *haute bourgeoisie* as with the court.

Since the *Tales* are so obviously unfinished and unrevised it is likely that Chaucer was working on them until he died. He does not seem to have been ill for very long: in December 1399 he took a long lease of his new tenement at Westminster. But he may have begun dying soon after and this might explain a crux in Chaucer criticism: the meaning of the retractation at the end of the *Parson's Tale.*

The *Parson's Tale* is singularly uncharacteristic of Chaucer: its flat long sentences have nothing in common with the rhythmic prose of the *Boethius* or of the *Melibee*; it is not even characteristic of the Parson, for it is oddly without charity and without trust. It seems to be a rather literal translation of some guide for confessors ultimately derived from the thirteenth-century *Summa Paenitentiae* of Raymond of Pennaforte. It is marked by a fear of Judgement and of 'the grievous malady of death'. It ends with an appeal to Christ, King of Kings, priest over all priests who has bought us with the precious blood of His heart, and with a retractation of all worldly vanities including even the *Book of the Duchesse* and *Troilus*. The attitude to religion and the sense of guilt is so unlike all that is otherwise known of Chaucer that it would be easiest to assume that all the *Parson's Tale* is an interpolation. But whose interest was it to interpolate? And how did it slip so securely into the manuscript stream? If it is not an interpolation it is only intelligible if Chaucer wrote it in 1400 in rough draft when he knew that he was about to die.

VIII

John Gower

Like Geoffrey Chaucer, John Gower would seem to have had a double public, in London and at the Court; as with Chaucer it was probably Gower's Court public that gave him most of his prestige. In the *Kingis Quair* James I of Scotland, who had been bred at the Court of Henry IV, wrote of 'My Maisteris dere Gowere and Chaucere that on the steppis satt of rethorike quhill thai were lyvand here superlative as poetis laureate'.[1]

But unlike Chaucer, Usk, Hoccleve and Lydgate, Gower was of independent standing. This is rather well conveyed by John Stow's description of his tomb at Southwark. 'He lieth under a tomb of stone with his image also of stone over him, the hair of his head, auburn long to his shoulders but curling and a small forked beard. On his head a chaplet like a coronet of four roses, a habit of purple damasked to his feet, a collar of esses gold about his neck. . . . His arms a field argent on a chevron azure three leopards heads gold their tongues gules.'[2] A similar impression is left by John Gower's will. He had founded a chantry in Southwark and made bequests to London hospitals and churches but he left his wife the rental from two manors as well as a hundred pounds and a quantity of silver ware.[3]

It is precisely because he was in no need of grants or annuities that Gower's life is so difficult to trace. It seems clear that he was related to Sir Robert Gower of Kentwell in Suffolk, who married Margaret Mowbray; perhaps he was a nephew and thought himself in some fashion Sir Robert's representative, for he is found re-purchasing Sir Robert's lands. But his frequent land purchases seem to have been a form of capital investment: he bought the manors of Multon in Suffolk and Feltwell in Norfolk on August the 1st, 1382, and on August the 6th he leased them for his life in return for an annual rent of £40 to be paid to him at Westminster. In the 1390s he had his lodgings in Southwark close to St Mary Overys. Possibly all his life had been spent in London or its suburbs. Perhaps he was living on a small legal fortune invested partly in land and partly in the wool trade; he may have been the son of the Gower who was a prominent lawyer in the 1350s. It is unlikely that he was born much before 1340 since he married in 1398 and was writing so vigorously after 1400. It is unlikely that he was born very much later, since he was already investing money in land in 1368. His will was proved on October the 24th, 1408.

It would be easy to place John Gower in the new literary movements of the late fourteenth century if only his *Cinkante Balades* and his *Confessio Amantis* are analysed. But his *Mirour* and his *Vox Clamantis* seem to belong to two different traditions. Perhaps the differences are partly due to three publics: the court, the London merchants and learned men.

The *Cinkante Balades*[4] have survived in a single manuscript of some elegance. It is noted on it that it was presented to Henry IV on his coronation. A dedicatory balade to the King states that the poems have been written as a court entertainment (*'Por desporter vo noble Court roial'*).

It seems likely that John Gower began as a lyric poet. In the *Mirour*[5] he writes that previously he had surrendered himself to mad delight and to vain joy, that he had dressed lavishly and made love songs which he sang while he danced. In the *Confessio Amantis* he writes that he had often made 'rondeal balade and virelai' and sung them in hall and chamber.[6] It is too often ignored that he was a lyric poet of power and of originality.

The *Cinkante Balades* are at times beautiful,[7] and they never seem to be derivative. They are composed in the new fashion prized at the Valois Court; metrically Gower is close to Deschamps. There are echoes from contemporary French verses[8] but, unlike Chaucer's translated poems, they are never derived from them. There are many parallels to twelfth-century provençal lyrics; but then the medieval phrases on romantic love were first minted in twelfth-century Provence. Romantic love is the subject of each Balade. Eight times this is termed 'fyn amour'—lasting

[75]

unselfish courtly love as opposed to the transient lusts of 'amour fol'. It is conceived as being compatible with marriage but the fact of marriage is irrelevant to it.

It is this 'fyn amour' which is the central theme in the *Confessio Amantis*. In its first version this is a court poem dedicated to Richard II. In its Prologue Gower states that Richard had invited him on to the royal barge on the Thames and charged him by his loyalty that he should write 'som newe thing'.[9] Later in the Prologue Gower emphasizes that he hopes to merit the King's thanks and could not have been excused if he had failed to obey.[10] The final dedication is to

> Richard by name the secounde
> In whom hath evere yit be founde
> Justice medled with pite
> Largesce forth with Charite.[11]

The description of the Company of Lovers is an idealized court scene; the garlands 'some of the leaf some of the flower', the great pearls and the new 'guise of Beawme'.[12] Beawme is Bohemia.

It seems established that the first version of the *Confessio Amantis* was completed in 1390.[13] Possibly it was begun as early as 1385. As it has survived in eleven manuscripts and is the basis of twenty more, it is likely this is the version current throughout Richard's reign. It is clear that Gower had another patron besides the King. Eight of the manuscripts contain two lines of Latin verse: 'Go chaste book to the Count of Derby, who is cherished by those well skilled in praise, rest your future upon him.' Henry of Bolingbroke, Earl of Derby, came back to England in the summer of 1393 and that autumn Gower accepted his livery and joined his household—at least that would be my interpretation of the entry in Henry's accounts for a collar for the 'esquier' John Gower.[14] A new version of the *Confessio* was prepared in which there was no reference to Richard and instead there are the lines

> I sende unto myn oghne lord
> Which of Lancastre is Henri named.

13   Thomas Hoccleve and Henry Prince of Wales.
British Museum Arundel MS.38, frontispiece.

Confessus Gemo si sit medicina sub
Omne morbis quos tulit ipsa Venus

14   The Lover making his confession.
From the *Confessio Amantis* of John Gower.
Bodley MS.294, f.9.

15 Chaucer reading *Troilus and Criseyde*.
Corpus Christi College, Cambridge, MS.61, f.1 v.

16 Venice.
From *Li Livre du Grant Caam*, Bodley MS.264, f.218.

This was not necessarily a new publication; it may have been written only on the presentation copy to a new lord which still seems to survive in a manuscript de luxe in the Huntingdon library.[15] Naturally after Henry's accession it would become the exemplar for a new family of manuscripts.

If Gower's first patrons were in the court circle his public was far wider than the court. There are forty-nine manuscripts of the *Confessio Amantis,* and it was translated into Portuguese and Castilian.

The attraction of the *Confessio Amantis* may have lain in its novelty of architecture and style. It should I think be read as an autobiography. John Gower, then about fifty, is the lover who is becoming old. He remembers the time when he danced as lightly as a roe, the futile jealousies of other lovers, the moments of envy and malice, the hours he had spent with his lady, reading her Troilus, or playing dice or watching her dance. He knows that he has been unfaithful to others but not to her. Cupid has left him wounded and Venus tells him to make confession to her priest of the sins against her law. There follows, through question and answer, an exposition of the Seven Deadly Sins, their servants and their remedies, illustrated by many stories and broken by many digressions. And in the end Gower is shriven and, looking at a mirror, sees his wrinkled skin and his bleared eyes. He knows that Cupid has passed him by because he is too old. The Green Tree has withered. There is chill ointment for his wounded heart and Venus gives him a rosary of black and gold inscribed 'To Rest' ('*Por Reposer*').

The framework is novel precisely because the *Confessio Amantis* is not an allegory and since it is more than a sustained metaphor. It is a recital of facts to be understood in their literal sense and illustrated by allegorical figures and the use of symbol. It is odd how far away it is from either version of the *Romaunt of the Rose.* Its contents were novel since they were a great sequence of stories forming part of a single plot and possessing an over-riding unity. The stories often branch into disquisitions, but this provided the instruction which so many medieval publics appreciated.

The style had no precedent and no immediate succession. It may represent court English[16] but if so it is court English as it was spoken not as it was sung. Dante would have recognized it as a *volgare illustre* for it is a polished, too polished, vernacular; but it is antithetic to the 'aureate' golden lines that Lydgate learned from Chaucer. If Thomas Usk foreshadowed the Euphuists, John Gower foreshadowed the Augustans—and at times, much more surprisingly, Jane Austen.

His concise restraint can give his English a chiselled strength. When Gower is asked by his confessor whether he had ever attempted to rape his mistress he answers

> Certes fader no
> For I mi ladi love so.[17]

When he wishes to convey the sense of Judgement he writes

> That dai mai no consail availe
> The Pledour and the plee schal faile.

But of course such strength is not sustained.

Gower was more than an English poet; he came of a bilingual culture and he wrote too easily in three languages. Perhaps shortly before 1398 when he married Agnes Groundolf he composed a treatise for married lovers: *Traitie selonc les autours pour essampler les Amants Marietz.*[18] This is a sequence of eighteen French balades, technically accomplished and heavy with the classical allusions that Othon de Granson had made so fashionable. The ideal marriage is that of a loyal friend with a loyal friend ('*Loiale amie avec loial amis*'). Too much space is allotted to adultery and its effects, but this had an appeal in devout circles; in about 1407 it was translated into English as a treatise against 'avoutrie'.

In contrast to all this there is the *Mirour de l'Omme*, a very different French poem which at first reading suggests a quite different personality as its author. The only manuscript that has survived is anonymous, yet it is clearly by the same author as the *Vox Clamantis*, which is certainly by John Gower. Besides, in the first version of the *Confessio* Gower refers to an earlier work of his as the 'Speculum Hominis'.

The *Mirour* belongs to a familiar fourteenth-century genre, a Complaint against the Three Estates of the Realm, or treatise on the iniquities of the times. It is written very consciously by a Londoner and was perhaps addressed to a group of devout merchants connected with the Wool Staple: there are forty-eight lines written to the glory of wool;[19] wool is a noble lady, she is the goddess of merchants, merchants of all lands seek her with passion, she is born in England. Lawyers are attacked for their low birth and their rapacity. There is much evidence for a nerve-racked distaste of the London Lombards.[20] The standpoint is rigidly anti-clerical and orthodox. The Pope as Pope cannot err,[21] but parish priests, monks, friars and Oxford scholars are sexually profligate. There is much strong invective in the *Mirour* but oddly little poetry. Yet it is certainly a source for the *Canterbury Tales*[22] and has some relation to the *Vision of Piers Plowman*. It was finished after 1378, since there is a reference to the Great Schism,[23] and probably after 1381, for there is a clear prophecy of the Peasants' Rising[24] and medieval prophecies are normally after the event.

The *Vox Clamantis* grew slowly between 1385 and 1402. In its final form it is dedicated to Thomas Arundel, Archbishop of Canterbury. Since it is written in Latin and in classical metre it must always have been intended for a public of learned men. It is itself elaborately learned; at times it is a pastiche from Ovid. Of the 2150 lines of the first book of the *Vox*, 247 are taken from seven of Ovid's poems.[25] Yet the background of the first book of the *Vox* is the second book of the *Aeneid*. He begins a disquisition[26] on kingship with a tag from Horace: '*Plectuntur Achivi*'. He knew his Livy well. He delighted in the genealogies of Gods and heroes. He tells an anecdote of Dante, the poet of Italy.[27] He had absorbed Brunetto Latini. He had in fact precisely the kind of erudition that might be expected from a learned poet in the court circles of late fourteenth-century Europe.[28]

Only he had so much more as well. He had a mass of old-fashioned English knowledge. It is natural that he should use the Dominican Nicholas Trivet as a source for his stories; Chaucer had done so too. But it is odd that he should rely so much on twelfth-century writers: on Nigel Wireker and Alexander Neckham; on Eustace of Kent and John of Salisbury. And there is much that is thirteenth-century in the certitudes of John Gower. In the *Mirour* he cites Master Aristotle 'the good clerk'.²⁹ He knew either at first or second hand Aquinas and Albert the Great. In the *Vox Clamantis* he incorporates passages from the *Pantheon* of Godfrey of Viterbo and from the *Aurora* of Peter Riga, handbooks that had been popular for two centuries. St Gregory the Great is a recurrent influence.

This second kind of knowledge is precisely that which he shared with William Langland; Gower knew in depth what Langland knew. This may explain a similarity in central themes between the *Vox Clamantis* and the *Vision of Piers Plowman*.

For Gower 'the beast called man' shares something in common with every form of God's creation; he exists like the stones, he has life like the trees, he has sensations like the animals, he understands like the angels.³⁰ In consequence he is 'the mirror of the world'.³¹ But alone in creation he retains the power of choice; angels and demons have already chosen for ever. Because all nature is linked with him the rhythm of nature is broken when he falls. There is the same concept in the C version of the *Vision of Piers Plowman*.³² 'Neither the sea nor the sand nor the seed yieldeth as they were wont in whom is the fault.' Man falls when he acts against reason for then he is no longer like the angels but only like the beasts. He acts against reason when he acts against justice since equity is reason made manifest. He acts against justice when he extorts that which is not his due. This is to become Gower's charge against Richard.

Like the *Vision of Piers Plowman*, the *Vox Clamantis* is conceived as the work of a prophet. It is the voice of one crying in the wilderness 'Make straight the path of the Lord'. But it is also the voice of the people clamouring that the common good was being destroyed by the lust for unlawful gain. It could be both, since in this case the voice of the people was the voice of God: '*Vox populi cum voce Dei concordat*'.³³ Gower, too, begins with a vision and enforces his teaching through long sustained metaphors. But unlike Langland his thought is never Christocentric, and in consequence there is none of Langland's emphasis on charity as the counterpoise to covetousness. His aim is to tell what happens when private profit is preferred to the common good; evil will come to those who do evil, good to those who do good. It is all very like the pardon that Piers the Plowman tore. There is little room in it for Christ's forgiveness or for the turning of fortune's wheel.

The first book of the *Vox Clamantis* is a vision of the Peasants' Rising in 1381. Through lusting after that which was not their own the peasants had turned into beasts. They had sacked London ('New Troy'); for Troy was without a Hector. In the books that follow Gower writes of the putrefaction of the other estates and closes with the 'Epistula', a letter to Richard II, which in its unrevised form could have been written by a moderate old-fashioned royalist with a strong distrust for the King's advisers. It is likely that the *Vox* was first made public about 1385. It was completed and revised between 1399 and 1402, for the Epistula is changed into an attack on Richard and his counsellors and the 'Cronica' are added dealing with the crises of 1387, 1397 and 1399. This is often in the form of an allegory in which heraldic emblems represent the men who bore them, like the Swan who is Thomas of Woodstock, the Northern Moon who is the Earl of Northumberland; and the Shadowy One who bore the Sun is Richard, who at last starves himself to death in despair. As a version of contemporary history it should have been very acceptable to Henry IV.

For the last eight years of his life John Gower was closely associated with King Henry's court. He was styled 'the King's esquire' when he received an annual grant of two pipes of Gascon wine on November the 21st, 1399. He dedicated French and English and Latin poems to Henry and called himself his 'oratour'.

But though Gower had had a public both in London and at the court it is unlikely that he conceived himself as a courtier and certain that he did not consider himself a bourgeois. He was consciously independent and individual. He was not only individual but novel in the depth of his human tenderness and in the loathing for war that sprung from it.

The day is goon, the night is dark and fade

.   .   .   .

The blod is schad which no man mai restore.34

Three poets of great originality were writing in London towards the end of the fourteenth century, Chaucer and Gower and Langland. It is customary to compare Gower with Chaucer but at least in his *Mirour* and in his *Vox Clamantis* he has far more in common with Langland.

Chaucer was a courtier and a diplomat writing primarily for that new sophisticated court circle in which he was himself established. It was a small world in itself, paralleled by the Valois court at Paris and the forerunner of that of Burgundy. Political manœuvres and cataclysms, disgrace and violent death occurred within it, but it seemed sheltered from the world without. By 1390 perhaps the fact about the Peasants' Rising most clearly remembered among the privileged was that it had failed so utterly. The figures of that world without could be seen moving as in the *Canterbury Tales*; they could be studied minutely with a profound and pleasured understanding and with secure detachment. There is much tenderness and much irony in the subtle nuances of the world that Chaucer knew. There is no horror. Nor is there a sense of guilt and evil until that strange afterthought, the *Parson's Tale*. But both in Gower and in Langland the purpose is primarily didactic and the moral values are simple, unchanging and contrasted like black on white or blood upon the snow. Horror alternates with beauty. There is corporate guilt and individual evil. England is conceived as a commune, the *Communitas Regni*, now grown sterile and frustrated because the rhythm of justice and equity which alone brings a commune into being had been broken.

Now faileth the folk of the flood: and the folk of the land
Shepherd and shipman: and so do the tillers
No more can they ken: the course of the seasons.35

IX

'Piers Plowman'

It has often been stated that the C Text of the *Vision of Piers Plowman* was composed during the last years of Richard II. Dr Skeat found references in it to the King's quarrel with the rich men of London in 1392 and to the use of his London 'Lombards', the Alberti; Professor Jusserand found a reference to the Shrewsbury Parliament in 1398; the dating 1398 to 1399 was supported tentatively by Professor Manly; Professor Coghill once found reason to suggest a date after 1394. None of these arguments seems conclusive though they should not be ignored.

Against this it has been urged that the C Text was cited before 1387 by Thomas Usk in his *Testament of Love*. The evidence for this too is inconclusive. There are three parallel sentences,[1] but when Usk writes that it is better to die than to live falsely; that when a man weens his own wit more excellent than others he scorns all manner of devices except his own; and even that the Tree of Charity is rooted in the heart; it is possible that he is quoting from a common stock of aphorisms rather than from the C Text. At the most these parallels would suggest that some variants now in the C Text were already current by 1387.[2]

Versions of the *Vision of Piers Plowman* have survived in fifty-five[3] manuscripts; it must have possessed the popularity of ballad literature and many of the variants in text and shape may be due to the fact that they had been transmitted through recitation. Though the main versions are commonly grouped under the headings of A, B, and C, textually this is rather an artificial classification; the three groupings remain abnormally fluid and sporadically they interpenetrate each other. Yet it seems clear that some text underlying A was the first draft of the poem, that it was logically continued in the text that underlies B and that C is based[4] on the final recension. In spite of so many ingenious attempts at exact dating all that can be held with safety is that all the versions seem to have been completed before 1399; that in some form the vision was current before 1381; that the B version seems to suggest the political climate of Richard's early minority and the C version that of Richard's personal rule.

Clearly there have been many alterations and some deliberate interpolations but it is simplest to believe that in the main all these texts have ultimately a single author;[5] for there is so vivid a contrast between them and all similar poems of a similar period—*Wynnere and Wastoure,* the *Jacke Uplande* series, *Mum and the Soothsegger, Pierce Ploughman's crede.* It seems probable from many of the texts that this author was named William.[6] There is some fifteenth-century evidence that he was named William Langland.[7] There is a statement of the same period that he was the son of Eustace de Rokayle of Shipton-under-Wychwood.[8] He was a clerk—according to medieval categories the *Vision of Piers Plowman* is essentially a learned poem—but if he was an academic he belonged to the academic proletariat. He gives details of his life in London, the hovel he shared in Cornhill with his wife and his chance work in the city chantries.

> The looms that I labour will my livelihood to earn
> Is the pater noster and my primer: Placebo and Dirige
> And my psalter sometime: and my seven psalms
> That I say for the souls: of such as me help
> And those that find me my food: vouchsafe I trow
> To welcome me when I come: otherwhiles in a month
> Now with him now with her: and this way I beg
> Without bag or bottle: but my belly only.[9]

Some of this may be in the literary convention of self-caricature that Chaucer used, but Langland's life was obscure enough; no contemporary refers to him and there is no reference in any document. The fate of his text suggests how slight was his prestige. No other poem of its rank has ever been so corrupted in manuscript transmission.

In his critical edition of the A text[10] Professor Kane has noted: 'Recension is not a practicable method for the editor of

17   The Tree of Jesse.
Alabaster in the Victoria and Albert Museum, London.

18 The Deposition from the Cross.
An ivory in the Victoria and Albert Museum, London.

the A manuscript, nor is the creation of hierarchy with some one copy elevated to a role of authority: while some of the manuscripts are certainly more corrupt than others all are corrupt to an indeterminate but evidently considerable extent.' Yet of the three versions the A text seems closest to an underlying original and the C Text the most distant. It would seem to be established that the poem that underlies C is by the same writer as that which underlies A, for there are original passages in it which could be by no other poet. But the C Text contains many citations from A and B in which the sense has been mutilated by the choice of an easy reading instead of a difficult one[11] and this is most easily explained by a scribe's revision. It is inconceivable that any text of Chaucer or Gower would have met with such treatment.

It seems likely that the variants in the manuscripts are due not only to alterations by scribes but to adaptations by minstrels. This has been queried by Professor Kane, but he lists the characteristics of oral transmission in Middle English Texts— 'compression at one point and expansion at another, dislocations of matter other than palaeographic, large omissions evidently made for abridgement or from defect of memory and marked unevenness in the accuracy of reproduction'. These seem to be precisely the notes of the corpus of Piers Plowman MSS. The reciter would naturally adapt his recitation to his audience. This would explain such alternatives as 'Wynchelsey' for 'Wynchestre'; the sudden reference to a 'Malwicke Strete'; the alternating names of trades; and above all the odd omissions —the changing of Pope into the less explicit 'clerk' or 'bishop', of monks and minstrels into minstrels and messengers, the erasure of 'Freris', the disappearance of an occasional grossness, and of a reference to the expropriation of monastic land. The tastes of an individual audience helped to shape the text of all vernacular verse in an age of recitation.

The variant readings seem to suggest two publics for the *Vision of Piers Plowman*: the devout middle class in London and in towns to the south and west; and the occasional religious house, serious-minded parish priest and devout landowner.

This seems supported by the history of the manuscripts in the fifteenth century.

It is obvious that Piers Plowman had an especial appeal in middle-class circles sympathetic with Lollardy.[12] This is shown by its influence on four Lollard tracts.[13] Yet the doctrine in the *Vision of Piers Plowman* is old-fashioned and orthodox and it is clear that the poem was also current in a right wing conservative milieu. This can be tested by an analysis of the manuscripts of the A text. The MS. belonging to the Society of Antiquaries was compiled about 1425 for a parish priest of conservative views, for it includes besides the *Vision* a manual on confession, a 'penitentiale' and instructions to the clergy on the application of ecclesiastical censures. Harley MS. 6041 was owned in the fifteenth century by the Benedictines of St Augustine's at Canterbury and then by William Hollyngborne, their Abbot's Chaplain. Dr M. R. James suggested that the Trinity College Cambridge MS. had once been in the possession of the Benedictines at Christ Church. The Lincoln's Inn MS. seems to me merely a common form of minstrels' repertory book; still, according to Miss Barnicle's hypothesis it comes from Wenlock Priory. Harley MS. 3954 was compiled in an anti-Lollard milieu; the *Vision* is added to *The Merit of hearing Mass*, *The Virtue of the Mass* and *The Seven Sacraments*. Dr Skeat has information that the Ingilby MS. now in the Pierpont Morgan Library had been in the possession of the Cistercians at Fountains. Digby MS. 145 in the Bodleian was copied in his own hand by Sir Adrian Fortescue of Stonor; he was a 'confrater' of the Oxford Black-friars and a knight of St John of Jerusalem. This accounts for seven manuscripts out of a total of seventeen.

The *Vision of Piers Plowman* is too scholastic to have appealed to a popular audience except when only sections were recited. Langland seems familiar with a London that even Hoccleve never mentions—'a ribibor, a ratoner, a raker of chepe',[14] (that is, a rebab player, a rat catcher and a Cheapside scavenger)—but he must have been trained in the schools, possibly at Oxford. He writes in the university categories of the 'quaestio', the 'distinctio' and the 'quodlibet' and their key words—'whether'

('*utrum*'), 'but against this' (*sed contra*)—echo in his vernacular.
He has some familiarity with Ockham's logic and possessed a
knowledge of the Fathers which could include quotations from
St Ambrose, St Augustine, St Gregory the Great, and St John
Damascene.

With such qualifications it should have been easy for Langland to establish himself in late fourteenth-century England had
he been a priest or found a patron. It was perhaps his marriage
that had made priesthood impossible and his personality that
prevented him from becoming some rich man's dependant. For
Langland was essentially a prophet: *Piers Plowman* combines
three distinct literary genres—the vision, the debate, and the
encyclopaedic satire[15]—but like the *Vox Clamantis* it is the voice
of one crying in the wilderness. Its message is not the Way to
Salvation but the Way to Perfection; perhaps because man can
only be saved by trying to become perfect.

In spite of corrupt, interpolated and possibly dislocated
texts, the plan of the *Vision of Piers Plowman* becomes intelligible
when Langland's conceptions of justice and charity are analysed.

Justice is the unswerving determination to give to each man
that which is his due,[16] a definition that the jurists had transmitted to Christianity from the Roman past. This is presupposed
throughout the *Vision* and is summed up in Christ's message
'render what you owe'. It is characteristically medieval that all
social problems should be phrased in terms of law, and to
Langland, as to John of Salisbury, law is not law unless it is the
voice of equity. Injustice is equity violated, and therefore a
blinding of that right reason which lies in the very nature of
created things:

> In sooth I saw reason ruling all beasts
> Save man and his mate and therefore I wondered.[17]

For within man there is a force that drives him to snatch from
others that which is their due; it is covetousness ('covetize'),
the desire for undeserved meed.

All the people have gathered to the wedding feast of Lady

Meed and False who hold the lordship of the seven deadly sins. For in the Community of the Realm the lust for Meed has become a common poison. 'Monks and minstrels are among her lovers, landless men and lepers in hedges. She is with the sheriffs that rule the shires.'[18] Men do evil knowing that it is evil; within them is Conscience, the Constable of God, preaching to them with the Cross; and in the fifth stage of the *Vision* all the Deadly Sins confess themselves and cry forgiveness. Yet the Pardon that St Truth has taught Piers Plowman cannot save them, for it is the sentence of the Athanasian Creed that only those who do good enter eternal life and those who do evil go to eternal fire. Piers tears the Pardon; without God's mercy it is not a pardon but a condemnation; even the just man falls seven times a day.

There is only one force strong enough to preserve justice among men and that is charity. Charity is the love of others as well as the love of God. It is the motive force of justice, as covetousness is that of injustice, for it is fired with the desire to give to the other that which is his due. This again was a patristic commonplace learnt through St Ambrose from Lactantius, but Langland brings it to a novel conclusion. If charity is the cause of justice, each man's due will be determined not only by his merits but by his need: 'Blessed be Piers Plowman who toileth to till alike for the wastrel and the wench of the stews.'[19] Charity is the champion who saves the sinner from drowning. Mercy and justice are fused through the charity of man just as they are one in the charity of God; human sins are quenched as completely by the divine compassion as the sparks from London chimneys that fall into the Thames. '*Deus Caritas est*' and therefore charity alone can give light and life to every other virtue.

> For though you be true of your tongue and earn truly
> And chaste as a child that weepeth in church
> Unless you love loyally and give in goodly fashion
> You have no more merit in Mass nor in Hours
> Than Malkin of her maidenhead: that no man desireth.
> Chastity without charity: lies chained in Hell
> It is a lamp with no light in it.[20]

It is the effects of the death of charity that lead to the filth, the horror and the stench of the London Langland knew. The preacher comes back from St Paul's Cross to gorge among the starving frozen poor.[21] The rich men feast on their dais with much edifying discourse, 'gnawing God in their gullets while their guts are full';[22] while beggars outside are being hued from their gates like hounds. The wrongs that are done are done to Christ Himself, for whatever is done to others is done to Him; many a man has met God among the poor and hungry 'in the apparel of a poor man and in a pilgrim's likeness'. Perhaps as in so many medieval legends this is an echo of Martin's meeting with the beggar. Only in Langland's experience Martin more often refused to share his cloak. 'Piers the Plowman' was painted all bloody, and came in with his cross before the common people, 'like in all limbs: to Our Lord Jesus'.

Since the evil of injustices lies in having filched from others that which is their due, injustice is naturally most apparent among the respected, the learned and the rich.[23]

> God is much in the gorge: of these great masters
> But among mean men: are his mercy and works.[24]

> Cobblers and tailors: and such lewd jots
> Pierce with a Pater Noster: the Palace of Heaven.[25]

Yet of himself Charity as much as Lady Meed can live in every group in the 'Commune'.

> I have seen him in silk: and also in russet
> In gray and in fur; and in gilt armour
> And gladly he gave: to all men that needed.[26]

But where he lives cannot be judged by pious discourse: 'He is the merriest of mouth: where he sitteth at meat. The love that lieth in his heart: maketh him light of speech. He is companionable and comfortable: as Christ Himself, God's champion and gentle as a good child.'

Wherever Charity may live he lives in three forms or grades. In the ninth article of the twenty-fourth question of the Secunda

Secundae of his *Summa,* Aquinas states that it is fitting to distinguish three degrees of charity: beginning, progress and perfection ('*Caritas incipiens et proficiens et perfecta*'). This is a common division among medieval scholastics and is derived ultimately from the saying of Augustine in his commentary on the first epistle of St John: 'As soon as charity is born it takes food, after taking food it waxes strong and when it is become strong it is perfected.' In the *Vision of Piers Plowman, Caritas incipiens, proficiens* and *perfecta* are seen in action as Do Wel, Do Bet and Do Best; Piers the Plowman, Piers the Teacher, Piers the Builder of the Barn.

The quest for perfection is the quest for perfect charity, and, as Aquinas teaches, when perfect charity is reached the gifts of the Holy Ghost become dominant over the Virtues. In the *Vision* the Holy Ghost is dominant in Do Best, just as Do Bet is marked by the readiness to suffer and Do Wel by the pursuit of the active virtues.

All three crown Christ, who through Charity has come 'to joust in Piers armour, in his helm and his habergeon humana natura'[27] in order to give to each man that which was his need. Charity is the Good Samaritan sitting on his mule, who stays to heal the wounded man whom Hope and Faith had left, and the incarnation is an act of personal love. 'For I that am Lord of Life: Love is my drink. And that drink today: I died upon earth. And I will drink of no deep ditch: and of no deep learning. But of the common cup: of all christian souls'; 'sitio'.[28]

'I thirst' (*sitio*); all the dreams in the *Vision of Piers Plowman* seem dominated by the realization of a double thirst: The thirst for Meed that leads blindly to violated justice and to a sterile anarchy of oppression; and the thirst of love which leads back to equity and unity, to the single Barn of the christian people and to the brotherhood of a common debt.

> For all we are Christ's creatures: and of His coffers rich
> And brethren of one blood: alike beggars and earls.[29]

Between these two desires there is a necessary conflict. For both there are quick but not lasting victories. The Vision of the harrowing of Hell, when Lucifer himself is blinded by the light of redemptive love, is balanced by the Vision of the coming of Anti-Christ when all the religious of the convent come out to greet him with their crosses.

It is perhaps a mark of the poem's realism that it ends leaving the issue still undecided.

X

Provincial Art

At least in the version that underlies the C Text, the *Vision of Piers Plowman* is contemporary with the new court culture but it is quite remote from it. It has no parallels among the work of the court miniaturists; Herman Scheere illustrated Gower, he could have illustrated Chaucer, he could never have illustrated Langland. Yet there are resemblances between the *Vision* and some of the few provincial panels that survive and some of the broken fragments of country wall paintings: the gross and detailed personification of the Deadly Sins, the meeting of the Living and the Dead, the sudden triumph of the rising Christ, the immediate threat of Hell's Mouth.

There must have been much panel-painting in England unaffected by court fashions. By accident ten oak panels of this period survived at Norwich: two, found in a cottage there in Huby's Yard, are now in the FitzWilliam Museum at Cambridge; three are in the church of St Michael-at-Plea; five are in the Cathedral, forming a retable 8 ft 6 in. long and 3 ft high. All seem from the same workshop, it could be that of Thomas of Ocle who was a painter at Norwich in 1388. The back of the retable bears the arms of Henry Despencer who was Bishop of Norwich from 1378 to 1407, and of five knightly families of the Shire.[1] The figure-work seems to be stylized with thin bodies and square heads; the dominant colours are blue-green, green-blue and purple-red. It is strong harsh painting with an element of fantasy in the contemporary dress, and occasionally a crafty brutality in the faces. All these details recur in the Lee of Fareham Crucifixion, a crowded crucifixion scene against a dull blue background in which the dominating figure is not Christ bu tthe centurion Longinus. But this must be a generation later than the Norwich panels and Hanseatic influences on it are much more marked.

The influence of North German Hanse painting on the Norwich school is intelligible if the school represented established burgess art, in spite of the knightly shields behind the Cathedral retable. The Hamburg and Lübeck Hanse merchants had houses at King's Lynn and Hull. It has been shown that a number of brasses of wealthy fourteenth-century East Anglian merchants were made in East Prussia: Robert Braunche who died at Lynn in 1364 was buried under a brass 5 ft 1 in. broad, 8 ft 10 in. long which came from the same workshop as that of Albrecht Hovener at Stralsund. It would be natural if the aesthetic standards of East Anglian and Hanse merchants gradually tended to coincide. In the museum at Stockholm I have noted a panel of Christ surrounded by the implements of the Passion which I would place as early fifteenth-century East Anglian. The Hanseatic influence is very obvious especially on the St Catherine of Alexandria who stands leaning on her wheel beside Christ; perhaps that was why it had an appeal to the Hanse merchant who imported it to some such town as Wisby. There is no evidence for influences passing from the capital to Norfolk but there are indications that influences from Norfolk reached London: all the known associations of John Siferwas are with the south or west, but his roots are in early fourteenth-century East Anglia and his figure-work has a relation to that of the Norwich school.

The Norwich panels survived by chance. Most large towns may have had a painter's workshop that served a public of local ecclesiastics and rich burgesses. In the ceiling of St Helen's Church at Abingdon there are a series of panels 4 ft 9 in. high and 9 in. wide which have been dated between 1390 and 1400. One represents the Annunciation and another the Crucifixion; the rest are single figures of kings and prophets treated monumentally. They are inelegant, unsophisticated and uninspired, but they are the work of a competent well-trained journeyman and two assistants. Presumably these would have come out from Oxford. Such journeymen must have been responsible for many of the English wall-paintings of the late fourteenth century.

There has been much careful and ingenious research on the

fragmentary paintings in fourteenth-century English village churches, but so far there has been no attempt to determine who commissioned them. One group must have been commissioned by the knightly families who were the lords of the manor and presumably the resident lords. This was marked by the use of their own coat of arms and those of associated families and patrons: the Vernons were clearly responsible for the paintings at Clifton Campville which bear their 'Argent a fret sable'; the Lorings placed twenty-one coats of arms in their church at Chalgrove near Dunstable; there are still thirteen shields that are heraldically decipherable in the church at Hailes in Gloucestershire. Again, the arms suggest that the paintings at Bedale in Yorkshire were ordered by a Stapleton who had married a Grey of Rotherfield; there are seven shields at Swinstead in Lincolnshire and at least three at Winterbourne in Gloucestershire. The paintings in this group would reflect the tastes of the patrons and could at times be the work of artists too expensive to be employed by the local miller or parish priest.

The wall-paintings at South Newington in Oxfordshire may be dated by style at about 1340–50. The arms show that they were commissioned by a Gifford who had married a De Mortayne. Among the subjects chosen were a St James and a St Margaret, a martyrdom of St Thomas of Canterbury remarkable for its heraldic detail and a beheading scene which almost certainly represents the execution of Thomas Earl of Lancaster in the spring of 1322. It is reasonable to suppose that St James and St Margaret were the patrons of Gifford and of his wife, that there was some family association with the Earl of Lancaster—perhaps Gifford had been bred in his household—and that the martyrdom of the twelfth-century Thomas had been chosen as a counterpoise to the fourteenth-century execution scene. It is more significant that Gifford was willing to pay two artists of rank to paint his village church. The Master of the St James and of the two beheading scenes may only have come from Oxford but the Master of the St Margaret and of the Virgin suggests the latest mannerisms of the Court. The slender Virgin of South Newington sways westward holding a green-stalked white lily in her left hand; there is a dark red halo behind her long gold hair, her light green cloak is elaborately folded above her pale red tunic. The Christ on her arm holds a red apple in His right hand while with the left he touches His Mother's neck. There are echoes from Siena which might have just reached London by way of Avignon.

Perhaps only a few landowners were ready to spend so much on the decoration of their manor church—the heavily heraldic paintings at Hailes are all in ochre—but it is likely that a knightly patron is presupposed by most of the fragments of fine work that survive, like the broken plaster painted in gold and costly pigments which was found beneath the floor in Milton Regis church and which has been dated about 1390, or the late four-teenth-century sophisticated girl saint with her long hair and purple tunic and blue cloak lined with pink, who is now in the FitzWilliam Museum and came from a church in Cambridgeshire.

It is very rarely that wall-paintings of this group have a didactic purpose. The east wall of Martley church in Worcester-shire is decorated with a rabbit and a deer, a fox and a wolf and grotesques; at Northmoor the Delamores seem to have painted their church primarily as a family chantry. More commonly the heraldry is interspersed with the isolated figures of patron saints.

The evidence for knightly patrons becomes much rarer in the late fourteenth century; it is perhaps at its strongest between about 1310 and about 1365. There are exceptions: at Horley in Oxfordshire St Osyth with her red cloak lined with white and her yellow nimbus has been dated about 1400 and seems to have been commissioned by a donor who bore as his arms 'Gules on a fesse sable a crescent argent'; and the paintings at Willingham in Cambridgshire which may be of the same period because of their representation of the Five Wounds, include a number of almost indecipherable coats of arms; but as a whole knightly patronage seems to have faded with the break-up of so many manorial units.

Perhaps wall-paintings in village churches became in-creasingly a form of peasant art, following no fixed iconographic pattern, often little better than daubs in ochre but at times possessed of a rough vitality. In contrast, especially towards the end of the century, there are long series of carefully planned figures painted in cheap pigments by uninspired but adequate draughtsmen. Usually the purpose of such a series was to teach a moral lesson: between 1390 and 1420 the most popular subjects were the Seven Deadly Sins and the Seven Works of Mercy; occasionally they told the life of a Saint—in this period the most popular narrative was that dealing with St Catherine of Alexandria. There are no heraldic emblems; rather they presuppose designs from a pattern-book. All this would be explained if they were the work of journeymen painters from a nearby town and had been commissioned by the richer men in the village or by some bailiff or parish priest.

It is only my own hypothesis that many wall-paintings in English village churches are a form of peasant art. But scholars may have exercised too much ingenuity in searching for consistent over-all designs among the jumbled fragments. The presence of some recognized iconographic detail cannot prove that the scheme to which it belongs was ever rendered in completion; it could be an isolated reminiscence from the paintings in some other church. Even if a subject has a literary source like the scene of the Three Living and the Three Dead it could have passed through sermon stories into an unlettered peasant milieu. The occasional inscriptions are not in themselves conclusive; they could have been added by the priest. But if my theory should be right it will become increasingly hard not only to decipher but to date some English wall-paintings; European peasant art has always been conservative in its use of motifs and it would be difficult to construct a stylistic sequence. Only a wide range in technical capacity can include the daubs in black and ochre at Edstaton church in Shropshire, the oddly proportioned angels at Purton in Wiltshire and the Hell's Mouth in the north aisle at South Leigh.

Yet none of this has anything in common with the carefully planned and controlled and rather pedestrian series of didactic wall paintings which have been dated between 1390 and 1400. Among the best drawn are those at Hoxne near Eye in Suffolk where a cycle of the seven deadly sins, the seven corporal works of mercy and probably the seven ages of man led inevitably to a Judgement scene. The ages of man would have been a rarity but the contrast between the works of mercy and the deadly sins was in common use in late fourteenth-century England in order to teach the difference between the way of Life and that of Death; there is a close link between such representations and the central themes in the *Vision of Piers Plowman*. This was a contrast taught by the wall paintings in St Nicholas's church at Arundel, at Cranborne in Dorset, at Dalham in Suffolk, at Trotton in Sussex, at Felstead, at Ingatestone and at Kentford; most of these have been dated between 1390 and 1400.

Perhaps these dates are too close, and between 1389 and 1430 might be safer. Details of dress characteristic of the last years of Richard II can only prove the date of the pattern-book from which they were derived and such sketchbooks were probably in use for decades. But at least it is established that it was the most popular form of didactic wall-painting under Richard II and Henry IV. It is harder to explain the appeal of the story of St Catherine of Alexandria of which so many fragments survive and which consisted of a cycle of twenty-five scenes.[2] Still it was crowded with the rather improbable adventures in which the late fourteenth-century public delighted and like the tales of the 'Constance group' it illustrated a woman's constancy. It must have been considered a seemly and inspiring system of decoration and perhaps at times replaced less conventional daubs.

There is need for research on the extent of over-paintings in village churches, for it would be natural if the system of decoration varied in the same church according to the changing social structure of the village. When I was working on the paintings at West Chiltington in Sussex I noticed traces of forceful daubs in ochre above a more sophisticated thirteenth-century cycle that might have been commissioned by a knightly patron. Or again Dr Tristram has recorded[3] that the late fourteenth-century cycle of the life of St Margaret of Antioch at Limpenhoe partially concealed an earlier scene of the Three Living and the Three

[97]

Dead. Such instances can be multiplied but they should be studied in relation to the evidence for the manorial tenure of each particular village.

The reigns of Richard II and of Henry IV coincided with the emergence of a new rural middle class, the 'kulak' peasant, the miller and the reeve who were so often to be the ancestors of the Elizabethan squirearchy. It would be natural if this grouping had come to share that zest for edifying narrative and straight moral teaching which marked the neighbouring burgesses and if they had fetched journeymen from the local town to make their churches seemly. Developments in painting are most easily intelligible as the reflections of changing ideals in a changing social structure.

XI

Social Ideals and the Social Structure

For Langland the 'Commune' means primarily the community of the kingdom conceived as a single organism,[1] living and diseased. It is only on occasion that he uses the term for the common people as opposed to the knighthood and the King.[2] There is the same sense of an over-riding unity in Gower's *Mirour* and in his *Vox Clamantis*. Yet sociologically fourteenth-century England seems deeply divided in standards of conduct and in ideals, in preconceptions and preoccupations.

It is hard to reconstruct the economic history of the last years of Richard II. There is so much evidence and some of it appears to be conflicting, yet it seems clear that at least the south and the north-east were passing through a phase of tangled economic maladjustment. There were sporadic labour shortages and quickly fluctuating rising prices. The breakdown of the manor unit and of the machinery of the manorial courts had synchronized with the growth of a town proletariat among those artisans who could not penetrate within the now top-heavy system of the guilds. All this was aggravated by systems of taxation that were corrupt and clumsy in their application.

At this period little can be known directly of the ideals of the great mass of the people, the unpropertied and the unprivileged, the peasants and the farm servants in the countryside, the poorer artisans there or in the towns. We still possess some catchwords from the Peasants' Rising and a few rude paintings in some village churches. In the Bodleian library there are some fragments of ale-house songs in Rawlinson MS. D 913 and Bodley MS. 692, and from an earlier generation some animal charms and stories in Digby MS. 86.

Yet indirectly it seems possible to pierce through folk-custom, folk-song and recorded folk-feast to a medieval substratum and to find evidence for the existence of a peasant culture in which fertility cults were central, in which pre-Christian beliefs may have survived as well as pre-Christian usages and which would seem to have possessed some continuity with the Stone Age. Digby MS.86 may be as early as the reign of Edward I; it contains a charm to be recited on meeting a hare.[3] On meeting a hare a man must lay his burden on the ground, bless him with the elbow and worship him and recite his names. The hare loses his power when this has been done and said, and the man may go where he wishes. It seems likely enough that the animal stories that survive in literary form came seeping upwards from the medieval peasant culture.

Again, the songs on the Holly and the Ivy seem to be echoes of peasant concepts of man and woman like the much later folk custom in east Kent of the Holly boy and the Ivy girl. Balliol MS. 354 is a commonplace book compiled by Richard Hill, 'Servaunt with Master Wyngar'. It was only begun about 1493 but it contains some fourteenth-century material as well as the most characteristic of all the poems on the Holly and Ivy:

> Holly bereth beris
> Beris rede enough
> Ivy bereth beris
> As blak as any sloe.

Throughout there is a prejudice in favour of the Holly, reinforced by the refrain:

> Nay Nay Ivy
> It may not be I wis
> For Holly must have the mastery
> As the maner is.

It seems tenable that fragments of peasant songs survive, though written down and therefore normalized, in some minstrel's repertory books. 'Maiden in the mor lay, in the mor lay sevenyght ful' is a likely example, which has been preserved by chance in Rawlinson MS. D. 913; in the Bodleian there seem to be many such echoes in MS. Eng. Poet *e.i.* compiled by some fifteenth-century minstrel in the Midlands, and some at least in Douce MS.

19 Bodiam Castle, Sussex.

20   Tiles from a kiln at Bawsey, Norfolk.
British Museum.

302 which includes the carols collected about 1426 by John Awdlay, a priest at Haughmond in Shropshire.

It seems clear that many of the outlaw ballads had their first source among the peasantry, however much they may have been conventionalized when they assumed a written form.[4] The *Littel Geste* of Robin Hood probably belongs to the late fifteenth century but it is based on four ballads that may have taken shape about 1400. When Hood says:

> Loke ye do no husbande harm
> That tylleth with his plough.

and again,

> These bishoppes and these Archbishopps
> Ye shall them bete and bind
> The Hye Sheriff of Nottingham
> Hym holde you in your minde,

he was outlining the practical programme of the Peasants' Rising in 1381. This is a link with the climax of the fourteenth-century East Midland tale of Gamelyn in which the outlaw hero hangs the judge and the sheriff and all the jurors.

It is very improbable that the peasant culture was homogeneous; there must have been marked regional differentiations. Dialects were likely to have been far more remote from each other than any literary evidence suggests, since all speech tends to be normalized when written down. It was only in some areas, too, that the village community was the dominant social unit.

Yet with all its variations it is likely that peasant culture was more autonomous in the late fourteenth and early fifteenth centuries than at any other period in English history. It was still true that every land had its lord, but the lord was often distant. Not only the great men of the land ('*les grants de la terre*') but the great men of the shires were gathering more and more scattered manors. Many manors were being split into moieties among absent lords. The Elizabethan pattern of rural England with its resident squire, literate parson and strong yeomen was still far away. Often the parish tithes were paid to a non-resident rector or to a monastic house, just as the manorial dues were paid to an absent lord, and the 'vicar' or 'chaplain' at the village church may have been essentially one with the peasantry among whom he lived. There is no evidence of any social cleavage in a village between the villein and the free man: the prosperous peasant who held his land by villein tenure in 1390 may often have been the direct ancestor of the Elizabethan squire, though perhaps it was more often the descendants of the reeve or the miller who began by farming the manor dues and ended as lords of the manor. Possibly by 1390 many reeves and millers were coming to belong to a middle class rather than to the peasantry.

In the fourteenth century there is a grouping throughout England that is best described as a middle class, though its exact limits are difficult to determine. The guildsmen in the towns were central to it, but it may be said to include those who possessed property and pride of status but who neither used nor aspired to use coat armour. This was a grouping that found its closest parallel in fourteenth-century Europe among the burgher class of the Hanse towns and Flanders. Partly this may have been the result of trade contacts and of the sustained economic predomin- ance of East Anglia—the life of Margerie Kempe suggests how naturally King's Lynn was orientated to Lübeck, Danzig and Cologne—but primarily it was due to the presence of similar economic factors in a similar setting and to the slow growth of a trading community consciously divorced from the ideals of a would-be international knightly class. It is suggestive that when the knightly romance *Octovian* was recast for a new audience in south-east England, about 1350, the *courtois* elements—most of the love matter and introspection—were replaced by a new emphasis on the shrewd triumphs of the butcher Clement and on the hero's skill in wrestling and in throwing the weight.

It seems possible to reconstruct some of the ideals current in this class from the great mass of literary evidence that remains; unlike the peasantry the burgesses were largely literate and therefore historically articulate. During the last years of Richard II religion was perhaps at its strongest within this grouping; it provided not only most of the great preachers and much of their audience but also much of the religious vitality of the Lollard movement. The boisterously orthodox Margerie Kempe and the Lollard martyr, the tailor Badsby were both born in this milieu. But it is curious how much of its didactic literature and of its popular gnomic wisdom turns avowedly upon a profit motive; strong in its emphasis upon objective right and wrong it yet suggests a world very remote from that of Froissart's public.

The verse treatise *How the Gode Man taught his Sone*[5] has survived in five manuscripts and is late fourteenth century in its present form. The good man tells his son to worship God and to pay his debts, to avoid holding office and serving on 'inquests', to talk little and to laugh little. There is the refrain, 'If you do not do this you will suffer'. The same values are inculcated in *The Child of Bristowe*, which seems to date from the last years of Richard II and which is the earliest version of the story of the industrious apprentice. The sombre proverbs of Hendyng were still current; there is a manuscript at Cambridge of about 1400:[6] 'If your foot aches tell not your foe quoth Hendyng'; and 'Dear bought is the honey that is licked from the thorn'. It is often possible to place a manuscript in its social context by some social detail; in *The Good Wyfe wold a Pylgremage* the girl is adjured not to run about the streets like a St Anthony's pig, nor to sit on the ale bench with the men. The hero is not the knight but the wealthy and devout merchant, as in *The Child of Bristowe*, but there is some evidence for a war-like national consciousness that is perhaps stronger than in any other class. Back under Edward III the songs of Lawrence Minot[7] were probably for a middle-class public, since their heroes are not knights like Sir John Chandos but a Master Archer, John of Doncaster, and a ship-master from Rye, John Baddyng.

> I praise John Baddyng for one of the best
> Bold came he sailing out of the west.

And they combine an intense English pride with a contempt for all foreigners—for "The Boy with the Black Beard" (the Doge Bocca Negra), for Philip of France and for all Scots 'both wild and tame'. This is a very different approach from that of Sir Thomas Gray in his *Scalachronicon*, or from that of the Chandos Herald, with their sense of international knightly solidarity.

Again the ideals of woman and of marriage seem to be in contrast with those of the knightly class.[8] The ideal of marriage is neither cynical nor ignoble, but it is prosaic. In *How the Gode Man taught his Sone* the wise father tells his son to choose his wife for her honesty and goodness; to cherish her and never to strike or curse her; to rule her gently and to remember that though she is his servant she is also his companion. There is a parallel piece, *How the Gode Wife taught her daughter*,[9] which survived in six manuscripts, of which the earliest is from the end of the fourteenth century. In this the Good Wife instructs her daughter in detail in the 'hausfrau' ideal. An identical impression is conveyed by *The thews of Gudwomen*,[10] by the Wycliffite tract 'Of wedded men and wives'[11] and by the verses on a girl's upbringing in *The Good Wyfe wold a Pylgremage*. It is an ideal quite compatible with the crude humour of the York guild plays, for the conception of the wife as a household shrew has always been the obverse to the ideal of the wife as a hausfrau.[12]

Apart from an economic interpretation of history it would be difficult to discern any adequate reason for the patent difference in ideals between the trading and the knightly class in the reign of Richard II. It is improbable that at this period there was any race distinction between them, though it seems clear that some such distinction was believed in.[13] The knightly class can only have been a very small minority;[14] its cadre was formed by the new court, the magnates with the gentlemen of their households, the small groups of knightly families in each shire who now controlled so much of the machinery of local administration[15] and the group of Welsh knightly families who raised the dues and levies for their absent lords. Consciously it was linked together by the use of heraldry, at a time when this was still restricted; and it was welded by the acceptance of French knightly custom and, in the case of many of its members, by similar training in some great lord's household or by some experience of the wars.

Social Ideals and Social Structure

But sociologically it was long possible in England to combine the existence of clearly-marked class distinctions with the fact that the classes flowed almost perceptibly into one another. In the late fourteenth century, however great the value placed upon the possession of good blood, social status was in fact determined rather by training and by employment than by descent; Chaucer was unique as a poet, but in his official career he is a type. Any attempt to estimate the significance of the ideals of the knightly class must take into account the fact that they would have possessed the prestige of fashion at a period when it was a commonplace of satirists that the soap maker's son would wish to be knighted and that the franklin wished his son to be like the knight's. These ideals would affect radically the ideals of the hero, the heroine, and those of marriage in English fiction. Preconceptions on knightly conduct and on the nature of the bonds of loyalty could also affect English history at a time when the court, the magnates and the knighthood of the shires held the immediate monopoly of political power. Among them the great magnates as a group held the chief political power and their households were inevitably centres of literary patronage.

XII

The Influence of the Magnates

A new form of higher nobility had developed in England during the fourteenth century. It had no French counterpart and was in sharp contrast to the great feudal baronage of the early years of Edward I. The Norman families who had dominated so much English history for two hundred and fifty years had now become extinct: the De Clares in 1314, the Bigods in 1306, the De Lacys in 1311, the De Redvers in 1293, the Warennes in 1347. Only the De Bohuns survived until 1373. The great magnates of 1390 were normally descended from the class beneath them: a century earlier the Montacutes and the Courtenays had been wealthy knights; the Staffords, Percies and Nevilles had been somewhere in the lesser baronage. The Fitzalans, Beauchamps and Mortimers had been politically more significant but even they had risen rapidly in the fourteenth century.

The higher nobility of the last years of Richard II were sharply differentiated from their predecessors by the nature of their political influence and by the organization and distribution of their estates. They consisted of about a dozen families. About fifty landowners were technically '*magnates Regni*', since they received a personal summons to Parliament from the King, but in 1390 the conception of a peerage was only beginning to develop.[1] Socially as well as economically the great majority of peers were indistinguishable from the wealthy knightly families with whom they intermarried. In Sussex Sir John Dallingridge of Bodiam Castle was as rich[2] as Thomas, Lord De La Ware, and lived in greater state. There were groups of knightly families like the Bonvilles and the Stourtons, the Tiptofts and the Hungerfords, whose landed power already merited the peerages which would normally come to them in the fifteenth century. The great men of the shires, whether knights or barons, formed a homogeneous grouping differing in kind from the true magnates—the great men of the realm who possessed a national and not merely a local significance, and who for the most part had lands scattered through England. The normal income in the first group would probably be between £100 and £200 a year;[3] thus Thomas, Lord Camoys, had £150 a year from his Sussex and Hampshire lands in 1412. In the second grouping of true magnates a normal annual income might be between £2,000 and £3,000; the Bohun inheritance was worth rather over £3,000 a year in 1384.[4] This must have implied quite different standards of living.

By 1399 all the greater magnates held earldoms, but not all earls were among the greater magnates: the earldoms of Wiltshire, Worcester and perhaps Gloucester, like the Marquessate of Dorset, had been court honours granted by Richard without an adequate basis of territorial power. It seems to have been Richard's policy to restrict duchies to the royal kin: though it was the highest titular honour, a dukedom did not necessarily presuppose great landed wealth. The political power of any magnate depended primarily on the extent of his estates.

The nature of political influence had altered with the disappearance of the English feudal system. Feudal tenures had been weakening through the thirteenth century and the practice of sub-infeudation had been ended by the Statute of Quia Emptores in 1290. A magnate would normally hold his lands from the Crown by feudal tenure as a royal tenant-in-chief[5] but he no longer had feudal vassals. In the 1390s a magnate relied on the support of his personal retinue, his tenantry and the lesser landowners who had bound themselves to him by temporary contract. A magnate's heritage consisted of the complex of his estates and jurisdictions; his affinity consisted of the whole body of his supporters; his household was the centre both of his heritage and his affinity.

The significance of the magnates' households for the development of English poetry is frequently ignored: they provided not only publics in need of winter entertainment but also the patronage to reward the entertainer; in the thirteenth century

Waldef had begun as a household romance of the Bigods, *Bevis of Hamton* of the De Albini's at Arundel, *Guy of Warwick* of the Mauduits at Warwick. As the last two examples suggest, it was the fashion to possess a household romance associated with a dynastic founder or possessions. Such romances merged with family histories, whether primarily factual like John of Erleigh's *Song of the Marshal* or primarily imagined like the *Song of Fulk Fitzwarren*. But there was also a demand for pure and improbable fiction like the fourteenth-century *William of Palerne*, a household romance of the Bohuns.

When a romance survives today in a manuscript de luxe it is very probable that it is from a magnate's household. *Floriant et Florete* may be chosen as an example. This has been preserved in a single manuscript de luxe owned by the Marquess of Lothian. Its sixty-nine leaves of vellum are ornamented with illuminated letters and grotesques, by a hand suggesting the end of the fourteenth century; the French is of some elegance. It is an adventure story centring on two courts, Cardigan in Wales and Monreal in Sicily. There are many details of courtly life— the singing and the dancing in hall (*le rondel; les caroles*),[6] the suppers of spiced cakes and wines. There is an episode about a white hart:[7] it is as white as silver, it enters the Hall; it is the pledge of immortality. It is not impossible that this is a reference to the white hart livery, and in such a case the poem might have reached its final form between 1390 and 1399 in Ralph Neville's household at Raby. This is a guess, but at least the manuscript suggests the kind of entertainment provided in a very wealthy household in the north in the last years of Richard II.

Floriant et Florete is one of many indications that French was maintaining itself among the magnates even when English was gaining ground at court. French remained the official language of their households: it is characteristic that when William de Montacute died in 1397 his will was in crude Anglo-French; and that between 1391 and 1398 the correspondence dealing with the Mortimer retinue and estates is in French, infiltrated by an occasional English or Latin word; and that Aubrey de Vere settled his estates in French in January 1399.

It was a help to the survival of French that it was the language of the law courts as well as of chivalry. But in practice it is likely that all magnates were bi-lingual: as early as 1354 John of Gaunt's father-in-law Henry of Grosmont, Duke of Lancaster, wrote in his *Livre de Seyntz Medecines*,[8] 'If the French does not happen to be good I ought to be excused because I am English and have not much practice of French'[9] (*n'ai pas moelt hauntee de Frenceis*).

Through the self-examination in the *Livre de Seyntz Medecines* it is possible to gain an intimate knowledge of one of the greatest of fourteenth-century English magnates, with his deep piety and his courage and his sexual frailty, his craving for honour, his itch to amass more lands and his vivid sophisticated sense of life. Henry of Grosmont knew that he had sinned through pride of the nostrils when he turned away from the poor.[10] But he had delighted in smelling flowers, fruit and women,[11] and even scarlet cloth.[12] He had also found delight in good spices and 'poignant' sauces and strong wine both white and red.[13] The bath was among his pleasures; he noted that it was best to bathe in tepid flowing water neither too chill nor too warm and that this should be followed by sweating in a hot room.[14] Hunting must have meant much to him, it recurs so often in his illustrations. Though he was quite un-Puritan, his conscience was perhaps a little sensitive: he knew that jousting and dancing were not sinful, but he believed that it was lewdness that made him stretch out his stirrups and dance with elegance;[15] he noted that he had gained more pleasure from the kisses of lewd women even if ill-favoured and poor than from the kisses of God-fearing women however great their rank or beauty.[16] His vivid personal faith had brought with it a certain egalitarianism; he wrote, 'We are all brothers and the sons of God'. No fourteenth-century English magnate had greater personal prestige than Henry of Grosmont. At least he set a standard to his grouping and one which was not too high to be attainable.

It seems likely that the fashions set by the generation of Henry of Grosmont were still prized in the 1390s by those who, like the Earl of Arundel and the Duke of Gloucester, scorned

the new court modes. Thomas of Woodstock, Duke of Gloucester, had shown rash courage in the French wars and ruthless-
ness when he led the opposition lords in 1387, but he was notably
devout: in 1393 he had founded a college of priests at his gates at
Pleshey; he had a devotion to St Mary Magdalen and twenty-one
books on spirituality, as well as his great vellum bible illuminated with his arms and with the Swan badge he had assumed from
the De Bohuns. He too, was bi-lingual: he wrote a short treatise
in French on the order of battle, but his bible was in English,
and so was the petition that he sent to Richard from Calais
before he was killed in prison there. In 1397 he had a library at
Pleshey[17] which contained eighty-three manuscripts: nine of
these were chronicles, five dealt with the law, six with philosophy, nineteen were romances; there is nothing to suggest
contact with the new literary movements of the court. His wife,
Eleanor de Bohun, had her own small library when she died in
1399: eleven manuscripts—books of devotion, a book on law, a
book on philosophy, two chronicles and a romance.

The household of a great magnate in the 1390s would seem
to have resembled a small old-fashioned court, very different
from the new court at Eltham or at Sheen, but rather like the
earlier courts of Edward III. It would consist of the great
officials, their deputies and assistants and presumably their
wives, and the young who were being bred in the household
as squires, pages or damsels. These would form a fairly homogeneous social unit since they seem normally to have been drawn
from the wealthier knightly families; thus the Earl of Salisbury
who died in 1397 had had a Loring, a Hungerford, a Stapleton
and a Mountford among his household servants; and the Earl of
Stafford who died in 1386 was served by a Shirebourne, a Corbet,
a Deyville and a junior Stafford. It is harder to determine the
relationship of this group to the *garceouns* or inferior servants, or
the chaplains, the herald, the minstrels, the physician. Much as
these differed, it may be suggested that they served the Household
rather than belonged to it.

The personnel of a household may be illustrated from that of
the de Montacutes, Earls of Salisbury, since it is one of the

best documented; the will made by the second earl in 1387 has survived[18] and there are a number of references both in the Close and Patent Rolls. The de Montacutes' main house was Christchurch Castle in Hampshire. Their chief household officials[19] were the chamberlain (who is left a thousand marks in 1387), the steward, the treasurer and the receiver-general (in this case the two offices are distinct). There were bequests in 1387 to an usher of the chamber and to seven squires who seem to rank beneath him. There is no reference to the number of pages, but there were twelve in the lesser household of Elizabeth de Burgh.[20] There are legacies to twenty-one servants, thirteen of whom are described as yeomen. Yeoman is a socially ambiguous term: the yeomen of the chamber and the buttery seem to rank with squires, but many were probably *garceouns*; prominent among these was the cook (the *garcion de ma cuisine*) who is left two pounds, the same sum as a chaplain. There were seven 'clerks of the chapel'. There had been a physician, Master John Bray, who had been hired at £5 a year.[21] Beyond the immediate household it is possible to trace a network of stewards, constables and receivers who administered the de Montacute inheritance throughout England.

For it was an essential mark of any late fourteenth-century magnate that his lands were scattered; this gave him his national significance but also weakened his military power. In 1390 the de Montacutes held land in Somerset, Dorset, Hampshire, Oxfordshire, Berkshire, Buckinghamshire and Kent. They owned Wark castle upon Tweed, had great estates in Wales and were lords of Lundy Island as well as the Isle of Man. The Fitzalans centring from three castles—Arundel, Reigate and Holt—had manors in Sussex, Surrey, Hampshire, Kent, Shropshire and Cheshire. The Beauchamps dominated Warwickshire, Worcestershire and much of Herefordshire from their great castle of Warwick; but they had manors in Kent and Essex, and owned Barnard Castle in the Bishopric of Durham and the lordships of Gower and Elfael in Wales.

The de Veres were in eclipse in 1390 but their heritage was restored in 1392. They had reached the first rank of the magnates through a fortunate marriage in 1336. Their household was at Castle Hedingham, but they held manors in Essex, Suffolk, Cambridge, Northamptonshire, Rutland, Leicestershire, Hertfordshire, Middlesex, Kent, Sussex and Wiltshire.

Outside the royal house there seem to have been eleven magnates of the first rank in the early 'nineties. Of these only the Percies and those newcomers the Nevilles had their power concentrated regionally. The Mortimers, who were the wealthiest among them, owned areas in Ireland, Wales and the Welsh Marshes, but they were also powerful in Dorset, Somerset and East Anglia; the Mowbray heritage had centred from Axholme in Lincolnshire, with lands in Yorkshire, Warwickshire and Leicestershire; the Bigod inheritance brought them manors in most of the shires. The two least wealthy of the great magnates were the Staffords and the Courtenays. The Stafford household seems to have been at Tonbridge Castle in Kent, while their landed influence was primarily in the Midlands. The Courtenay estates were scattered in Cornwall, Devon, Dorset, Somerset, Hampshire, Berkshire and Buckinghamshire. Both the Percies and Nevilles had been rising to power in the fourteenth century through the intermittent Scottish wars along the Northern March; they were the English counterpart of the house of Douglas. Their military power was concentrated from Yorkshire to the Scottish border, and they could mobilise and strike quickly. Richard was dethroned by the Percy and Neville heritages acting in support of the old Lancastrian affinity.

For, as this analysis will have suggested, the political history of the last years of Richard II cannot be interpreted in terms of a struggle between the King and the magnates. No royal government could have survived had the great magnates united against the crown; but in every crisis the majority stayed neutral and perhaps indifferent, since their own interests were not affected. As I have already suggested, the real parallel seems to lie with the manœuvres of the Fronde in seventeenth-century France: the Court, with some support among the magnates, was opposed to a small fluctuating group of magnates with supporters who had deserted from the court; personal motives explained the political alignments, and pretexts were drawn not from constitutional issues but from the conventions of knighthood and loyalty which were held in common by the knightly class. Shared ethics and common ideals knit together the country knights, the magnates and the Court.

XIII

Chivalry

Ideals of knighthood and of knightly conduct had a crucial significance. It is probable that for the majority of the ruling class they formed a standard of values at times consciously followed, at times consciously sinned against, but always pre-supposed. They are first clearly identifiable in the years of Henry II; they received a classic expression under Henry III in the *Song of William the Marshal*; they were to survive past Malory, first fluctuating and then modified into the code of honour. They were never so formalized and so precise as in the last years of Richard II.

These ideals carried with them theories of personal loyalty that influenced both history and fiction, for such conceptions were to have direct political consequences, and could provide the avowed motive for political action, while at the same time they helped to stylize the hero of a romance and form the framework of its plot. It was perhaps a central tension in late fourteenth-century English culture that its economics, its politics and its fiction were all too complex for so simple and individualistic a code.

In the reign of Richard II, knighthood and knightly loyalty combined into a system of ethics which seem to presuppose a class society in which personal relationships held primary importance, and in which the emotional content was provided by a romantic—perhaps rather adolescent—conception of personal loyalty, friendship and adventure. Some of its quality is best conveyed by the delight in clear bright colours and fine stuffs which characterize the literary sources for it: the gold and azure, the argent, gules and sable, and the fine silks of the Chandos Herald; or else, as in the story of Sir Degrevant, sapphire and red-gold, violet and azure and the jewels of Melidor; honour and dishonour had the sharp contrasts of heraldic colours. Some of its individualism is suggested by another note in contemporary metrical romances: the perpetual sense of the forest, the absence of horizon.

During the last years of Richard II it is possible to reconstruct the standards of knightly conduct in minute detail. This can be illustrated from three English manuscripts and their value as sources largely depends on the precision with which it is possible to determine their provenance, the public for which they were intended and the exact contemporary sense of the epithets that they employ.

A manuscript in the library of Worcester College, Oxford,[1] contains a verse account of the life and deeds of the very noble prince of Wales and Aquitaine who had by name Edward— King Richard's father, the 'Black Prince'. Its purpose is explicitly didactic:[2] it aims at teaching the hearer how to know the good and to gain honour.[3] The manuscript is in an admirable hand and carefully rubricated, and is by a good professional scribe, probably about the beginning of the fifteenth century. It was possibly commissioned for some lord's household: a note '*defic hic*' written in the scribe's hand (on f.37r) makes it clear that it is a copy of another manuscript; it is stated in the text that the author had been herald in the household of Sir John Chandos.[4] Later it seems likely that either he or his patrons had some connexion with the affinity of John of Gaunt, Duke of Lancaster, since there is an apparent bias in the Duke's favour.[5] But the original poem has been handled by a redactor who added the descriptive titles, composed the verses on the officers of the prince's household, and on some occasions may have altered the text. This redactor was probably linked with the household of the Devereux—the name of Sir John Devereux is inserted at the expense of a rhyme;[6] he used an already old-fashioned Anglo-French and his work is the more easily traced since the main body of the poem is in a French similar to that of Froissart.[7] The conflation had already taken place in the manuscript from which that at Worcester College was copied, for similar scribal errors occur in the French verses and in the Anglo-French additions. The original poem was certainly composed after 1376.[8] It has been suggested that it was written before the death of the Princess of Wales, Joan of Kent, in 1385, since she is referred to in the present tense,[9] but this is inconclusive since the present tense is also used for the Queen of Navarre who died in 1373.[10] It seems most likely that the poem assumed its present form between about 1384 and 1400, perhaps nearer 1400.

The second manuscript can also be studied with some exactness. British Museum MS. Cotton. Nero A. X ff. 37–126[11] was bound into its present volume of miscellanea by Sir Robert Cotton. It had come into his possession from that of the Yorkshire antiquarian Henry Savile of Bank (1568–1617),[12] and this already suggests a northern provenance. Two annotations[13] in fifteenth-century hands seem to imply a secular rather than a monastic ownership. It contains four poems in Middle English: *Gawain and the Grene Knight*, *Pearl*, *Patience* and *Cleannesse*; all are in north-west dialect. The collection is clearly intended to be recited for the instruction and entertainment of some lord's household. Closely as all four poems are interwoven, they represent three different literary genres: in spite of echoes from Mandeville and from the *Romaunt of the Rose*, *Patience* and *Cleannesse* belong to an antique tradition of Bible paraphrase and homiletic verse; *Pearl* is part of the new literary movement in the fourteenth century, a didactic elegy by a learned man *fictio rhetorica musice composita*; *Gawain*[14] is a metrical romance portraying the conduct of the perfect knight, and unlike the other three it is not by fourteenth-century standards the work of a learned author. *Pearl* seems the poem of a clerk and trained rhetorician, *Gawain* that of a knight or of an esquire in some great household, a master of courtly manners and of hunting techniques. Yet the similarities between all four poems are so close that if they did not have a single author they had a single redactor: possibly the original manuscript was a repertory book composed by the author of *Gawain and the Grene Knight*, who included not only his own poem but *Pearl*, a favourite piece of recitation that had influenced his own verse very strongly, and *Patience* and *Cleannesse* which he had interpolated and polished.

21 The 'Black Prince'.
From the effigy in Canterbury Cathedral.

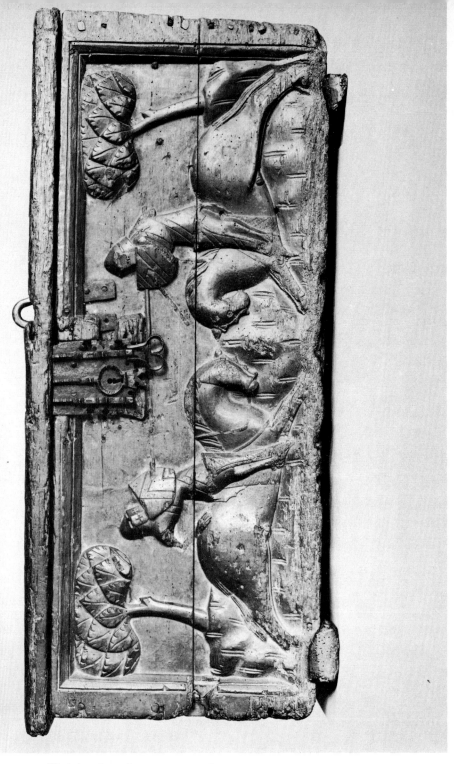

22 Knights jousting.
Wood-carving on a chest in the Victoria and Albert
Museum, London.

The one surviving manuscript was prepared, written and illuminated professionally and clumsily. It is possible that it was the work of a professional scribe in some such town as Chester; from the hand the period would seem to be early fifteenth century. Only the illuminations[15] suggest the kind of manuscript of which it is a copy:[16] slovenly executed, with figure-work curiously out of proportion, they are yet obviously related to the new experiments in the representation of natural scenery and of architectural background which marked sophisticated French court art at the turn of the century; they can be best explained as the clumsy copies of larger illuminations in a contemporary manuscript de luxe. On such an hypothesis the lost original behind the Gawain manuscript was a repertory book commissioned by a magnate of wealth; it was composed for the use of a household where the primary language was a rather archaic dialect of Middle English surcharged with a class dialect and grammar.

Even though both the Chandos Herald and the author of Gawain wrote for recitation, the public that they envisaged must have been far smaller than that of many of the minstrels' romances, for it was a public familiar with courtly usage, courtly grammar and the nuances of knightly epithet. This would also seem true of the author of *Sir Degrevant*, a romance which described in over 1900 courtly verses the motives and manners of the perfect knight.

It is entitled *Sir Degrevant and theynke and thanke* and is preserved in a rather odd manuscript at Cambridge,[17] which consists of 159 leaves copied rapidly and negligently, possibly about 1440. It seems primarily a song book. Annotations show that in the fifteenth century it was in the possession of families of established knightly rank—Hungerford and Shirley and perhaps Calverley—but it could well have been the rough copy from some *chansonnier*, compiled as was the French custom for some wealthy patron. It is certain that it seems to reflect the tastes of the court circle. There are roundels and ballades and many lyrics: the *Parliament of Love*, the *Parliament of Birds*, *La Belle Dame Sans Mercy*, and the *Complaint of Venus* translated from Othon de

Granson. *Sir Degrevant* is there in its entirety[18] and its northern dialect reads rather curiously among so much London English; perhaps it was included because it had household associations for the patron for whom the song book was first compiled.[19] It is commonly held to have been written in the north towards the end of the fourteenth century, but its 'north' was surely closer to the Welsh Marches than to the Scottish since the peril that is envisaged is that from 'wild men of the west'.

Identical standards of knighthood are portrayed in these three very different manuscripts. It is prowess that marks the good knight and brings him honour; chivalry has now become its exercise. For the Chandos Herald[20] it is the possession of 'proesce' which merits the term *bon chivaler* or *chivalerous*. *Bon chivaler* has ceased therefore to possess its moral connotation and shed its earliest association with horsemanship.[21] Prowess implies the possession of two natural qualities, rashness and indomitability (*audacia* and *magnanimitas*), and also an acquired habit of skill at arms. It is *audacia* that is emphasized by the Chandos Herald; he praises Sir Ralph Hastings because he did not value death at two cherries[22] and Sir William Felton because he threw himself among the enemy like a man without sense and without counsel.[23] 'Outrageus' (rash) is used as a term of praise.[24] The same emphasis can be found in most fourteenth-century metrical romances; in *Amis and Amiloun*[25] where Amiloun fights madly, as if 'wode', and in the battle scenes in *Rowlande and Otuel*[26] and in *William of Palerne*.[27] The glory of Sir Degrevant is his persistent '*audacia*'. There was thought to be something shameful in flight from any danger, a point brought out by Sir Thomas Gray in his *Scalachronica* when he is describing the deaths of Sir William Deyncourt and of Sir Giles de Argentine.[28] Indomitability, like rashness, was a part of fearlessness: in *Gawain* fearlessness was illustrated most often by indomitability.

The skill at arms which was presupposed by chivalry was commonly illustrated by good swordsmanship; the quality of being a 'good lance' was already prized but this was to develop in the fifteenth century. There may still have been some feeling that it was fitting that knightly feats should be performed on horseback: in the *Scalachronica* Sir Thomas Gray says to Sir William Marmion, 'Sir Knight you have come here as a knight errant to make your helm known, when it is possible it is a more fitting thing that chivalry should take place on a horse' (*que chevalerie en soit fait a cheval*), but this is an obvious play of words and Gray was writing about 1367; in a warfare of sieges, ambushes and night attacks, prowess would more normally be displayed on foot. Fair fighting was conceived as the condition of its exercise; this not only excluded foul blows but implied the acceptance of an intricate code of war which reached its most elaborate developments in the late fourteenth century;[29] this, if frequently broken was broken knowingly.

But the ultimate test of prowess remained adventure. Sir Gawain proved his hardihood alone in the forest.

> High hills on each half and holt woods under
> Of hoar oaks full huge a hundred together[30]

or while climbing cliffs in an unknown land ('many klyf he over-clambe in contrayez strange'). Sir Degrevant had fought

> In Hethenesse and in Spayne
> In ffraunce and in Brittayne.[31]

The emphasis placed by the Chandos Herald on the campaign in Spain may be partly due to the conception that when the Black Prince crossed the Pyrenees he had passed beyond the boundaries of the fully known world.

Geoffrey Chaucer was at his most conventional when he described the ideal knight in the prologue to the *Tales*.[32] It is significant how much he emphasized adventures in Egypt, Russia, Spain and Asia Minor:

> At Alesaundre he was whan it was wonne
> In Lettow had he reysed and in Ruce
> No Cristen man so ofte of his degree.
> In Gernade at the sege eek hadde he be
> Of Algezir and ridden in Belmarye
> At Lyeys was he and at Satalye
> Whan they were wonne; and in the Grete See.

Fiction reflected and helped to create fashion: patient and rather futile research has uncovered a number of contemporary knights whose adventures had been almost as far flung, some coming from the highest circle of the court.[34]

Though the primary object of adventures was to gain glory (*los e pris*) the exercise of prowess still preserved one moral implication. The knight was conceived as by nature a righter of wrongs, a 'justicier', an epithet which had survived from the primitive conception of the hero of the *chansons de geste*. For John Gower the function of the true knight is to give battle against injustices.[34]

For the author of *Piers Plowman* an essential note of true knighthood was to put down wrongdoers. Such knights would act for God not for a written law; their obligation was to preserve or to restore equity. The Seraphim were the first knights, their prototypes.

> When God began Heaven, in that great bliss
> He made knights in his Court. Creatures ten
> Cherubs and Seraphs. Seven such and another.[35]

It is this and not glory that is seen as the justification of knight errantry.

> Riding and roaming, the realm around
> Taking transgressors, and tieing them fast
> Till Truth has determined, their trespass to the end.
> That is the proper profession, that pertaineth to knights
> And not to fast on Fridays, for five score winters
> But to help him and her, that hold by the truth
> And never leave them for love, or for lacking of silver.[36]

The knight as a righter of wrongs was in no sense a magistrate; his function was a supplement or substitute for magistracy. The wrongs he righted were personal and individual wrongs, but the implications of his role were political as well as moral.

It is significant that the songs of the de Montfort faction seem to form the link between the *chansons de geste* and the reign of Richard II; it is also fitting since in so many ways Simon de Montfort was the last *chanson de geste* hero.

Chivalry

In the *Song of the Barons*,[37] in 1263, Sir Roger de Clifford is praised precisely as a righter of wrongs:

> *Et de Cliffort ly bon Roger*
> *se content cum noble ber*
> *si fu de grant justice*
> *ne suffri pas petit ne grant*
> *ne arere ne par devant*
> *Fere nule meprise.*[38]

(And de Clifford, the good Roger
bore himself like a noble baron
he was of such great justice
that he suffered no one whether small or great
whether behind his back or before his face
to accomplish any wrong.)

Simon himself was also primarily esteemed as a righter of wrongs:

> *Il eime dreit et het la tort*
> *Si avera la mestrie;*[39]

(He loves the right and hates the wrong
he will have the mastery)

but this in turn was conceived as part of his chivalry (*si ad grant chevalerie*[40]). Above all he was to be remembered by his supporters as the flower of knighthood: as in the hymn for his office

> *Salve Symon Montis Fortis*
> *Totius Flos Militiae.*

And it was a knighthood based on prowess, so that the lament for his death at Evesham[41] could have as its refrain, 'now is slain the flower of price who knew so much of war':

> *Ore est ocys*
> *La Flur de Pris*
> *Qe taunt savoir de guerre.*

This could lead naturally to a black-and-white approach to political situations; to the hymn on Gaveston's death in 1312;

> *Pange lingua necem Petri qui turbavit Angliam;*

to the hymn on Thomas of Lancaster's death in 1322,

> *Pange lingua gloriosi comitis martyrium.*

[121]

It could bring support for the Lords Appellant as well as for the Lords Ordainers. The concept that it was a knightly ideal to right wrongs not necessarily in accordance with the King's writ, and if necessary in despite of it, was a serious threat to the fourteenth-century English monarchy. Bolingbroke was to utilize it in 1399 when he landed at Ravenspur to claim his rightful inheritance.

In the late fourteenth century an emphasis on the quality of 'pitie' affected the conception of the knight as a righter of wrongs. In the thirteenth century the knight like the hero of a *chanson de geste* would seem to have righted wrongs from a sense of personal justice, the determination that every man should have that which was his due; in the late fourteenth he rights wrongs because of personal compassion.

'Pitie' in the late fourteenth century means compassion for an individual which finds expression in immediate action: John Gower writes that Pitie, *la doulce et debonnaire*, has mercy as her secretary;[42] the Chandos Herald notes that the prince found his pleasure in giving aid to him who asked it;[43] 'Pur Pitie' is a motive for the prince to undertake the Spanish campaign to restore King Pedro to his throne.[44] The frequency of the use of 'Pitee' by Chaucer seems typical of the period; even when it is used sardonically in the *Marchantes Tale* ('Lo Pitee renneth sone in gentil herte')[45] it is to emphasize that it is at once followed by action. Yet it is essentially part of a personal relationship. It is recorded that the Black Prince wept over and consoled an orphan; but he had sacked Limoges.

To summarize, in the 1390s chivalry was conceived as prowess, a combination of rashness and skill at arms: both were to be exercised according to a code of fair fighting and were to be tested by adventures; and it was fashionable that these adventures should be far flung. It was held seemly that chivalry should lead to the righting of wrongs through the motive of a personal compassion. But there were three other qualities that were not part of chivalry and yet were essential to the ideal knight: 'largesse', 'franchyse' and 'cortaysie'.

Largesse is a prodigal generosity. It is primarily valued

because of the detachment from possession and the disregard for
wealth that it implies: Chandos Herald illustrates it by the fine
gifts given by the prince, 'beal dons' of gold and silver and rich
jewels,[46] and by the 400 men that he entertained daily at his
table at Bordeaux; its moral is suggested by the statement in the
Livre des faicts of Jean Boucicault that the good knight must be
without the desire to amass treasures and riches; largesse is a
marked characteristic of Sir Degrevant. No epithet is more
closely illustrated in the fourteenth-century metrical romances,[47]
or had passed through more evolutions since the *chansons de
geste*.

For an epic hero largesse is essentially an act of justice; he
shares his spoils freely with his war band, as his recognition of
their due.[48] It has been suggested that for the hero of a *roman
courtois* largesse is a social accomplishment used to ensure esteem.
For the fourteenth-century knight it is a sign that he sits lightly
to all possessions. Its antithesis is 'covetesse'.

By this period 'franchyse' had taken the place of the 'debon-
neirete' of the early *romans courtois*. In the *Romaunt of the Rose*
it had been the arrow winged by courtesy and by courage.[49]
It remained the mark of the well bred ('the frely fode'), and it
implied a freedom and naturalness in manner and in form of
approach. Franchise was the antithesis of 'wrecced churlishness',
as in the *Frankeleyn's Tale*. A form of generosity of spirit, it was
close linked with 'fellowship' as in *Gawain*. It was controlled by
courtesy.

The sense of 'courtoisie' had been slowly narrowing. At
this time it primarily means good manners, whether in action as
in the 'cortaysie' books[50] or in conversation—the 'teccheles termes
of talkyng noble' as in *Gawain*[51] and in the careful courtliness of
Degrevant.[52] Yet it still retained some of its earlier moral
implications through its association with a gentle heart and a
fair welcome (*'coer gentil'* and *'bel accuiel'*). Thus the Chandos
Herald is recording examples of the prince's courtoisie when he
relates that he attempted to do squire's service to the captive
King of France,[53] and that he thanked his own knights very
humbly [*'moult humblement'*), and that he would say to his

household, 'Fair sweet Lords you are more than a hundred times welcome.'[54] It is Sir Gawain's courtesy that leads him to thank in turn the servants of his host.[55] But the possession of courtesy was shown at least as much by action as by words: it was a sign that Chaucer's Squire was 'curteys' that he carved before his father at the table;[56] the courtesy of Chaucer's Knight was illustrated by his bearing as well as by his speech.[57]

A class attitude to women was inextricably involved in such good manners. Courtesy was expected to find its expression in acts of service and its primary object in *dames et demoiselles de noble lignée*.[58] But ideally it was held that all women should be honoured and spoken well of. The fourteenth-century English allegory on the Castle of Love[59] contains a disquisition on courtesy. Its climax is the couplet[57]

> *Toutes femme deit honorer*
> *Toutditz le bien de eux parler.*[60]

'Druerie' is the personal courteous service of women. When Sir Gawain says to the wife of his host,[61]

> 'And soberly your servaunt my soverayn I holde you
> and your knight I becom—'

he was offering her 'druerie', instead of adultery. By the end of the fourteenth century 'druerie' was far wider than love, though it could include it. It was the fashion at the court to conceive marriage in terms of love service and of *amour courtois*. This had been stressed by the marriages of the Black Prince with Joan of Kent,[62] of John of Gaunt with Blanche of Lancaster,[63] of Richard II with Anne of Luxemburg.[64] Perhaps the fashion had been set in the early years of Edward III and Philippa of Hainault. In fiction also marriage was commonly associated with romantic love,[65] but such love was perhaps more closely linked with prowess than with courtesy, for it was conceived to be the stimulus of achievement.[66]

The physical beauty of a knight and his power of vivid sense perception were both valued, qualities which could be inter- woven with that of courtoisie. Gawain was a knight 'of bewté and debonerté and blythe semblaunt'.[67] He was found faultless in all five senses.[68] The pentangle that he bore as coat armour symbolized the five wits as well as franchyse and fellowship, cleannesse, cortaysie and pitie.

If a knight was to be *courtois* it was essential that he should be educated ('*enseigné*'), but this implied the mastery of accomplishments rather than of letters. Chaucer ascribes an ideal education to his squire:

> Wel coude he sitte on hors and faire ryde
> He coude songes make and wel endyte
> Juste and eek daunce and wel purtreye and wryte[69]

But this is perhaps a court education; it is noteworthy that the squire is in King Richard's livery, red and white:

> Embrouded was he as it ware a mede
> Al ful of fresshe floures whyte and rede.[70]

There is no suggestion that Sir Degrevant could compose poems or write, but he could play on the lute and sing sweetly, as well as having a mastery of hunting technique.[71] And like Sir Gawain he had also a mastery of forms of speech: even heroes of metrical romances were lettered on occasion:[72] the capacity for listening to fine books seems to have been generally admired.[73] But almost imperceptibly the ideal of accomplishments merged with the ideal of good manners.

At the end of the fourteenth century a man could be a good knight because he was of good courage and well born and well bred. It was chivalry's association with the quite distinct concept of loyalty that gave it an over-riding moral force; a man could not be a loyal knight without spontaneous constancy.

After so much analysis this chapter might end with a summary of the three most lucid accounts of the varying ideals of knighthood in medieval England, from the thirteenth, the fourteenth and the fifteenth centuries.

William the Marshal had been the second son of a baron with lands in Berkshire and Wiltshire and had first won fame when he was a landless knight. He had served in the household of the 'Young King', Henry II's eldest son, and had had adventures as far as Sicily and Palestine; he had made a great marriage with Isabel de Clare; had been guardian of the Kingdom for King John and *Rector Regis et Regni* for the boy Henry III; and had died at his manor of Caversham near Reading on the 14th of May 1219. His career had had many of the characteristics of medieval fiction and yet is well documented: sometime before 1231 his squire, John of Erleigh, left an account of his life and qualities which was put into verse by a professional minstrel.[74] Its purpose is didactic; the qualities to be learnt from William are illustrated by anecdotes.

William is a good knight, there was no better 'chivalier' in Christendom but *bonne chevalerie* still retains much of its primary sense of good horsemanship. It is linked with prowess, not with courtesy, and prowess is not yet analysed; it is enough that William is shown to be *vaillant et proz*. He is 'sage'; this implies that he is quick witted, resourceful, wise in council, but not crafty or subtle—he says of the King of France that he 'is as subtle as a fox'. He is accomplished, but his accomplishments are essentially social; he could sing and dance in full armour and he bore himself like an Emperor of Rome. All this merges into the fact that he had good manners (*'francs et dous'*). He has 'pitie' —pity on the old woman before her burning house at Le Mans, pity on the wounded thief—but he is not a redresser of wrongs. His largesse is still primarily the generosity of a leader to his war band,[75] but it already implies the exclusion of personal avarice and possessiveness: 'He knew how to give to others that which he himself had gained.' When he was dying he said, 'I will give no lands to my son Anselm because I love him so much.'[76] Here there must be something of the ideal of knight errancy: he had said as a young man 'England is a good country for vassals who have no heart to wander, but I go to different countries to seek adventures.'

Above all he is shown as loyal (*'leial'*); loyal to his pledged word as when he supports the young King against his father Henry II; loyal to the lords from whom he holds his lands. He is loyal to his followers; he is loyal to his friends, as when he shelters William de Braose from King John. His religion is primarily conceived as loyalty to his God; God had been a good lord to him ever since he was knighted. On his deathbed after he had been shriven he was asked to make restitution of his gains from tournaments. He refused and said, 'These clerks shave us too close.'77 'I have confessed. I surrender myself to God.' 'I have no fear of God for he is my courteous Lord.'

There must have been occasional conflict in such a network of loyalties. But at least it was not complicated as so often in the fourteenth-century fashion by the ties of affinity or by romantic friendship or by romantic love. He had married Isabel de Clare because she was 'Sage, of high lineage and of great possessions'. When he lay dying he said to her, 'Fair friend this is the last time we shall kiss each other.'78 This does not sound an unsuccessful marriage.

All his life he had had complete spontaneity and an absence of any kind of gêne; this is illustrated from his childhood, when as a hostage he had played conkers with King Stephen.79 It had been accompanied by and perhaps founded on the quality of joyousness (*Joie*), and it was a quality that stayed with him to the end. He said on his deathbed, 'For three days I have had the desire to sing. It is over three years since I had so great a desire to sing as I have now.'80 His daughters Mahaut and Jehanne sat by his bed to sing to him; he said to Jehanne, 'Sing with a full mouth, it spoils good singing to be shamefaced.'

The *Song of William the Marshal* reflects the ideal of knighthood in thirteenth-century England. A study of Edward of Woodstock, the 'Black Prince', suggests the essential continuity of the tradition and some changes in emphasis and in nuances.

Edward of Woodstock died in the palace at Westminster on the 8th of July 1376. He had been born in 1330 and had been famous as a knight since he was sixteen; perhaps at his death he still retained many of the characteristics of adolescence. Through the Chandos Herald and Froissart it is possible to discern a living personality beneath the crowding epithets. He had a love of jewellery, in especial of rubies and of bright red coral; he was a gambler—all his life he enjoyed taking risks; he 'took great delight in battle' and especially in close personal combat. He lived spontaneously and joyously ('in Gascony he reigned seven years in joy'; 'never was such good entertainment with jousts and with revels from Bordeaux to Angoulême'). He was not unlettered. He was vividly conscious of beauty and not unaware of his own; as he noted, 'Where now is my great beauty? My flesh is wasted'. He delighted in praise ('my heart craves and burns to win honour'), but he was never self-righteous ('I have done many great misdeeds'). It is likely that he was vividly imaginative and that this led to his sudden acts of compassion—from the sixty sous he gave to the small boy, to his waiting at table on his captive. He loved and served his wife with *amour courtois*. He was loyal to his friends. He was financially quite irresponsible.

William the Marshal represents the ideals of the thirteenth century; Edward of Woodstock those of the fourteenth; the classic summary of all the traditional qualities of knighthood was formulated in the fifteenth century by Sir Thomas Malory, in the lament over Lancelot by his brother Sir Ector de Maris:

Thou were the courteoust knight that ever bare shield and thou were the truest friend to thy lover that ever bestrad horse, and thou were the truest lover of a sinful man that ever loved woman, and thou were the kindest man that ever struck with sword, and thou were the goodliest person that ever came among press of knights, and thou was the meekest man and the gentlest that ever ate in hall among ladies, and thou were the sternest knight to thy mortal foe that ever put spear in the rest.[81]

But John of Erleigh and the Chandos Herald assumed that they could phrase their ideals of knighthood by describing a contemporary. Malory did so by imagining a past.

✑ XIV ✑

The Heroine and Marriage

The ideal of the knight was paralleled by that of the heroine of the romances; inevitably they share in some of the same qualities —constancy and courage and a loyal heart. But in the fiction of the knightly class and of those who wished to imitate its manners the heroine was commonly conceived as not only more beautiful but wiser, more self-controlled and better lettered than the hero. The appeal of romantic fiction seems to lie in the self-identification between the audience and the hero or the heroine. The heroines of metrical romances therefore probably represent either the type to which woman members of the audience wished to belong or the fashion in which they conceived themselves.

The type remained oddly conservative. A late fourteenth-century public could still find its satisfaction in earlier romances. Felice of Warwick is one of the most permanent factors in medieval English fiction. The author of *Gui de Warewic*[1] created her about the year 1240. Quite apart from the lasting popularity of the Anglo-French original there were four English versions, two apparently belonging to the last years of Richard II.[2]

Felice is not only very beautiful but very lettered. Her father had fetched tutors for her from Toledo to Warwick and they had taught her astronomy, arithmetic and geometry.[3] She is always wise ('*sage*'); she has a well-bred self-control—speaking to her lover she is almost unbearably didactic;[4] she is proud—pride which is unseemly in a knight is an admired quality in a heroine. Above all she is free: she is free to withhold her love or her marriage; she has refused counts and dukes before she marries Guy, the son of Siward of Wallingford, her father's seneschal. Marriage and childbirth are for her the natural fulfilment of love. She is loyal: when Guy leaves her to fight for God some weeks after the wedding she spends herself in charity; when years later she hears that he is dying in the forest of Arden she finds him before death and mourns over his body fifty days, then dies herself, and has joy with him in Paradise in the company of the Mother of God. Her life had always been accompanied by ceremony; she was both wedded and buried richly.

It is excessively improbable that there was ever any woman in medieval England who was exactly like Felice of Warwick. It is possible that there were many who would wish to be exactly like her. The fact that great learning was an admired quality in a woman[5] may have had its effect. It must have been possible for a girl in a great household to learn some letters from her father's chaplain and conceivable that she might become more lettered than her brothers. In the court culture learned poets would find patronesses like the Countesses of Westmorland, of Stafford and of March.

La Fiere is another early medieval heroine who remained fashionable in the reign of Richard II. She had been created in Herefordshire about 1185 by Hugh de Rotelande in his *Ipomedon*, but this was translated into English verse, apparently in Lancashire, and in the reign of Edward III another version was made somewhere in the East Midlands between about 1390 and 1410. There is a prose *Ipomedon* which has been ascribed to about 1400. There are three fourteenth-century manuscripts of the Anglo-French original.

It is notable in *Ipomedon* how very closely the hero and the heroine approximate to each other. When he comes into a hall Ipomedon illuminates it by his beauty. He has fair hair, clear eyes and a red mouth and it is significant that he is described in detail according to the rhetorical convention of the *Descriptio Puellae*.[6] He is very well lettered; he has a quality of sweetness and of emotional susceptibility (*si doz si soffrant*); he avoids the common sports; keeping his own counsel he loves 'fine silence' (*le bel taisir*; *Le bel teisir est curteisie*). It may be suggested very tentatively that the popularity of *Ipomedon* lay in its continual appeal to a woman's public.

Ipomedon is the lover and then also the husband of the

heroine La Fiere. Bright haired and white as a lily, '*sage*', reserved and proud, she is in every way his counterpart except in his prowess. But then his prowess is inspired by her; it was she who had wakened him to chivalry. La Fiere is a Felice of Warwick who has partly come alive.

Both have much in common with Ydoine, the heroine of *Amadas*; just as Amadas in his adolescent beauty is a less forceful variant of Ipomedon. Ydoine is auburn haired, with grey-green eyes and white as a hawthorne; she is '*debonaire*', well instructed and quick witted; above all she is of great loyalty ('*grant leaute*'). Her story remained a classic in the late fourteenth century: in *Sir Degrevant* it is embroidered along the coverlet of Melidore's bed; there is a similar reference in *Emare*. Whoever invented Ydoine, possibly about 1230, had been influenced from Provence. In his analysis of the joy-anguish of love and in his mounting series of frustrations there is much that echoes out of the world of Arnaut Daniel, whom Dante had seen in the *Purgatorio* as the symbol of joy and anguish mingled, and who had written

> I am Arnaut who garners air
> And with the oxen chase the hare
> And ever swims against the stream.

Influences from late twelfth-century Provence still remained in late fourteenth-century England through the survival of the thirteenth-century English heroine and of the love analysis that accompanied her. It is this that abruptly differentiates the heroine and the hero: Sir Gawain is of his own generation and would be at home in the wilderness of Wirral but not in Carcassonne; the idealization of Blanche of Lancaster is to its least detail Provençal.

Two qualities rendered the Provençal heroine lovable: her beauty ('*beautat'z*) and her courtesy ('*cortezia*'). Both had become stylized. Fair hair and whiteness of skin were highly prized— Chaucer ascribes both to the Duchess of Lancaster;[7] this was ultimately a literary legacy from Hellenistic Alexandria. Even in a predominantly dark haired society it was not an ideal impossible of achievement. In the fourteenth century the combination of

fair hair and dark eyebrows was most admired; which suggests
that the hair may have become fair artificially.

The Provençal conception of the 'courtesy' demanded of a
heroine can be illustrated from Guilhem de Cabestanh,[8] a
Roussillon poet all the more representative because he is of the
second rank. Courtesy implies the quality of *'franca'*, the predecessor of the fourteenth-century English 'fraunchyse', an
open-hearted absence of any gêne. It includes the quality of
'douz' which is perhaps most nearly translated as 'gentle'; he
loves his lady because of 'her gentle glances and her courteous
eyes'. It presupposes accomplishments and self-control, but
above all it is accompanied by gaiety, by the readiness to give a
'fair welcome' and by a 'laughing face': Peire Vidal[9] emphasizes
that gaiety is a part of courtesy, since laughter is the accompani-
ment of joy; the Duchess of Lancaster laughs and looks 'so
friendly', dances and carols and sings.[10]

There is hardly a phrase used by Chaucer to describe the
Duchess which could not be paralleled from a Provençal poem.
It would be a mistake to underestimate the influence of medieval
fiction upon medieval fact: his court poem must have been
recognizable enough and perhaps the Duchess herself conformed
to an ideal upon which she had been bred. Froissart's description
of her has been quoted often—'who died fair and young at
about the age of twenty-two years; gay and glad she was, fresh
and sportive, sweet and simple and of humble semblance, the
fair lady whom men called Blanche'.

In the court circle of Richard II, remote Provençal influences
were being reinforced by fresh Provençal echoes from contemporary French poems, notably from those of Othon de
Granson. But the emotional context in which they were em-
bedded seems to be altering: towards the end of the fourteenth
century the fashionable English heroine—slender, fair-haired,
clear eyed and self-controlled—descends from the heroine of the
earlier *roman courtois*, but like Dorigen in the *Frankeleyn's Tale*
and Melidore in *Sir Degrevant* she has reached terms of equality
with her lover; there is a new emphasis on a reciprocal need.
In a poem in an early fifteenth-century manuscript in Cambridge

23 A heroine.
From the tapestry 'La Dame à la Licorne'.
Musée de Cluny, Paris.

24 A Virgin at Winchester.
From a window in Thurbern's Chantry in the Chapel
of Winchester College, Hampshire.

University Library[11] it is the heroine who writes to the hero, 'You are my death and my life' (*'vous estes ma morte et ma vie'*); but this is what Guy had said to Felice and Amadas to Ydoine. Hero and heroine increasingly share the same adventures: there was no more 'curteyse creature ne cunnyngere of hire age' than Melior in *William of Palerne*, but disguised in a bear skin she flies to the forests with her lover; in *Sir Isumbras* the wife puts on a knight's armour and fights by her husband's side; in *Floriant et Florete* it is Florete who kills the dragon.

The readiness of the heroine to face physical dangers which were unknown to Felice of Warwick was emphasized by the new demand for stories that would illustrate her enduring constancy under quite unmerited and improbable trials. During the last years of Richard II this is the plot of *Emare*, perhaps the most accomplished and *'courtoise'* of the heroines of the metrical romances and twice cast adrift in an open boat, which is of course a variant of the Constance story told by both Chaucer and Gower. But Emare is also closely related through her adventures to Margaret, the heroine of the early fifteenth-century *Sir Triamour* and to La Bone Florence of Rome who came into existence in the North Midlands most probably between 1390 and 1410. There is a link with Chaucer's Griselda, but she was an Italian import and too passive for a French or English heroine. There had been rather similar exemplary tales in earlier medieval fiction, like the *Lai de Fresne* of Marie de France and the *Eric and Enid* of Chretien de Troyes, but the sudden vogue towards 1400 seems significant. The motif of the testing of the heroine's courage reached its consummation in the fifteenth century with the Nut Brown Maid's response to the challenge to

> cutte your here up by your ere
> Your kirtel by the knee
> With bowe in hande for to withstonde
> Your enmys if nede be.

The marriage of the heroine was held to have been dictated by romantic love. It has sometimes been asserted that romantic love was conceived as essentially adulterous, but it is difficult to maintain this in view of any close analysis of medieval texts. It is explicit in fiction that romantic love could exist in adultery, in marriage, or without either—possibly because it was also true in fact.

A fourteenth-century Anglo-French allegory preserved in the Arundel MSS.[12] treats of the relationship between such love and marriage. The imagery is influenced both by the *Romaunt of the Rose* and by Ovid. Love is a naked boy, yellow-haired and blind; he holds a dart and roses fly from him like sparks; his castle is raised on loyalty and its keep is a loyal heart; his three enemies are mistrust and treason and their father falsehood, while jealousy is the mangonel with which they attempt to breach his castle wall. He who loves worthily must be loyal and have a loyal heart; he must have courtesy and always speak courteously; he must honour all women and always speak well of them; he must be able to keep his own counsel and to keep chaste and to keep his mind from 'lecherie et ordure'. If his love is answered he will know himself to be unworthy and will do all things to increase the pleasure and honour of her who has answered it. They will take each other in holy church, but being married they remain '*amys et amye*' and such good loving rightly used can please and serve God and bring them to a joy without end.

Within the milieu of the knightly class the conventional theory of marriage assumed not only that it was compatible with romantic love but that ideally it was the expression of it. Owing to the conscious acceptance of French fashion such love was phrased in terms of that *amour courtois* first clearly formulated in twelfth-century France.[13]

The place of *amour courtois* in medieval theory is linked with the treatises *De Amicitia*: however deeply Ovid influenced its literary expression, its roots are with Cicero; ultimately it seems based on the Ciceronian conception of friendship, the love of another for the other's sake. Because it is the love of another for the other's sake it finds its expression in giving and serving, not in getting; and is frustrated not when it fails to get but when it ceases to give. Therefore love service is the essential expression of *amour courtois*. In contrast to a blind and transient passion ('*amour fol*'), courtly love was conceived as '*amour voulu*', an unchanging disposition of the individual will; it was an expression of an instinctive connaturality between two individuals and therefore could be conceived as part of the lovers' nature. This led to a stress on the vivid increase in all forms of sensibility which was held to follow from an experience that had affected the nature of the lover and to an emphasis on an unchanging loyalty. Chaucer describes the marriage of John of Gaunt in phrases of pure *amour courtois*.

> In alle my youthe in alle chaunce
> She took me in hir governaunce.[14]

William of Palerne[15] reached its present English form in the household of the De Bohuns in the reign of Edward III; the love symptoms of William and Melior are those uniformly characteristic in French '*courtoise*' poems; they marry and have sons.

A similar union of a romantic love and marriage is assumed in the majority of the knightly romances that took shape in the last years of Richard II. Under Henry IV, Degrevant saw Melidore standing on her castle wall and knew that he would rather possess her than 'alle the gold in the Reyne'; they live married for thirty years and have seven children. Sir Torrent of Portyngale at last marries Desonel; Sir Eglamour, Christabelle; Sir Triamour, the daughter of the King of Hungary; by 1400 the story of Sir Otuel has been altered so that he can marry Belyssant. The elaborate composite romance of *Partonope of Blois*[16] may perhaps be dated soon after 1400; the plot centres on Partonope's disobedience to Melior and his eventual pardon. Almost inevitably 'knytte in wedloke to gedre thei be', a generation later the elaborate marriage plots in *Generydes*[17] illustrate how much the union of love and marriage has come to be assumed.

The ideal of a constant love finding its expression in an unchanging love-service logically altered the ideal of marriage from that of the husband's calm rule into one of mutual service and mutual obedience.

> When maistrie comth the god of love anon
> Beteth hise winges and farewel he is gon.[18]

This finds its most explicit formulation in the *Frankeleyn's Tale*. Arviragus had resolved when he married Dorigen to 'hir obeye and folwe hir wil in al as any lovere to his lady shal'.[19]

> Thus hath she take hir servant and hir lord
> Servant in love and lord in mariage
> Than was he bothe in lordship and servage
> Servage? Nay but in lordshipe above
> Sith he hath bothe his lady and his love
> His lady certes and his wyf also
> The which that lawe of love acordeth to.[20]

Such marriage is a form of friendship, and as Chaucer noted friends must obey each other if they are to stay long in company.[21] It was an adage quoted by John Gower that woman was drawn from man's side—not from his head or foot—since she was to be his equal companion; as he taught in his *Traitie* for married lovers, each was to be a loyal friend with a loyal friend. Of her nature a woman desires liberty and not to be constrained as a thrall.[22]

This conception is more explicit at the court and in the knightly class under Richard II than at any other medieval period. It is expressed in the *Knightes Tale*.

> And Emelye him loveth so tendrely
> And he hir serveth al so gentilly
> That never was ther no worde hem bitwene
> Of jelousye or any other tene.[23]

In contrast there is a massed literature of disillusionment and of irony, but this is also perhaps a witness to the prevalence of the ideals from which it was the reaction.

There can never be sufficient evidence to determine the exact extent to which the ideal of love and marriage in the romances either influenced or reflected contemporary social custom. Though child betrothals and family alliances were clearly common enough in the knightly class, neither were necessarily unaffected by it. At least those who listened through

the long-drawn chivalrous romances can never have forgotten
the existence of an ideal of the relation between love and
marriage. It was a lesson almost monotonously inculcated by
the barely individualized heroes and heroines as they flitted
through plots formed by the tensions of conflicting loyalties
and surcharged with the fantastic adventures and severances
that are the tests of constancy.

XV

The Conflict of Loyalties

Constancy was conceived as the result of loyalty, and loyalty was considered primarily as a quality of the soul—a '*dispositio animae*', a loyal heart. A loyal heart ('*coer loial*') is a recurrent phrase in the verses of the Chandos Herald;[1] in the *Allegory of the Castle of Love* all right-loving is guarded by the Keep of Loial Coer. It was a quality that could only be exercised or violated in a personal relationship between two individuals. I can find no medieval example of the conception of loyalty to an idea or to a cause. The fact must have been there often enough, but it would not be phrased or thought of as loyalty. Even fidelity to the pledged word is fidelity to the man or woman to whom the word was pledged.

But in that cat's-cradle of social relationship which marked the late fourteenth-century knightly class, there were many ways in which loyalty could be violated or exercised. These fall into four main divisions, each with its own law. There was fidelity to the pledged word which was held to last until the pledge had been fulfilled. There was loyalty to an individual owing to a transient relationship such as guest and host, retainer and lord; this lasted until the mutual relationship which had given rise to it had ended. There was the solidarity of the kin. There was loyalty to an individual because of love or friendship ('*amour*' or '*amistie*') at a time when love was conventionally phrased in terms of friendship, and friendship in terms of love. Ideally this was held to be irrevocable and of its nature incapable of change.

Amis and Amiloun with its high-wrought emotion is the medieval English classic on loyalty between two friends. It retained its appeal in the last years of Richard II. The Anglo-Norman version, *Amis e Amilon*, was composed about the year

1200. It is preserved in three manuscripts: the first is of the thirteenth century, the second is of the reign of Edward III, the third late fourteenth-century.[2] In this last manuscript the story is still growing; there are fresh interpolations and a new character, Florentyn. The English version, *Amis and Amiloun*, is found in the Auchinleck MS., of which the most likely date is about 1360,[3] in Egerton MS. 2862 (1390–1400); in the fifteenth-century Douce MS. 326 and in Harleian MS. 2386.

The Anglo-Norman poem began by promising that it would be a song of love, of loyalty and of great sweetness and that it would be about two youths. Their physical beauty is described, their mutual love is shown to transcend the love of women, but there is no suggestion of any homosexual element in their relationship. The idea of sodomy was of course very familiar in thirteenth- and fourteenth-century England. It formed a most damaging political charge. But in theory it was conceived as the antithesis of romantic friendship, for friendship was essentially an equal relationship; according to a familiar Latin adage it either found men equal or made them so.

Sodomy was considered to be a relationship between a man and his pathic, one active, one passive, both unequal. Most usually it was a relation between an adult and a boy and this would seem to be the form to which William Rufus and Richard Cœur de Lion were addicted. It was considered particularly revolting in the time of Edward II that the king was surmised to be the pathic of fellow adults, Gaveston and Despencer. Richard's persistent efforts to procure Edward II's canonization[4] were as much an attempt to clear his memory as to brand his deposition as a crime. Richard's own relation with Robert de Vere was suspect among his political opponents[5] but the charge was not pressed and was never repeated. It is very unlikely that there was ever anything consciously sexual in Richard's extravagant friendships; possibly he was too conventional.

Friendship could only exist if it was mutual. Aquinas wrote—'A mutual loving is required, for a friend is a friend to a friend',[6] and again, 'We apprehend our friend as our other self.' Augustine remarks that well did a man say to his friend 'Thou half of my soul'.[7] A close connaturality knit two friends together as personalities. In the *Romaunt of the Rose* Reason taught the lover that 'Love of freendshipe' was 'of wille knyth bitwixe two, that wol not breke for wele ne wo.' Aquinas recurred sporadically to the problem *'Utrum similitudo sit causa amoris'*. He summarized his conclusion in the third article of the twenty-seventh question of the Prima Secundae of the Summa. There he takes as his text 'every animal loveth his like'. 'The very fact that two men are alike having as it were one form makes them to be in a manner one in that form . . . hence the affections of one tend to the other as being one with him.' This connaturality may be due to the possession of the same qualities or to the possession of quite different qualities in the same proportion. As Aquinas notes in the answer to the second Objection in the article 'if a good singer loves a good writer the similitude of proportion is to be noted there'. Possibly this might be best expressed in terms of rhythm and of music. It is the antithesis of the discordant. The emphasis on 'fair harmony' was a legacy to medieval thought from Boethius and Isidore and Bede. This conception could be used to explain sudden friendship as well as sudden love.

But though friendship could be sudden it was held to lead to an unchanging loyalty. St Jerome could be quoted, 'A friendship that can be broken was never a friendship'. Aelred of Rievaulx had added, 'I would have you believe that he was never a friend who could hurt one he had received in friendship'. This was a concept that was only strengthened by the new learning of the fourteenth century. Petrarch wrote to Francesco Nelli, 'Friendship that Divine Thing is for ever, there is within it no room for suspicion, no possibility of error'. Two friends could be considered one.

Through all the versions of *Amis* the emphasis is laid on the union between the two friends, a union so close that it leads to unity.[9] The plot consists in the testing of their mutual love: Amiloun chooses leprosy and poverty rather than desert Amis in an unjust quarrel; Amis kills his two small sons in order to heal Amiloun—and he could not know when he killed them that they would be restored to him by an angel. It had been an essential element in their friendship that they were

> to hold to gider in eueri nede
> In word in werk in will in dede.[10]

This high-wrought ideal of friendship seems characteristic of didactic Anglo-Norman literature.[11] It is notoriously difficult to distinguish between advice to friends and advice to lovers, but it seems clear that in the early fourteenth-century poem *La Lessoun a leals amants*[12] the loyal lovers are two men who are friends even though their friendship is described as '*fyne amour*'.

Like so much else in medieval culture the strength of this friendship was due to the fact that it had double origins, in Rome and in the Heroic Age. In the twelfth century the classical Ciceronian conception of '*amicitia*' as a central virtue in social relations had gained a quite new emotional content from the memory of the duties of blood-brotherhood and of the mutual obligations of fellow-members of a war band. It was a fresh synthesis; the early medieval Cicero is as divorced from the last century of the Roman Republic as the early medieval Ovid of the *Art of Love* had been divorced from the Augustan Age. Behind the repetition of his careful phrasings there lay echoes from the *Song of Roland* ('for love of thee here will I take my stand, together we endure things good or bad, I leave thee not for all incarnate man') or echoes from the *Song of Maldon* ('Aelfwin remember your vows over the mead').

At least from the twelfth century it had been assumed in vernacular literature that the betrayal of a friend was the ultimate villainy, the act of an Iscariot. It was noted in the Anglo-Norman *Amis e Amilon* that nothing worse can come to pass than when one friend is ready to betray another.[13]

Loyalty in friendship was of its nature reciprocal, but loyalty in love could be equally irrevocable though unrequited. It seems to have been the fashion to stress this at the court of Richard II, perhaps under the influence of the court of Paris. It was the theme of the turtel's speech in *The Parlement of Foules*[14] and it was the lesson that was taught to Troilus:

Many a man hath love ful dere y bought
Twenty winter that his lady wiste
That never yet his lady mouth he kiste
What shulde he therfor fallen in despeyr
Or be recreaunt for his owene tene
Or sleen himself al be his lady fayr
Nay Nay but even in oon be fresh and grene
To serve and love his dere hertes quene
And thenke it is a guerdoun hir to serve
A thousand fold more than he can deserve.[15]

But this was not the kind of loyalty in love that the audiences of the metrical romances cared to hear about; their favourite plots centred on the mutual loyalty of a reciprocated love. Such mutual loyalty is tested by enforced separation in one of the earliest forms of the novel. This had had its origin with *Daphnis and Chloe* among the Hellenistic romances of the third century A.D.; it had been revived at twelfth-century Constantinople with *Hysmenias and Hysmene*; from there it had passed north, perhaps through Sicily; and it had been naturalized in France with *Aucassin and Nicolete* and in England with *Floris and Blaunchflur*. It still retained its vogue in the last years of Richard II; the most complete manuscript of the English *Floris and Blaunchflur* was written between about 1390 and 1400.[16]

But constancy could also be tested by a conflict of loyalties: heroines like Melior in *William of Palerne* and Melydor in *Sir Degrevant* are forced to choose between loyalty to their fathers or to their lovers; it is clear that convention demanded that they should always choose their lovers. In parallel the hero was at times forced to violate loyalty to his lord, and although it is assumed[17] that this will happen it is not condoned. This seems constant from the twelfth century to the fifteenth: it is not the adultery but the betrayal of a knight's natural lord which brings the sense of a doom-laden tension to the lives of Tristram and of Lancelot.

There could also be a conflict between the loyalties of love and friendship. This is the primary plot of the *Knightes Tale*: Palamon warns Arcite that he will be false and a traitor if he hinders him in love, since they were sworn friends;[18] it is an appeal to which Amiloun would have answered, but to Arcite love is the greatest law.[19] This was an attitude very consonant with the Angevin Court of Naples where the story had its origin, but it is likely that the English audience rightly assumed that it was Palamon who after many trials would marry Emelye.

For in fact, as well as in fiction, romantically conceived friendship between men remained a fashion in the court circle. Richard II would seem to have cared deeply for several women in quite different ways—for Joan of Kent, for Anne of Luxemburg, for the child Isabelle of France; but the strength of his very personal friendships for Robert de Vere, for his cousin Edward, at times for Thomas Mowbray and perhaps for Simon Burley and John Holland were primary political factors in his reign. The 'plot' of the political history of late fourteenth-century England was conceived like that of contemporary English fiction to be a conflict of loyalties.

The forces that moulded fourteenth-century English history were ultimately economic, finding their expression through changes in the social structure; in their turn these changes affected the political organism by altering the balance of power. So too, new economic factors also shaped English literature by creating new publics with new demands. But how were the political changes of the reign of Richard II conceived by those who lived through them? The political party had not yet been thought of. The conflict between the King and groups of the magnates can hardly have been considered as a constitutional issue, for there was no constitution, only groups of precedents pointing different ways.[20] Feudalism had been dead since 1290.[21] The transition from feudalism to political party was the affinity, and this had brought with it a new and complex network of loyalties.

Membership of an affinity implied the free choice of some more powerful man to be 'good lord' and patron. It was a contract for mutual profit; a man commended himself to his lord for maintenance or perquisite, salary or preferment. In the genealogical tree of medieval loyalties it seems derived from the temporary fealty that a guest owed to a host; but though it lacked the stability of feudal vassalage, it could on occasion be surcharged with other and older forms of loyalty, just as friendship could be compatible with it.

An affinity might have been strengthened by the organization of an indenture company.[22] It had become a custom for individual magnates to raise companies for archers and men-at-arms under their leaders on an indenture system. Primarily this would be for the French, Scottish or Irish wars but a cadre might be maintained in England; men could join such a company not only because of the magnate's wealth but because of his reputation in skill at arms. Here there would be another kind of loyalty derived ultimately from the epics and the link between the war band and its chief, and this was a form of loyalty that would extend far beyond the limits of the knightly class; there could be an echo from the *Song of Maldon*: 'I am old in age and I will not hence for I purpose to lie by the side of my lord, the man so dearly loved.'

Again a knight or squire might owe loyalty to a magnate because he had been bred in his household. Here the bond of fosterage might still remain and an echo from the *Song of Roland* whose last thought had been with Charlemagne, 'his lord who nurtured him'. Thus loyalty to a later contract could conflict not only with the loyalties of personal friendship but with the remembered bonds of an earlier affinity and with the close solidarity of the family unit.

All this might supersede a loyalty to the King. When the Neville and the Percy levies followed Westmoreland and Northumberland to join Bolingbroke at Doncaster, it is unlikely that any of them had any qualm in placing their loyalty to their natural lords above their loyalty to Richard. Two factors had undermined any conception of an unswerving loyalty to a sovereign: it was a legacy from the feudal past that all men knew that they had the right to disavow a lord who did them wrong, and there was the familiar conception of the Felon King. This is already apparent in the *chansons de geste*: in the *Song of William*, William leaps on the table and cries '*Ce Roy est Fel*, let us make war on him, free valiant knights'; it was strengthened by the cult of Simon de Montfort and Thomas of Lancaster; it is marked in such a characteristically fourteenth-century romance as that of *Fulk Fitzwarin*. Richard II's livery of the white hart was perhaps the first attempt to create a body of cavaliers. It proved to be premature.

Professor Plucknett wrote in his *Legislation of Edward I*,[23] 'The idea of inheritance was one which all accepted without question as part of the natural order'. This was Richard's strength in 1399: he was the last King of England, for one hundred and ten years, to rule by undisputed right. But Professor Plucknett added, 'The most telling charge that could be brought against a tyrant was to say that he had thrust men out of their inheritance'. This was the charge that could be made against Richard, and his regime collapsed not merely by treason but in the paralysis of conflicting loyalties.

XVI

The King's Policies

Richard's policies are best studied in detail during his period of undisputed rule from the spring of 1389 to the summer of 1399. These ten years that followed have sometimes been divided by scholars into a phase of appeasement and a phase of tyranny. It has been suggested that the King suffered from mounting neuroses, but there is no evidence that Richard was ever neurotic; he expressed his emotions vividly but that was late fourteenth-century convention. His ten years of personal rule seem to possess an essential unity, and their history is intelligible enough once it is assumed that Richard was intelligent, an opportunist, not particularly scrupulous and had a gambler's trust in his own luck.

The *coup d'état* of May the 3rd had not been a revolution. The Chancellor and the Treasurer were removed from office, but they were replaced by two venerable ministers of Edward III, William of Wykeham and Thomas Brantingham. Gloucester and Warwick were removed from the Council; Arundel ceased to be Admiral and Captain of Brest. But Thomas Mowbray, now Earl of Nottingham, was confirmed as Captain of Berwick and Warden of the East Marches of Scotland and rewarded by the promise of great grants; Henry of Bolingbroke had a place on the Council; perhaps the *coup d'état* had been possible because Richard had detached these two younger appellants from the others. There was one novel appointment; Edmund Stafford was made Keeper of the Privy Seal, an office which he was to hold until 1396, when he became the Chancellor. He was perhaps the ablest of Richard's ministers and possibly the most influential; it is significant that he had been well trained in Roman Law.

In October 1389 the King's uncle, John of Gaunt, Duke of Lancaster, returned from Spain with his small multitude of household knights. This may have added to the stability of the new regime: he was the greatest landowner in England and had the wealth to maintain a private army; he was known to be courageous and reputed to be astute. But the nineteenth-century theory that he represented some 'Lancastrian' principle of constitutional opposition has been discarded. In fact, he seems to have held a high view of the prerogative and to have been consistently loyal to his young nephew. They were on demonstratively affectionate terms[1] and their two households interpenetrated each other.[2] Nevertheless, John of Gaunt's use of the collar of SS as his household badge may have stimulated Richard to the distribution of his own white hart; it was part of the new policy that no magnate should provide so great 'a livery and maintenance' as the King;[3] in January 1390 Parliament had attempted to limit by legislation the use of a lord's livery.

The war with France had long been only desultory; now there were series of truces and protracted negotiations for a lasting peace. The Parliaments of 1390 and 1391 seemed subservient: but there was evidently still some sense of insecurity. A couplet inscribed in a manuscript now at St John's College[4] Oxford describes 1390–91:

> The axe was sharp, the stock was hard
> In the fourteenth year of King Richard.

Intrigues within the court were perhaps becoming more significant with the rising importance of the Small Council. Parliament was no longer an arena: there were seven Parliaments between 1389 and 1397 but their average duration was only three weeks.[5] Old members of the opposition were promoted: Thomas Arundel received the Chancery in 1391, and was raised to Canterbury in 1396. Perhaps only his brother the Earl of Arundel remained irreconcilable. One of his two chief strongholds was Holt Castle on the Dee, and it was suspected that he was implicated in the Cheshire rising of the spring of 1393, which in turn seems to be linked with a rising in Yorkshire. Neither of these was technically a peasant revolt—the first was led by Sir Thomas Talbot and the second by William Beckwith, an outlawed forester who had once held office from John of Gaunt. All the same they may have had a similar recruitment to the great rising of 1381 and be symptoms of a lasting ferment among the peasantry.[6]

In 1394 on June the 7th Queen Anne died suddenly at Sheen palace; she was aged twenty-seven. Richard had been slowly organizing a great expedition into Ireland; he left for Wales in August and landed at Waterford on October the 2nd. He marched slowly north through Leinster and kept Christmas in Dublin, returning to England in May 1395.[7]

Richard's Irish policy was intelligent and constructive. He had aimed to reassert the personal authority of the King; none of his predecessors since King John had visited the island. He had planned to re-people the English 'Pale' along the east and to overawe the Gaelic chiefs beyond it by a great display of magnificence and force while wooing them with new titles and accustoming them to Anglo-French usages. It is characteristic that he knighted four 'Kings' during a feast at Dublin, and he seems to have regarded the Anglo-Irish lords with courteous suspicion. It is possible that had he reigned longer this policy might have met with some success.

There had been Lollard demonstrations in London[8] while the King was in Dublin; perhaps this was one of the reasons for his quick return.[9] Fifteenth-century Lollardy is now being studied exhaustively but it is still difficult to determine what the term meant exactly between 1390 and 1399. Its first known use is in 1387. It was a slang phrase[10] that could describe a number of different moods. In its widest sense it could represent a pietist movement primarily among the middle class of the towns. It was essentially a lay movement characterized by strong personal devotions tinged perhaps by revivalism, marked by the practice of meditating on scripture and combined with a high standard of sexual morality. The last factor often led to a suspicion of celibacy and to much speculation on the unnatural vices practised by monks and nuns. The lay character of such groupings developed naturally enough into anti-clericalism and anti-

25 Richard's army in Ireland being revictualled.
British Museum Harl. MS.1319, f.7b.

26 Archbishop Arundel inciting the people against Richard.
British Museum Harl. MS.1319, f.12.

27 Richard returns with a favouring wind.
British Museum Harl. MS.1319, f.18b.

28 Northumberland cozens Richard at Conway Castle.
British Museum Harl. MS.1319, f.50.

institutionalism. Their emphasis on the hearing and the preaching of the Word of God might lead to anti-sacramentalism and
to a scorn of images. They mingled with the great mass of the
orthodox devout laity and in time helped to discredit them. In
the height of the anti-Lollard reaction Thomas Hoccleve was to
write:

> Hit is unkyndly for a knight
> That shuld a kynges castel kepe
> To babble the Bibel day and night
> In restying time when he shuld slepe.[11]

It was a further complication in the 1390s that all Wycliffites
were termed Lollards, though all Lollards were not Wycliffite.[12]

John Wycliffe had died in 1384. He should always be studied
in a fourteenth-century context; he was an English Marsilius of
Padua not an English Luther. A brilliant scholastic and a
talented pamphleteer, he had won influential sympathy by his
championship of the secular power and by his suggestion that
the Church might be profitably disendowed. He had sacrificed
his career in the royal service and alienated his patrons by
developing his personal and unorthodox theory of the Eucharist.
Again neither 'Lollard' clerks at Oxford nor 'Lollard' knights
in the court circle were necessarily pietist. Oxford masters
might be Wycliffite because it was considered *avant garde*;
Knights like Sir Lewis Clifford, Sir John Clanvowe and Sir
Thomas Latimer might be Wycliffite because they were anti-
clerical and eager for the expropriation of Church land.

It was perhaps this last grouping that lay behind the Lollard
crisis of January 1395.[13] Placards containing twelve clauses or
conclusions were nailed on the doors of Westminster Abbey and
St Paul's. The immediate effect of this demonstration was to
strengthen the King's position as a champion of the Church.
He had come back from Ireland at the request of the bishops;
it was noted that at his coming Lollards drew back into their
shells like tortoises.[14] Richard was never to burn a heretic but
his strictly conventional orthodoxy was beyond any suspicion.

In July 1395 Richard began the negotiations for his marriage
with Isabelle, daughter of Charles VI. She was then only six,

but it could be hoped that she would bring a great dowry and that the truce with France would be changed into alliance. In fact, she brought £50,000 as a first instalment, the truce was prolonged for twenty-eight years, and the royal house of France promised to sustain Richard with all their power against any of his subjects. Isabelle made her state entry into London on the 23rd of November, 1396.

On February 1st 1397 the Westminster Parliament considered a Bill introduced by Thomas Haxey. Haxey was not a member of the Commons but a royal clerk of long standing; it has been suggested convincingly that he was an obvious man of straw set up by some sinister but unknown power in the background. His petition demanded the annual appointment of new sheriffs and criticized the defence of the Scottish borders and the expenses of the Court. This gave Richard the opportunity to defend his growing practice of appointing sheriffs for long periods and led the Lords to declare on the 5th of February that it was treason for any man to excite the Commons in Parliament to reform anything affecting the person, government or regality of the King. Haxey was condemned to death, but received a full pardon and returned to lucrative Crown employments. Granted that he was a man of straw it seems likely that he had been set up by the King.[15] It is perhaps significant that in the previous autumn he had been associated as one of Mowbray's proxies with Sir Thomas Bagehot who was about to become one of the King's confidential ministers.

It would have been only natural if the steady growth of the royal authority had led to counter measures among some of the magnates. If so Richard dealt with them adroitly. On the afternoon of the 10th of July, 1397, he arrested Thomas Beauchamp, Earl of Warwick, during a feast at the palace. Then he rode through the night to Pleshey where he arrested his uncle, Thomas of Woodstock, Duke of Gloucester. The Earl of Arundel had shut himself up in the castle at Reigate when he had refused the invitation to the banquet on the 10th; he was induced to surrender. The Earl's brother, Archbishop Arundel of Canterbury, was arrested later, as were Sir Thomas Mortimer and Lord

Cobham. It seems very likely that all these were concerned in a plot:[16] the Earl of Arundel was beheaded on the 21st of September; the Duke of Gloucester was removed to Calais and almost certainly privately executed there; Warwick saved his life by an abject confession; the Archbishop of Canterbury was exiled. Still it was recorded that when Richard arrested the Duke of Gloucester he had said, 'By St John the Baptist fair uncle, all this will turn out for the best for both of us,' and that he had sworn by John the Baptist[17] that no harm would come to the Earl of Arundel. In future, men would have rather less trust in his assurances.

In September 1397 Richard was more powerful than he had ever been. His white hart badge was now without dispute the greatest livery in England. Its bearers formed a nucleus for a private army; Richard had massed them at Kingston on the Saturday before he opened the September Parliament. The author of *Richard the Redeless* stresses the pride with which the badge was borne—those 'that had hertes on her brestes . . . bare hem the bolder ffor her gay broches'.[18] The core of the opposition had been liquidated with Gloucester and Arundel. Richard's international position had never been so strong; he had a close family alliance with the Valois; the Archbishop of Cologne and the Elector Palatine were in his pay; he was being wooed by Pope Boniface IX. Only—his government was insolvent.

Richard's need for personal magnificence had probably always been combined with a ravaging extravagance. It is characteristic that he delighted in jewellery. By 1397 he was maintaining one of the largest and most luxurious courts in Europe. The white hart was a royal maintenance as well as a royal livery; it was kept in being by a series of pensions and grants. His foreign policies presupposed a lavish expenditure. In 1397 he spent at least £2,000 in pensions in Germany and perhaps much more in France; he had distributed £7,000 in presents during the festivities for his second marriage. Possibly a vivid realization of his own splendour compelled him to make great gifts; it is characteristic that on the 3rd of May, 1399, he sent £2,000 to the Byzantine Emperor and allotted to the Marquess of Dorset over £2,000 in future customs dues.[19] Between 1396 and 1399 he made fifteen grants to John Holland, twenty-one to William Scrope and twenty-five to Thomas Holland.[20] All through his Patent Rolls there runs a torrent of lesser presents for dependants for whom he cared, such as his nurse Mundina, her husband the royal tailor, Walter Raufe, and the royal clerk, Richard Maudelyn,[21] whom perhaps he cherished because of his physical resemblance to himself. This unbroken flow of personal largesse was quite apart from the expenses of the Court which in the fairly characteristic year 1396–7 cost Richard £32,231.[22]

A delight in giving was a personal trait of Richard. It is more doubtful how far he was responsible for the three policies that give consistency to his reign from 1389–99. These may have been largely due to an able group of Ministers and Secretaries— Edmund Stafford, Richard Clifford, Guy Mone, Roger Walden, John Macclesfield. They came from different milieus—Stafford from that of the great magnates, Clifford from that of the baronage and Walden, a butcher's son, from Saffron Walden. Possibly none of them had a personal attachment to the King; nearly all were to serve Henry IV; but it is probable that all were attached to the conception of a strong kingship and likely that they had been led to this not only by self-interest but by the study of Roman Law. The policies of Richard and his Ministers were intelligently conceived and well executed, but cumulatively they imposed too great a strain on the King's finances.

The first plan was to provide the King with a strong striking force armed with the most modern weapons. Randolph Hatton, the Keeper of the Privy Wardrobe who died in 1396, had seventy-three cannon cast for Richard by William Woodward and left a stock of 4,000 lb. of gunpowder. These new weapons could be used in battle as well as in sieges; one of them weighing seven hundredweight had eleven barrels and could fire ten lead bullets at the same time as its stone ball.[23] When Richard went to Ireland in 1399 he left thirty-nine brass and iron cannon in the Tower as well as 1,353 bows.[24] Besides the Chamber Knights and the four hundred Cheshire archers of the guard there were paid reservists throughout England, particularly in the west and north. Richard first distributed his badge of the white hart at the Smithfield tournament in October 1390.[25]

A second policy was to create a group of great magnates through whom the King could act securely. This scheme seems foreshadowed by the vast grants made to Robert de Vere in 1386 and may explain those made to John Holland in 1389 and planned for Thomas Mowbray; it reached its climax in the autumn of 1397. For the last two years of the reign all the chief offices of state were monopolized by nine magnates who owed their titles and in six cases most of their wealth to Richard. None of them could be attacked as upstarts; John and Thomas Holland, Edward of Rutland, John Beaufort and Thomas Mowbray were of the royal kin; Thomas Percy was the younger brother of the Earl of Northumberland; Thomas Despencer and Ralph Neville belonged to the greater baronage; even William Scrope was of a baronial house. All except Neville were courtiers and Richard's friends. This was a policy that immediately impoverished the Crown. The bulk of the estates confiscated from the Earls of Arundel and Warwick and the Duke of Gloucester were distributed among members of this group instead of replenishing the King's resources, and they also received substantial grants of royal land.

The third policy was to increase the royal authority in the local administration. The representation and administration of the shires had come to be controlled by small groups of knightly families. Richard attempted to create his own party or affinity among them. At the same time minor royal officials, frequently lawyers, were sent into the shires on small commissions or served there as Justices of the Peace.[26] An analysis of thirty-five careers in the Patent and Close Rolls and the Calendar of Inquisitions suggests that this policy began about 1390. But it gathered momentum and in the spring of 1399 eleven shires were ruled by eight sheriffs who were members of the King's household.[27]

Richard's interest in politics is probably usually overestimated and consistency in policies is more likely due to the Council than to the King. The Small Council was turning into a Privy

Council dominated by experts, with the Privy Seal office closely linked with it and therefore also growing in influence; there was renewed activity in the Signet Office; there were developments in the Great and Privy Wardrobes. The Rolls provide evidence for the existence of a much larger number of minor officials; Richard had to provide for a centralizing bureaucracy that was increasing rapidly through its own momentum.

For all this he had only the haphazard resources of the fourteenth-century English monarchy. His father, his grand-father and his great-grandfather had all been financially irrespon-sible. He had inherited a cumbersome and corrupt financial administration. The last three years of Richard's reign are most easily explicable as a series of ingenious and hazardous financial expedients. In turn these caused his deposition.

In the summer of 1397 Richard began to raise forced loans; rich men and corporations were compelled to lend to the govern-ment. By the following Easter this had brought in £20,000. There was something to be argued in favour of forced loans and there were respectable precedents like the loan of 1387. They were to have a long history. It is clear that they were intended to be repaid, letters patent under the Great Seal being offered as surety, and it might be thought therefore that the creditors had an interest in maintaining the security of the Government. But it was the extent of Richard's forced loans that was so exacer-bating; it was the £6,570 raised from London and the £5,550 raised from other towns that probably alienated the rich bur-gesses from him.

Nothing but its ingenuity could be urged in favour of the new system of 'La Plesaunce'—fines imposed that the King's good pleasure might be regained. The Parliament of late 1397 had begun at Westminster and been continued at Shrewsbury; it had been notably subservient and it was said that it had been overawed by the Cheshire archers of the royal guard. It had granted the King the wool and leather duties for his life; it had voted him one-and-a-half subsidies to be raised at intervals of six months; it had placed an extra tax on aliens. All this was useful if inadequate. But it had also recognized the Fronde of

1387–88 as treason and this opened a new financial possibility; for in that case, all who had supported a Lord Appellant were liable to forfeiture and could be forced to compound. The King responded by granting a free general pardon with some un-named exceptions. The sequel is stated perhaps too dramatically in the twenty-first article of his deposition, which asserts that the King had forced the people of seventeen shires to submit them-selves to him as traitors and by this means had extorted great fines to recover his pleasure. In theory, La Plesaunce should have ceased to be levied on the 24th of June, 1398, but some negotia-tions were still proceeding as late as the 27th of February, 1399.[28] It should be noted that La Plesaunce was never levied in the north or west, the regions in which Richard counted for support, and that it brought in useful sums of money: London and the shires of Essex and Hertfordshire compounded for £1,000 each. But it must have induced a strong sense of insecurity among the property holders of the south and east.

This must have been enhanced by the odd episode of the Blank Charters. It is clear that at least the proctors for the compounding shires and for London had signed and sealed blank documents which were then handed in to the royal clerks. These had not been filled by the time of the deposition. It is most likely that they would have been filled by a new oath of allegiance and possibly by acknowledgement of past guilt, but it was natural that it should be suspected that they might be used in some new form of extortion.

The excessive quantities of the forced loans and the legal chicanery of La Plesaunce were both political mistakes even though they may have been financial necessities. But there were political as well as financial reasons for Richard's next scheme, the absorption of the great Lancastrian inheritance.

John of Gaunt, the fourth son of Edward III, had been born at Ghent in the spring of 1340. When he was a child his father had created him Earl of Richmond and the original nucleus of his power was centred in Yorkshire. When he was nineteen he had married his cousin Blanche of Lancaster, the heiress to great estates which centred in the North Midlands. When he was twenty-two his father had created him Duke of Lancaster and Earl of Lincoln and of Leicester and of Derby. At his death his English revenue was £12,509 a year.[29] Certainly he was the greatest subject of the crown, and his position in late fourteenth-century England was comparable to that of Douglas in early fifteenth-century Scotland. So many problems would be solved if on his death his lands were to pass to the King. He was fifty-nine when he died, but it is not known how long he had been sickening. If he was already in ill-health in the spring of 1398,[30] it is possible that the exile of his heir Henry of Boling-broke was part of a royal manœuvre.

In January 1398 Henry of Bolingbroke, who had recently been created Duke of Hereford, would seem to have charged Thomas Mowbray with an attempt to implicate him in a plot against the King. If Mowbray had really attempted to implicate him in a plot it was possibly at the King's suggestion. Further, Bolingbroke charged Mowbray with causing the death of the Duke of Gloucester in the Calais prison. This was an indirect attack on Richard since the official version was that Gloucester had died naturally. The charges were referred to a committee of eighteen set up by the Parliament of Shrewsbury. It was decided that the evidence was insufficient and that the case should be settled by trial by combat at Coventry on September the 16th. The King cancelled the combat and sent both Bolingbroke and Norfolk into exile. Mowbray was banished for a hundred winters but perhaps Adam of Usk was correct in suggesting that the King had arranged to recall him at the first opportunity.[31] Bolingbroke was banished only for ten years. Still, even if John of Gaunt was in good health it was likely that he would die while his heir was in exile. On the 3rd of February, 1399, John of Gaunt died at Ely House in Holborn. On the 18th of March Richard took possession of all his estates.

All that spring Richard had been mobilizing an army for a second expedition to Ireland. He sailed from Milford Haven and landed at Waterford on the 1st of June, accompanied by promin-ent courtiers and some of the most trusted of his magnates.

Henry of Bolingbroke was then at the French Court. He had

been received with honour; the Hôtel Clisson had been assigned to him; he was in treaty to marry the daughter of the Duke of Berri; and he had formed a private alliance with the Duke of Orleans. He had been joined by Archbishop Arundel and by young Thomas Fitzalan. It might be expected that within the next few months he would be allowed to make a descent on England to assert his claims to his inheritance.

Yet Richard's expedition to Ireland was not ill-timed since it enabled him to keep a fully mobilized army under his control during the critical months. Otherwise it achieved little: the King marched from Waterford to Kilkenny and then to Dublin and then back along the coast to Waterford. It was then that Richard heard that Henry of Bolingbroke had landed. He had left a strong and apparently trustworthy administration in England: his uncle Edmund, Duke of York, was keeper of the Realm—a cipher, appointed only because of his rank—but Edmund Stafford was Chancellor and Richard Clifford was keeper of the Privy Seal. Both were able, both had been close in the King's confidence since 1389. William Scrope, Earl of Wiltshire, was Treasurer, assisted by three members of the Household, John Bushey, Thomas Bagehot and Henry Green. There was no danger that any of these four would be admitted to a compromise by any opposition; they had been too closely associated with the King's financial extortions, and contemporary lampoons suggest that the last three were particularly hated as upstarts.[32] The administration was to put up a very incompetent resistance, but this was at least partly due to Bolingbroke's well-planned feints.

Henry of Bolingbroke was thirty-two. He was already famous as a knight. He was handsome—to Froissart he is '*beaux*' —and possessed a cultivated sensibility; he was sophisticated and intelligent; all through his career he showed a capacity for quick movement and an admirable sense of timing. He left Paris about the middle of June by the St Denys road, probably announcing that he would take a ship from Brittany. He made for Boulogne, seized some small ships and sailed to Pevensey. Then he passed up the Channel and went north to Ravenspur on the Humber where he landed his small force, probably on July the 4th. He marched through Knaresborough raising his father's Yorkshire tenants, and at Doncaster was joined by the Percies and the Nevilles with their levies. It seems that he asserted, possibly sincerely, that he had only come to seek his inheritance. Inevitably he had become the champion of property rights: if the Lancaster estates could be sequestrated with impunity no magnate could feel secure. It is probable that he could rely on the town middle class, for he had sent circular letters to the boroughs asserting that Richard was about to abolish all town charters and impose fresh taxes. He marched south to Leicester as if taking the London road; there he swerved west to the Severn valley in order to cut off Richard's returning army from the Council at London.

The Council had first heard that Bolingbroke was lying off Pevensey, for William Scrope led a royal force to Dover. Then when the news came that Bolingbroke had raised the north and was advancing on London they attempted to mobilize an army at St Albans in order to cover the capital. When they heard he was making for the Severn they rode west; Scrope, Bushey, Bagehot and Green to Bristol, and the Duke of York to Berkeley castle. So far they had shown a rather flustered energy. But when Bolingbroke reached Berkeley on July the 27th the Duke of York joined forces with him. It is improbable that he thought that he was betraying the King; more likely that he felt that he was about to negotiate a compromise solution between his two nephews. But the apparent adhesion of the Keeper of the Realm gave Bolingbroke some legal sanction. On the 28th of July Sir Peter Courtenay yielded Bristol to him; on the 29th Scrope, Bushey and Green were executed.

It is likely that Richard first heard that Bolingbroke had landed in the south of England. It is clear that he planned to disembark his main force in south Wales and march on Bristol while John de Montacute, Earl of Salisbury, was sent to Conway with a strong detachment in order to raise forces in north Wales and Cheshire. He left Waterford on July the 24th, landed at Milford Haven and at Haverfordwest heard of the fall of Bristol.

On a sudden decision he rode north to join Salisbury's army in Cheshire. Perhaps he planned to strike south from Chester to London as his friend de Vere had attempted twelve years before. Meanwhile, his southern army might have engaged Bolingbroke's forces. It is likely that Bolingbroke heard of this new plan from his agents since by a brilliant forced march he reached Chester on August the 9th.

Richard met Salisbury at Conway, but there was no army; most of it had scattered on a rumour of his death. Meanwhile, the southern army had disintegrated;[33] when its leader, the Duke of Albemarle, declared for Bolingbroke. But Richard's position was not hopeless: Conway was a strong castle and there were ships in the harbour; he could have sailed back to Dublin or made his way to France. Instead he chose a last gamble. The Earl of Northumberland came to him as an envoy from Bolingbroke, probably on August the 13th. The terms offered were reasonable: Richard was to remain King but he was to restore John of Gaunt's estates to Bolingbroke, agree to his appointment as hereditary High Steward, and surrender five members of the Council to trial. It is likely that Northumberland offered them in good faith; on his own suggestion he swore to them on the Host. But when Richard agreed to them he was placing himself in his enemies' power and there was only a chance that he might assert his authority when he was back in London. On August the 19th he rode to Bolingbroke's camp at Flint and next day went with him to Chester. There he issued letters patent and sent out writs to summon a new Parliament to meet at Westminster at the end of September.[34]

Richard's final month as King is the most obscure in his reign. The *Annales* state that he was treated 'with reverence and honour' as he travelled to London with Bolingbroke. He was lodged in the Tower. All through September the Government was still carried on in his name. It is even possible that he was still attempting to negotiate and being driven from surrender to surrender. On the 3rd of September he gave the Treasurership to John Norbury who had been with Bolingbroke in Paris. Two days later he ordered Edmund Stafford to surrender the Great

Seal and appointed John Scarle in his place; Scarle had once been in John of Gaunt's Chancellery. Richard Clifford remained Keeper of the Privy Seal but then he had quietly acceded to the new administration. On Tuesday the 30th of September, 1399, it was announced that Richard had abdicated. On the 13th of October Henry of Bolingbroke was crowned in Westminster Abbey by Archbishop Arundel.

∞ XVII ∞

The Revolution

It is possible to make a tentative analysis of the motives and pretexts of the leaders in the revolution of 1399. By all fourteenth-century standards Henry of Bolingbroke's enterprise was justified by its avowed purpose and spectacular through the odds against him: he had come to claim his just inheritance and he had only fifteen 'lances' with him. He was accompanied by Sir Thomas Erpingham, John Norbury, young Thomas Fitzalan and his uncle Archbishop Arundel. Erpingham and Norbury belonged to Bolingbroke's retinue, and their loyalty to him was to be well rewarded; Norbury became Treasurer of England in September. Thomas Fitzalan, who was about eighteen, was to prove brave, passionate and revengeful; he came not only to claim his inheritance but to avenge his father's execution and the insults that he himself had suffered from John Holland and his steward John Shelley. It is odd that Archbishop Arundel was with them instead of waiting in the security of Paris; it must have been his aim to re-establish the Fitzalans and to regain his see of Canterbury; and Henry may well have valued highly his considerable political experience.

It is natural that Bolingbroke should have raised his father's tenants at Pickering and Knaresborough and it is not surprising that he was joined by his cousins the Percies. Henry Percy, first earl of Northumberland, was then aged fifty-seven. His father's marriage with Mary daughter of Henry of Lancaster had placed his house among the greater magnates. He was first cousin to Blanche, the subject of Chaucer's *Book of the Duchesse*, had served under John of Gaunt in 1369 and 1373, had acted with him during the crisis of 1377 and owed him his earldom of Northumberland. His eldest son Sir Henry Percy, Warden of the East Marches, who was to be famous in border legend as

'Hotspur', was then thirty-five and had been a Knight of the Garter since he was twenty-four. He had been in Bolingbroke's retinue in 1391, and may have persuaded his father to join him at Doncaster. During the next four years the father seems to have followed the son as he passed swiftly to the final gambler's throw that led to his death at the Battle of Shrewsbury. The Percies had their own grievance against Richard, who had interfered with their administration of the Scottish March since 1397.[1]

The adhesion of the Percies to Bolingbroke is intelligible enough. It is harder to understand why he was also joined at Doncaster by Ralph Neville, Earl of Westmorland. Unlike the Percies, Neville owed personal loyalty to Richard, who had made him Warden of the Royal Forests North of Trent and Deputy Constable of England, had created him Earl of Westmorland in September 1397 and granted him the royal honour of Penrith. He had been prominent during Fitzalan's trial and had recently strengthened his links with the court circle by marrying his son John to Elizabeth Holland, the Duke of Exeter's niece. In 1380, when he was sixteen, he had been in the retinue of Thomas of Woodstock and had been knighted by him; the fact that Thomas had been privately executed could hardly have been a motive for disaffection but it might be a pretext. His mother was a Percy, just as 'Hotspur's' mother was a Neville; his wife was Bolingbroke's sister; in theory he could be justified in supporting his brother-in-law's just claims. In practice he may have been won over by the promise of the great honour of Richmond which would link his Wensleydale and Teesdale lands; this was granted to him in October 1399. But all his later history suggests the possibility that Henry of Bolingbroke was not only his brother-in-law but his friend.

The revolution succeeded primarily through the support of the northern magnates but partly through the hesitancy of Edmund of Langley. Richard had been mistaken when he appointed his uncle Edmund of Langley, Duke of York, to be Keeper of the Realm; it would have been wiser to have taken him to Ireland. It is likely that he trusted him because he was the father of his friend the Duke of Albemarle. Edmund was handsome and addicted to hawking and had never taken independent political action; he had always followed an elder brother, sometimes John of Gaunt, sometimes Thomas of Woodstock. He was now aged fifty-eight, the respected figure-head of a rather disreputable council: it is improbable that he felt at ease with Bushey, Bagehot and Green. Richard and Henry were both his nephews. Richard had trusted him, but he had also executed his brother Thomas and by confiscating the lands of John of Gaunt had destroyed the security of the royal appanages. Perhaps Edmund fumbled for a compromise solution when on July the 27th he joined Henry of Bolingbroke at Berkeley.

When on July the 28th Sir Peter Courtenay surrendered Bristol Castle to Henry this could not be justified by any medieval standard, even though the townsmen had already opened the city gates. He was not only surrendering the King's strong castle without resistance but he was handing over his three guests, Scrope, Bushey and Green, to immediate execution. Still, he had begun his career as one of the de Bohun affinity, of which Bolingbroke was heir; his grandmother Margaret de Bohun lived until 1391 and in 1371 he belonged to the retinue of Humphrey de Bohun, Earl of Hereford,[2] Bolingbroke's father-in-law. He must have been opposed to Richard in the crisis of 1387 for the Lords Appellant appointed him Chamberlain in place of Robert de Vere; perhaps Bolingbroke was his link with them. When Richard had resumed personal power he had removed the Chamberlainship from Courtenay and given it to John Holland. Now he was only Constable of Bristol. All this may make his action understandable.

The fall of Bristol made Henry's victory inevitable, and self-preservation could become sufficient motive for changing sides. But in the debacle that followed there was often some colour of conflicting loyalties. This could be illustrated by the case of Thomas Percy, Northumberland's younger brother, who belonged to the inmost circle of the court, and had been Steward of the Household since January 1393; before that he had been Vice-Chamberlain. He was also famous as a knight and was one of Froissart's patrons. On October the 10th, 1397, Richard had given him the Beauchamp's London house Warwick Inn, eighteen manors in Shropshire belonging to the Earl of Arundel, and seven manors belonging to Thomas of Woodstock,³ so it was to his interest that the confiscations of 1397 should never be repealed. He was also created Earl of Worcester. He went with Richard to Ireland, sailed back with him from Waterford, and together with the Duke of Albemarle was left in charge of the army at Haverfordwest when Richard heard of the fall of Bristol and rode north towards Cheshire.

It would be unrealistic to suggest that Thomas Percy would have been aware of conflicting loyalties if Richard had been winning; yet if he fought for Richard he would be fighting against his elder brother and his own house, and he had made his career as a member of the Lancaster affinity, serving under John of Gaunt in Spain and Portugal. The French sources, Creton and the *Traison et Mort*, describe him as a traitor; it is more likely that he was hesitant. He did not stop the southern army from disintegrating but then he must have ridden north to join Richard, for Walsingham and the *Annales Ricardi II* state that he was with him at Conway. Henry deprived him of his Steward-ship of the Household.

Richard failed not so much from treason as from paralysis of support. His troops did not desert to Henry, they disbanded. The safeguarding of inheritance and property-rights was an essential function of medieval kingship, so Richard had alienated his natural supporters outside the court circle. There are three clear cases of treason within the court—Edward, Duke of Albemarle, Richard Clifford and John Stanley—all of which occurred after it became apparent that Richard would be defeated.

The Duke of Albemarle was cast for the role of Iscariot in the legend of the revolution precisely because he was the King's close friend. Creton states that Richard loved him more than any other man; after Chaucer, he was probably the most interesting personality in the court circle. He was the son of Edmund of Langley, the king's uncle, by a daughter of Pedro the Cruel, King of Castile; he had had a continental childhood and had

29 Henry of Bolingbroke brings Richard back to London.
British Museum Harl. MS.1319, f.53b.

30 The vacant throne.
British Museum Harl. MS.1319, f.57.

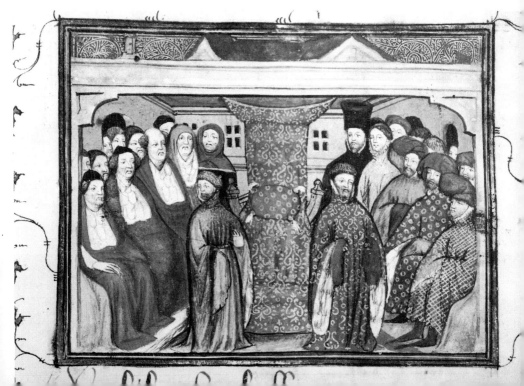

31 Henry IV.
From the effigy in Canterbury Cathedral.

been married in the Cathedral of Lisbon to Beatrix of Portugal, but the marriage had been annulled and he had returned to the English court. From 1389, when he was sixteen, he would seem to have succeeded Robert de Vere as Richard's closest friend; perhaps he resembled de Vere in good looks and charm and courage and in failure of nerve but there are indications that he was considerably more intelligent. He was created Earl of Rutland in 1390, and was the most powerful of the courtiers by 1396: Admiral, Warden of the Cinque Ports, Lord of the Isle of Wight, and Warden of the Forests South of Trent. In 1397 Richard made him Duke of Albemarle and Constable of England and revived for him the old office of Justice of the Forests. All the courts under his control had quickly extending jurisdictions marked by Roman Law procedure, which at least suggests that he could choose energetic and modern minded clerks. He would also seem to have been in charge of the King's foreign policy and had close contacts with the Paris court and carried out the negotiations with the Elector Palatine and the Archbishop of Cologne. Like de Vere he was not homosexual; he made a rather improbable and clearly disinterested marriage with Lady Golafre who was the widow of an Oxfordshire landowner and by birth a Mohun of Dunster. Like de Vere his whole power was dependent on the personal friendship of the King; it is inconceivable that he should have acted so much against his own interests as to plot Richard's downfall. Besides, he stood to lose so much if the confiscations of 1397 were annulled; he had gained the lordship of Clun from the Fitzalan inheritance, the lordship of Holdernesse from that of Thomas of Woodstock, and Flamstead and a group of manors from the Beauchamps. I would therefore ignore the unsupported statement in the French sources that he was plotting against Richard when Bolingbroke landed. Still, sometime about August the 3rd, he deserted Richard's army in Pembrokeshire and rode across central Wales to join Henry of Bolingbroke on his march to Chester. It was an attempt to save what he could of his own fortunes as he saw the regime collapse. He saved very little but at least he survived to die at Agincourt.

The case of Richard Clifford seems simpler and less interesting. He was a courtier clerk and in the fourteenth-century phrase 'a sublime and literate person' who had been an intimate of Richard's since 1387, when he had been imprisoned by the opposition lords. He was appointed Keeper of the Wardrobe in 1390 and later Keeper of the Privy Seal. He was one of the ablest of Richard's ministers, an executor of his will and a member of the Council left in charge of England in the summer of 1399. He was probably loyal to Richard until he had surrendered, but by September the 5th he had given in his adhesion to Henry and had been confirmed in his office; as a northern Clifford he was a cousin of the Nevilles and Percies.

There were no conflicting loyalties for Sir John Stanley. He belonged to a knightly family in south-west Lancashire and had been in the service of Robert de Vere. He became prominent at Court and in 1396 was given the Controllership of the Wardrobe which brought with it the responsibility for the military organization of the Chamber Knights and of the bearers of the white hart badge. His services to Henry of Bolingbroke must have been considerable, for in the winter of 1399 he was granted the castles of Mold and Hope and the Lieutenancy of Ireland. In 1405 he became a knight of the Garter and King of the Isle of Man.

I have a theory that Sir John Stanley was the patron of the Gawain Poet. The poem ends '*Hony Soyt qui mal pence*' and this suggests that it was written for a knight of the Garter; the dialect suggests that it was written in south-west Lancashire,[4] and at this period Sir John Stanley was the only knight of the Garter in south-west Lancashire. It is also possibly relevant that he was hereditary forester of Wirral and had links with North Wales and Man. Loyalty is a recurrent theme of the Gawain poem. Sir Gawain searches the wilderness for the Green Knight that he may offer himself to be beheaded rather than break his word; the sub-plot in the castle in the forest turns on the loyalty due from guest to host. If *Sir Gawain* was composed for Sir John Stanley it would be a useful reminder. It is always possible to determine the ideals of a society from its literature; it is never possible to be sure when these ideals will be put in practice.

Henry the Fourth

The revolution that began in July 1399 was not completed until the Parliament of 1406 and its results can only be analysed if it is studied as a whole. Henry of Bolingbroke seems to have shared the same conception of kingship as Richard and pursued the same policy in administration;[1] he was served by many of the same ministers. He was a characteristic product of the international court culture of the late fourteenth century and had an experience of foreign courts that Richard lacked. He was the patron of Geoffrey Chaucer and John Gower and invited Christine de Pisan to his court at Eltham. In the spring of 1400 he seemed secure in the tenure of the throne. The character of his reign and of the revolution was determined by his financial embarrassments and this was due partly to a foreign policy that had been forced upon him and partly to the drain of the Welsh rising.

In the autumn of 1399 Henry was divided from Richard not by any divergence in policy but by a well rooted distrust of the King's word. It was this that rendered a compromise ultimately impossible: if Richard was to retain the royal power how long would Henry keep the Lancastrian inheritance? The Duke of Gloucester and the Earl of Warwick had both been arrested by surprise. It is probable that Henry had already determined on a deposition; all through September he was busy buying support and men learned in the law had been appointed to examine the monastic chronicles, presumably in the search for precedents.[2]

There is a curious story in the *Annales*[3] that on the morning of September the 29th Richard was visited in the Tower by lawyers and by representatives of the Estates and that when they came back in the afternoon accompanied by certain lords Richard 'with a smiling face' abdicated from his Kingship, signed a document asking that Henry should succeed him and sent

Henry his signet ring. The story in this form seems incredible, but the account seems too circumstantial to be a complete fabrication. It is possible that on the afternoon of the 29th Richard offered to resign the rule of the Kingdom not the Kingship, the *'regimen'* not the *'regnum'*, signed a document suggesting that it should be entrusted to Henry and sent him his signet ring as a token. Such a compromise might have served Richard well; there were still magnates on whom he could rely; he might have detached the Percies from Henry; and after a short interlude he could have resumed power by a *coup d'état*. It was precisely the presence of Richard's faction among the magnates which would have made such an offer too dangerous for Henry to accept.

Next day a Parliament summoned by Richard met in Westminster Hall. It did not follow parliamentary forms: no Speaker was elected, nor any Triers and Receivers of petitions, and a London mob mingled with the Members. It was declared that Richard had abdicated and that Henry had succeeded him as King. According to the *Dieulacres Chronicle* and the *Traison et Mort* there were protests. Thirty-three articles were read aloud to show that Richard had deserved deposition, and throughout the emphasis was on his perjury. Henry asserted that he claimed the vacant throne 'by right of descent vindicated by conquest'. On October the 1st, proctors renounced their homage to Richard at the Tower. Henry issued new writs and Parliament met again on October the 6th. On October the 13th he was crowned with great splendour in the Abbey, and anointed with the sacred oil which the Virgin was reputed to have given to St Thomas of Canterbury. On October the 16th he made his first move against Richard's supporters and imprisoned John de Montacute, Earl of Salisbury, Thomas Despencer, Earl of Gloucester, John Holland, Duke of Exeter and Thomas Holland, Duke of Surrey.

Politically they were still a formidable grouping. John de Montacute, Earl of Salisbury, must have been aged about fifty, for he had won honour in the French wars as early as 1369. He was a courtier and a lyric poet who had close links with Valois Paris. Wealth had come to him late: in 1394 he had inherited the Monthermer lands from his mother; in 1397 he had succeeded his uncle as third Earl of Salisbury. He was now one of the greatest landowners in England. The fact that he was a patron of the Lollards must have made him suspect among the strictly orthodox, but it also must have made him the leader of a section of opinion that was otherwise still politically inarticulate. He had been consistently loyal to Richard throughout the crisis.

Thomas Despencer, Earl of Gloucester, was aged twenty-six and a courtier. He was by birth a magnate of the second rank but had married Constance the sister of Edward of Rutland, Duke of Albemarle, and had risen with his brother-in-law's fortunes. In the autumn of 1397 he had been created Earl of Gloucester, a title to which he had some claim through his great grandmother Eleanor de Clare. He was with Richard in North Wales in August 1399. He had given his adhesion to Henry on October the 1st but there may have been some reason to suspect his sincerity; his uncle Henry Despencer, Bishop of Norwich, was still one of the two leaders of Richard's party among the bishops. His military significance lay in his possession of Glamorgan and of a network of strong castles in the Welsh Marches.

John Holland, Duke of Exeter and Earl of Huntingdon, was about forty-seven. He was the son (perhaps the favourite son)[4] of Richard's mother, Joan of Kent, by her first marriage with Sir Thomas Holland, who had begun his career as steward in the Montacute household. John Holland had won fame as a knight during the war in Portugal. On his return to England he must at first have taken the side of the magnates of the opposition since it was they who procured him his earldom in 1387 and an annuity of 2,000 marks. Then he joined the King's party and must have had some share in the re-assertion of the royal authority in May 1389, for he was rewarded by being appointed Chamberlain, Admiral of the Fleet in the Western seas, Constable of Brest and of Tintagel and a member of the Council. He seems to have been flamboyant and he could be brutally passionate; it was in a private quarrel that he killed young Ralph Stafford.[4] He was the Mars of Chaucer's *Compleynt of Mars* according to a fifteenth-century note in the manuscript at Trinity College,

Cambridge,⁵ and it is possible that he was the 'royal tercel' in the *Parlement of Foules*. He had been a Knight of the Garter since 1381, was married to a daughter of John of Gaunt and was reputed to have been the lover of the Duchess of York.⁶ Richard created him Duke of Exeter in 1397, perhaps as a recognition of his semi-royal status as his elder half-brother. Next year he handed over to him the great Lancastrian inheritance in Wales⁷ and by the summer of 1399 he ranked among the greatest magnates.⁸

His nephew Thomas Holland, Duke of Surrey and Earl of Kent, was aged twenty-five. He seems to have been a conventional young courtier whom Richard regarded with a rather feverish affection: in 1397 he was created a Duke and given Warwick Castle⁹ and the Beauchamp stud of horses;¹⁰ in 1398 he succeeded Mowbray as Marshal and gained tracts of land in Lancashire that had belonged to John of Gaunt; in the spring of 1399 he was given County Louth, the town of Drogheda and two Irish baronies. As a third generation Holland he was ensconced among the magnates; his mother was a Fitzalan and his wife a Stafford. Froissart praised his skill at arms. He only seems abnormal in his piety, for when he was twenty-four he founded the Charterhouse of Mountgrace; but it should be noted that the Carthusians were favoured by King Richard.¹¹

These were the four lords who attempted to reinstate Richard in January 1400. They had been released early in November 1399. This was attributed to the intercession of King Henry's sister Elizabeth, Duchess of Exeter, but perhaps it had only been intended to imprison them while Richard was being removed from London to the security of a Yorkshire castle; Richard was taken to the north on October the 28th. All four had been among the 'appellants' who had charged the Duke of Gloucester and the Earls of Arundel and of Warwick with treason in 1397; but that was not a charge which could be pressed too closely since Henry himself and Ralph Neville had been so actively on Richard's side during that crisis.¹² Still it was rash of Henry to release them without having conciliated or bought them.

A double policy can be traced in Richard's confiscations in 1397 and 1398. Like the forced loans they helped to relieve his pressing necessities and they enabled him to build up a Royal Palatinate in Chester which could be a basis of military power. But by handing over so many of his newly acquired lands to his friends he was also able to create a group of magnates of the first rank on whose fidelity he was convinced he could rely. It was inevitable that in the autumn of 1399 even those friends who had deserted him were forced to disgorge. It would have been difficult for Henry to have offered them compensation but it was perhaps a mistake to deprive them of their new titles; in November the Hollands lost the Dukedoms that marked their royal rank, and so rather surprisingly did Edward of Rutland, Duke of Albemarle. Thomas Despencer ceased to be Earl of Gloucester. They now had a private grudge to stimulate their loyalty to Richard.

On December the 16th the two Hollands, now known as the Earls of Huntingdon and Kent, met the Earl of Salisbury at Westminster to plan Richard's reinstatement. They were joined by Sir Ralph Lumley, Sir Benet Sely and Sir Thomas Blount; it was said, probably enough, that they were also joined by Edward of Rutland who then once again lost his nerve and informed Henry. They mustered their men at arms at Kingston on January the 2nd and marched on Windsor planning to seize Henry, who had gone there for the Twelfth Night jousts. But when they reached Windsor they found that Henry had ridden past them to find shelter in London. They rode on to the child Queen Isabelle at Sonning, presumably meaning to secure her person, but at Sonning they changed plans. John Holland seems to have left them there and gone to Essex, the rest going north to Woodstock and then west to Cirencester; probably they were making their way to Despencer's Welsh castles, from which they might have negotiated terms with Henry. They reached Cirencester late in the night of January the 6th. They had had a successful skirmish at Maidenhead, but no one had joined them and they must have lost many of their men during two days' hard riding. At Cirencester they were attacked by the townsmen, who seized John de

Montacute, Thomas Holland and Ralph Lumley and beheaded them in the market-place on the morning of January the 7th. Thomas Despencer cut his way out and went on to Glamorgan.

Ten days later the rising had flickered out. John Holland was captured at Pleshey and was beheaded there on January the 16th in the presence of the young Earl of Arundel and perhaps at his instigation. Thomas Despencer had first gone to his castle at Cardiff; then he had boarded a ship, probably intending to go to France, but he was taken into Bristol by the ship master and beheaded there by the burgesses. Henry's ride to the security of London and the violence of the burgesses at Cirencester and Bristol suggest how completely Richard had alienated the town middle class but he may still have had support among the knights. A passage in the Calendar of Close Rolls proves that there had also been a 'stir' in Cheshire in January in connection with the rising in the south.[13]

The January rising made Richard's execution inevitable. He had been imprisoned first at Leeds Castle in Kent, then at Pickering, then at Knaresborough and last at Pontefract. He died at Pontefract, aged thirty-three, sometime between the 9th and 17th of February. It is probable that he was either starved or suffocated. On February the 9th a Council minute recommended that if Richard was dead his body should be shown to the people; perhaps this was his death warrant. On February the 17th payment was made for the carriage of his body from Pontefract to London. It was the government version that he had starved himself to death but it was added that he had attempted to take food when it was too late, thus clearing his memory of the charge of self-murder. He was buried at Kings Langley. Henry held a solemn requiem for him at St Paul's and ordered that a thousand masses should be said for him. The first phase in the revolution had ended.

If the revolution had ended then it might not have had any lasting effects on English history. Henry was a strong king and able and self-controlled. Economically he was in a better position to maintain the royal prerogatives than Richard had been in 1389, for the possessions of the Crown had been augmented by the whole Lancastrian inheritance and by over half the inheritance of the De Bohuns. His cardinal mistake was in foreign policy, but that was forced upon him.

It would seem that Henry had at first intended to continue Richard's policy of peace with France. On the 29th of November, 1399, he sent an embassy to Paris to ask for a French princess for his eldest son. It might have been wiser to wait another three months until his position was secure, for the Valois court refused to recognize him as King of England. It was a misfortune that Henry knew Paris so intimately, for this suggested the alternative policy of playing one French faction against another. War was declared in 1401. Then there were Henry's intrigues in Brittany that led to his rather unsuccessful marriage to Joan of Navarre in 1402; also his private feud with the Duke of Orleans and the Count of St Pol. Later, after desultory fighting, there was his alliance with the Duke of Burgundy against the Armagnacs and finally his alliance with the Armagnacs against the Duke of Burgundy. The year before he died he planned to lead an army into Aquitaine. This was the policy that led to his son's triumphs and ultimately to the collapse of his grandson's government; it was intelligent and well-informed but it over-taxed English resources.

The ending of the truce with France brought on a new war with the Scots. Henry led an army from York to the Firth of Forth in the summer of 1400. He achieved nothing and on his return he heard of the Welsh rising. This seems to have been the result of social and economic tensions within late fourteenth-century Wales. The reign of Edward III had coincided with the emergence of a new Welsh class who as Seneschals, deputy Constables and Receivers administered the Welsh estates of English magnates. They had adopted knightly usage and coat armour, but had retained Welsh as their first language. The poet Dafydd ab Gwilym and his patrons were characteristic of this milieu. They were to show a remarkable tenacity as stocks, most of the historic Welsh families being descended from them. But their position was radically insecure since it was dependent on the patronage of distant magnates who, with the exception of the Mortimers, showed little interest in their Welsh lands. The confiscations during the last years of Richard with the consequent quick changes in patronage must have heightened their insecurity. The revolution gave them the occasion to rise in arms for a secure tenure of lands; a private quarrel between Lord Grey of Ruthyn and Owain Glyndwr provided them with a leader. In so many ways Glyndwr was typical of his class; though a patron of Welsh poets he was culturally much anglicized, had served in the Fitzalan household and had been one of Henry's squires. He was marked out for leadership by the fact that he held his lands in central Wales as a tenant-in-chief of the crown, by his descent from the thirteenth-century princes of Powys and by his indomitable ability.

The rising may have begun as a movement among the knightly class; it soon became also a peasant revolt. The peasants, the common 'Welshry', had been the main sufferers from the Edwardian conquest of Wales which had called the knightly class into existence as entrepreneurs; they had been exposed to taxation, extortions and levies which were quite unsuited to their usual tenure of land by the family unit. It was their adhesion to Owain Glyndwr which enabled him to keep the field until 1411, for already by 1402 a number of 'uchelwyr', the 'nobles' among his supporters, were suing for their pardons. The very disparate elements in his revolt were knit together by a common Welsh consciousness, but it would perhaps be truer to say that Welsh nationalism was created by the Glendower rising rather than that the Glendower rising was created by Welsh nationalism.

On the 19th of September, 1400, Henry IV summoned the levies of ten shires to join him in the invasion of Wales. This was the first of four very costly and quite inconclusive campaigns. The French court sent arms and men to help the Welsh and recognized Owain as sovereign Prince of Wales in 1404.

It is likely enough that there were supporters of Richard among the leaders of the Welsh revolt in 1400. It was proclaimed in 1402 that Owain intended to restore the throne to King

Richard if he were still alive and that if he were dead the right heir was the Earl of March. There were persistent reports that Richard was still living. Somewhere there was a false Richard, perhaps the King's clerk, Richard Maudelyn, though no one seems to have taken his claims very seriously. It could be argued that Edmund Mortimer, Earl of March, had a right to the throne since he was the grandson of Philippa of Clarence, only daughter of Lionel of Antwerp, the second son of Edward III. Edmund Mortimer was only eleven in 1402 but this would give a group of magnates the opportunity to act as his Council of Regency; Henry Percy, 'Hotspur', the Earl of Northumberland's heir, was his uncle by marriage and is likely to have considered himself a suitable Regent. Henry Percy and his uncle Thomas, Earl of Worcester, raised a revolt in Cheshire among Richard's partisans and marched south in the summer of 1403 in order to join forces with Owain Glyndwr, who was then in Monmouthshire. Henry IV made a forced march from Lichfield and intercepted them outside Shrewsbury. Henry Percy was defeated and killed on July the 21st. Shrewsbury was the decisive battle in the revolution of 1399.

Northumberland submitted and then rose again in 1405 with Thomas Mowbray, Earl of Nottingham, Lord Bardolf and Archbishop Scrope, but the second rising collapsed without a battle. The revolution of 1399 had been finally concluded by 1406. Henry was clearly secure.

He was also insolvent. It was this rather than the circumstances of his succession which again weakened the powers of the English Kingship. It is a myth that the house of Lancaster owed the throne to a parliamentary title and it is one that Henry would have found repugnant. He was very conscious that he was of the Royal House, holding that he was King by right of descent vindicated by conquest and acclaimed by the whole '*Communitas Regni*', a wider conception than the estates of parliament. It could not be denied that on Richard's death he was the next heir by the male line.[14] But every historic myth has some foundation and under Henry IV parliaments gained new powers and a fresh significance.

This was first apparent at the Parliament of 1401 where a party was organized by the Speaker, Sir Arnold Savage, a knight of the shire for Kent, and where it was demanded that supplies should be preceded by the redress of grievances. Henry coped with this successfully and used every obvious expedient to save himself from parliamentary control. Arnold Savage was won over and was made a member of the Council and all lawyers were excluded from the Parliament that met at Coventry. Henry raised £14,000 in private loans on the 11th of May, 1402, and had increasing recourse to foreign money-lenders: to the Florentine Alberti, to Andrea Giustiniani of Genoa, to a man from Como, to some German Hanse merchants.[15] But though he had come to the throne as a champion of property rights he was increasingly forced to default on his obligations.[16] In 1406 there was a Parliament of quite unprecedented length, its first session opening at Westminster on the 2nd of March, its second session closing on December the 22nd. The King was forced to submit to the audit of his accounts and to the reform of his household, and new and independent powers were given to the Council.

Henry reigned for another seven years, dying when he was aged nearly forty-six on the 20th of March, 1413. Though hampered by ill-health he never lost his adroitness or his sense of timing, and he was perhaps one of the most intelligent of English Kings. At the time of his death the Welsh revolt had ended at last and both his French and Scottish policies seemed to promise success.

The revolution had resulted in the collapse of Richard's policy of peace with France and the end of the attempt to assert the royal authority in Gaelic Ireland. It had occasioned the Welsh revolt and had strengthened the power both of parliament and of the Council. Its cultural effects reflected the dwindling influence of the court. There had been no sudden break in 1399 and the quality of court life at Eltham stayed unaltered. There is a continuous tradition in court poetry: the *Cuckoo and the Nightingale*, *La Belle Dame Sans Mercy*, Lydgate, *The Flower and the Leaf*, *The Assembly of Ladies*. The work of the court miniaturists reaches its climax under Henry IV. The Lancastrians were continuing to give their patronage to movements in painting and poetry and aesthetics that had come into existence in the last years of Richard II. But the scale of the court had altered; the first creative phase in the court culture had ended.

Notes

I

pp. 3-11   *The International Court Culture*

1   *Troilus and Criseyde*, ll. 1791–2.
2   *The Legend of Good Women* (B text ll. 249–63). I would like to clarify the system of quotations in this book. These lines are quoted as they are printed in *The Complete Works of Geoffrey Chaucer* edited by W. W. Skeat (Oxford University Press, 1931, p. 356). For convenience, all the quotations from Chaucer are taken from this volume, although I recognize that the Skeat spelling was unduly simplified. The Skeat text has also been used for *Mum Soothsegger* which he named *Richard the Redeless*. For the Gower quotations I have followed G. C. Macaulay and for Hoccleve F. Furnival and T. Wright. Both Hoccleve texts could be improved. For the *Parlement of Thre Ages* I have used the definitive edition by M. Y. Offord. All the quotations from the *Vision of Piers Plowman* have been modernized and in many cases I have used the modernization by Mr Christopher Dawson. I have also modernized one of the citations from *Sir Gawain and the Grene Knight*, one from *Sir Degrevant* and two from the poems of Laurence Minot.
3   It may be noted that the C version of *Piers Plowman*, although a learned poem by medieval standards, represents a quite different and more speculative and archaic type of learning. The new fashion perhaps affected the *Pearl* poet and certainly dominated Hoccleve and Lydgate and Thomas Usk. These texts are discussed in Chapters 6–9.
4   It seems likely the twelfth-century Byzantine love romances like *Drosilla and Charicles* and *Hysmenias and Hysmene* formed the link between the North French *roman courtois* and third-century Hellenistic romances like *Daphnis and Chloe*.
5   This might explain why Chaucer cites 'Daunt' and 'Petrak' as authorities while he never cites Boccaccio from whom he borrowed so much more.
6   In contrast there was a cult of Augustine among some learned men at the Paris Court like Jacques de Nouvion.
7   Note his devotion to the Carthusians.
8   *The Knightes Tale*, ll. 1951–2.
9   *The Legend of Good Women*, Text B, ll. 1–6.
10   Though it should be noted that at Paris Jean de Montreuil valued

Petrarch as *Philosophus Illustrissimus* and that Christine de Pisan refers to '*Virtus*', though I think in the sense of valour.

11 For details of the court organization, cf. M. Thibault, *Isabeau de Barière*. Paris, 1903.

12 *The Legend of Good Women,* Text B, ll. 496–7.

13 Cf. A. Coville, *Gontier et Pierre Col.* Paris, 1934.

14 Cf. a poem on Jacques de Nouvion by Nicholas de Clamanges printed in Coville, op. cit., p. 96.

15 Cf. M. J. Pinet, *Christine de Pisan* (1927).

16 *Christine de Pisan,* ed. M. Roy (1886), vol. I, p. 153.

17 Op. cit., p. 277.

II

pp. 12-20   *The English Court*

1 F. Devon, *Issues of the Exchequer* (1837), p. 193.

2 For details on the wall paintings in St Stephen's, cf. E. W. Tristram, *English Wall Painting in the Fourteenth Century* (1955), p. 48 seq.

3 Cited in E. W. Tristram, op. cit., p. 49.

4 Cf. E. W. Tristram, op. cit., p. 46.

5 It seems not impossible that in some fashion Richard II identified himself with the youngest of the Magi.

6 For the names and wages of those employed on St Stephen's, cf. the accounts printed in E. W. Tristram, op. cit., pp. 282–7.

7 From the accounts cited in E. W. Tristram, op. cit., pp. 267–8.

8 Since the King paid £16 for his ransom from the French on March the 1st, 1360.

9 For full details cf. *Chaucer Life Records,* ed. M. Crow, C. C. Olson, 1966.

10 The quality of franchyse is discussed in detail in Chapter XII on 'Chivalry'. For its especial association with the Black Prince, cf. *Romaunt of the Rose,* ll. 1246–50.

11 E.g. *Gawayn and the Grene Knight,* l. 652.

12 *Eulogium Historiarum,* III, p. 378. Cf. Anthony Steel, *Richard II* (1941), p. 278.

13 Cf. Freytag von Loringhoven, *Europaische Stammtafeln* (1958): T.108.

14 E. Perroy, *L'Angleterre et le grand Schisme* (1933), p. 145.

15 In the Act legitimating the Beauforts.

16 For these German negotiations, cf. E. Perroy, op. cit., pp. 342 seq; *Annales Ricardi* (Rolls Series, 1866), p. 199 seq.

17 Adam of Usk, *Chronicon* (ed. 1904), p. 9.

18 For the organization of the Chamber Knights by Burley and Raddington, cf. Anthony Steel, *Richard II* (ed. 1952), pp. 114–15.

19 For the early association of Mowbray and Richard, cf. Thomas Walsingham, *Historia Anglicana* (Rolls Series, 1863–4), II, p. 156. From 1389 he was to be heavily loaded with grants, favours and privileges. He had his

own apartments in the palaces at Eltham and Sheen (cf. Chapter 4).

20 Cf. M. V. Clarke, *Fourteenth Century Studies* (1937), p. 117. The valuation of his household stuff at Chester came to more than £435.

21 For a brilliant reconstruction of the Radcot Bridge campaign cf. J. N. L. Myres in the *English Historical Review*, XL, 111, pp. 20–3.

III

Life at the Court

1 Cf. the panel portrait now in Westminster Abbey and perhaps originally painted for the palace.

2 Cf. the Royal effigy in Westminster Abbey completed in 1397.

3 Cf. BM. MS. Royal 20 B vi, f. 2.

4 R. R. Betts, 'English and Czech influences on the Hussite Movement', *Transactions of the Royal Historical Society*, 1939, p. 81.

5 It seems odd that he did not recall de Vere from exile in the autumn of 1390, and Mowbray in the spring of 1399.

6 E.g. the case of Thomas de Beauchamp.

7 E.g. the physical onslaught on Richard Fitzalan in 1394.

8 E.g. when he arrested his uncle Thomas of Woodstock.

9 For the high value set on the quality of being 'outrageus' cf. the praise of Sir Ralph Hastings and of Sir William Felton in the Chandos Herald ll. 2729–30 and ll. 2739–40: for praise of 'largesse' in the metrical romances, cf. *Sir Degrevant*, ll. 81–7; *Sir Isumbras*, ll. 19–24; *Sir Cleges*, ll. 13–72; *Sir Amadas*, ll. 50–61.

10 F. Devon, *Issues of the Exchequer* (1837), p. 213.

11 *Rotulus Expensarum*, 9–11, Ric. II, cited in M. V. Clarke, *Fourteenth-Century Studies* (1937), p. 122.

12 M. V. Clarke, op. cit., p. 120.

13 Printed by J. Nichols, Printer to the Society of Antiquaries, 1780.

14 A 'vyander' is a provider of viands.

15 Recipe 20.

16 E.g. Recipe 35.

17 E.g. Recipe 83.

18 Recipes 41, 90, 120.

19 Recipe 132.

20 E.g. Recipes 20, 148.

21 Recipe 28.

22 Recipe 20.

23 The only exception that I could find was peacock eaten with ginger.

24 It would be more accurate to call this poem *Mum Soothsegger* (silence truth teller) but I use the title that has been popularized by Skeat.

25 The edition used is that of W. W. Skeat, *Piers the Plowman and Richard the Redeless* (ed. 1954), p. 603 seq. Cf. *Mum and the Soothsegger*, ed. M. Day and R. Steele, 1936.

[26] Op. cit., Passus III, l. 162 seq.

[27] Op. cit., Passus III, l. 145 seq.

[28] Op. cit., p. 619. Passus III, l. 128 seq.

[29] M. V. Clarke, *Fourteenth-Century Studies* (1937), p. 120.

[30] For the intricate financial transactions suggested by the *Book of Forfeitures* of 1388, cf. M. V. Clarke, op. cit., pp. 122–3.

[31] Passus III, l. 152.

[32] E.g. in the description of Youth in *Parlement of Thre Ages* (ed. M. Y. Offord, E.E.T.S., 1959), l. 109 seq.

[33] Ibid., l. 114.

[34] The tint of red mulberry.

[35] *De Regimine Principum* (ed. T. Wright, Roxburgh Club, 1860), p. 26.

[36] E.g. f. 50.

[37] The descriptions of the dress (ll. 122–8) suggest that the *Parlement of Thre Ages* was written towards the close of the century. It is obviously by a different author than the earlier *Wynnere and Wastoure*, though both are in the same fifteenth-century manuscript (B.M. Add. MS. 1042).

[38] Cf. M. V. Clarke, op. cit., p. 277.

[39] Ibid.

[40] Richly jewelled collars are recorded as belonging to the Dukes of Exeter, York and Gloucester and the Earl of Westmorland.

[41] Cf. Anthony Steel, *Richard II* (1952), p. 147.

[42] *De Regimine Principum* (1860), p. 19.

[43] *9–11 Ric II*, P.R.O. E 101. 401. 15, cited by M. V. Clarke, op. cit., p. 117.

[44] Cf. *Eulogium Historiarum* (1858–63), III, p. 378.

[45] Cf. *Floriant et Florete* (ed. Francisque Michel, Roxburgh Club, 1873), ll. 1376–9.

[46] *Eustache Deschamps* (ed. G. Raynaud, 1891), vol. 7, pp. 266–93.

[47] Op. cit., p. 270.

[48] Balade II, 4, 1.3; *The Complete Works of John Gower, The French Works* (ed. G. C. Macaulay, 1899), p. 337.

[49] *Chaucerian and Other Pieces* (ed. W. W. Skeat, 1897), pp. 347–58.

[50] Op. cit., ll. 283–4.

[51] *The Knightes Tale*, ll. 1339–49.

IV

pp. 32–7   *The Royal Palaces*

[1] H. M. Colvin (ed.), *The History of the King's Works* (1963), vol. 2, pp. 930–7.

[2] For Edward III's occasional presence at Langley, cf. T. F. Tout, *Chapters in Medieval Administrative History* (1920–33), IV, pp. 176, 180.

[3] Cf. *The History of the King's Works*, vol. 2, pp. 970–7.

[4] Two large bronze taps 'for the King's Bath to bring hot and cold water

into the bath' were in use at Westminster Palace too. Cf. *History of the King's Works*, vol. I, p. 550.

⁵ For Sheen, cf. accounts in the *History of the King's Works*, vol. 2, pp. 994 seq.
⁶ Ibid., p. 1008.
⁷ Cf. *The History of the King's Works*, vol. i, pp. 491 seq.
⁸ It is only my conjecture that the White Hall was a timbered building.
⁹ Geoffrey Chaucer, *The Book of the Duchesse*, l. 321 seq.
¹⁰ Ibid., l. 251–4.
¹¹ Quoted in *The History of the King's Works*, vol. 1, p. 499.
¹² E. W. Tristram, *English Wall Painting of the Fourteenth Century* (1955), p. 49.
¹³ Ibid., p. 38.
¹⁴ Cf. J. Harvey, *English Medieval Architects* (1954), pp. 130–1.
¹⁵ For its architectural significance, cf. G. F. Webb, *Architecture in Britain: The Middle Ages* (1956), p. 189 seq.
¹⁶ But it should be noted that this includes the expenses for the coronation of Queen Isabelle on the 7th of January, 1397.
¹⁷ For Richard's expenditure at the Tower, cf. *The History of the King's Works*, vol. 2, p. 728.
¹⁸ For the discoveries in the Byward Tower, cf. E. W. Tristram, *English Wall Painting of the Fourteenth Century*, pp. 36–7.

V

pp. 38–50   *Court Art and Aesthetics*

¹ Printed in F. Palgrave, *Ancient Kalendars and Inventories of the Treasury of the Exchequer* (1836), vol. III, pp. 313–58.
² F. Palgrave, op. cit., pp. 358–61.
³ Ibid., pp. 364–5.
⁴ Cf. A. Matejcek and J. Pesina, *Czech Gothic Painting, 1350–1450* (Prague, 1950), p. 21 seq.
⁵ Margaret Rickert, *Painting in Britain. The Middle Ages* (1954), p. 152.
⁶ Cf. the Queen's effigy at Westminster.
⁷ Cf. Margaret Rickert, *The Reconstructed Carmelite Missal* (1952).
⁸ Cf. M. Rickert, *Painting in Britain. The Middle Ages* (1954), p. 174.
⁹ B.M. Add. MS. 16998.
¹⁰ B.M. Royal MS. 2.A.XVIII, f. 23.
¹¹ Lambeth Palace Library MS. 69. This was at one time in the possession of Archbishop Chichele but all that is certain of its date is that it is earlier than 1416.
¹² B.M. Royal MS. 1.E.IX.
¹³ Bodley MS. Lat. Liturg. F. 2.
¹⁴ Cf. the mutilated inscription on f. 19 v or the style of the deposition of Christ on f. 10.
¹⁵ f. 146v.

[16] f. 147 seq.
[17] B.M. Harl. MS. 7026, f. 4 v.
[18] Richard Medford was Secretary to Richard II from 1385 to 1388 and remained among the King's close intimates. He was perhaps Siferwas's patron at the Court.
[19] Pepysian Library MS. 1916. Cf. M. R. James, *An English Medieval Sketch-book* (1924–5).
[20] Cf. J. A. Herbert, *The Sherborne Missal* (Roxburgh Club, 1920).
[21] B.M. Harl. MS. 7026.
[22] Bodley MS. 264.
[23] Cf. Joan Evans, *English Art 1307–1461* (1949), p. 84.
[24] Now in the National Gallery, London.
[25] Joan Evans, *English Art 1307–1461* (1949), p. 105.
[26] Op. cit., Plate 52.
[27] For details of these royal tapestries, cf. Joan Evans, *English Art 1307–1461* (1949), pp. 93–4; for the new vogue for tapestries, cf. Margaret Wood, *The English Medieval House* (1965), pp. 402–4.

VI

pp. 53–60   *Thomas Usk and Thomas Hoccleve*

[1] *Art Poétique* 3, l. 391.
[2] Cf. T. F. Tout, *Chapters in Medieval Administrative History* (1920–33), vol. 3, pp. 479–81.
[3] Burley had borrowed money from a pelterer, a tailor and a draper. Cf. M. V. Clarke, op. cit., p. 122.
[4] Most of the leading city families of the 1390s can be traced back to the reign of Edward I. This must be partly due to the fact that it was not yet the custom for the rich citizen to leave London and become a land-owner.
[5] Edited by W. W. Skeat in *Chaucerian and Other Pieces* (1897), pp. 1–145.
[6] Since it was printed in 1532 it may have been known to Robert Lyly.
[7] *Testament of Love,* I, x.
[8] Ibid, II, iii.
[9] Ibid., I, ii.
[10] Cf. T. F. Tout, *Chapters in Medieval Administrative History* (1920–33), vol. 5, pp. 106–10.
[11] Cf. the Introduction to his edition of the *Anonimalle Chronicle*, Oxford, 1927.
[12] *La Male Regle,* ed. J. Furnival (E.E.T.S., E.S. 61, 1892), ll. 110–12.
[13] *De Regimine Principum,* ll. 1866–7.
[14] Ibid., l. 4978.
[15] Ibid., l. 1403.
[16] Ibid., ll. 1451–3.
[17] Ibid., l. 1561.

[18] *The Letter of Cupid*, ll. 286–7.
[19] *Male Regle*, l. 51.
[20] Ibid., l. 121.
[21] Ibid., l. 95.
[22] Poem in the Ashburnham MS., printed by J. Furnival in his edition of the *Male Regle* (1892), p. xxxviii
[23] *De Regimine Principum*, ll. 1905–6.
[24] *Temple of Glas*, l. 755.
[25] Ibid., l. 701.
[26] Cf. B.M. Harleian MS. 367, f. 127 r.
[27] *Temple of Glas*, ll. 179–214.
[28] *Life of Our Lady*, Bk. II, l. 1628 seq.
[29] *As a Mydsomer Rose*, ll. 81–4.
[30] *Fall of Princes*, Bk. VIII, ll. 80–1.
[31] *St Edmund*, Envoi 12.
[32] Aureat is often used more narrowly for the unexpected adjective or noun which is a Latin loan word.

VII

pp. 64–72   *Geoffrey Chaucer*

[1] The body of evidence that Chaucer's wife was sister to Katherine Swynford and that Thomas was their son is only cumulative, but I think that it is conclusive.
[2] *Compleint to his empty purse* (ed. W. W. Skeat, 1931), p. 126, ll. 22–4.
[3] *Legend of Good Women*, Version B, ll. 496–7.
[4] Op. cit., l. 441.
[5] Op. cit., l. 416 seq.
[6] Trinity College Cambridge MS. R. 3. 20.
[7] Cf. Mario Praz, *The Flaming Heart* (1958).
[8] *Legend of Good Women*, ll. 1012–14.
[9] I owe this reflection to Professor Nevill Coghill.
[10] Fragment A, ll. 1–1705.
[11] *Boethius*, Bk II, Metre 3.
[12] *Boethius*, Bk II, prose 2, ll. 78–80.
[13] Ibid., l. 76.
[14] *The Monk's Tale*, l. 409 seq.
[15] Ibid., l. 401 seq.
[16] Ibid., l. 385 seq.
[17] Ibid., ll. 775–6.
[18] *Anelida*, ll. 18–19.
[19] Frontispiece of Corpus Christi College Cambridge MS. 61. Plate 15, fac. pp. 76–7.
[20] *Troilus*, Bk II, l. 147 seq.

21 *Troilus*, Bk I, l. 810 seq.

22 Ibid., I, l. 1078.

23 Bk III, l. 1775.

24 Ibid., l. 1790.

25 Ibid., l. 1781.

26 Ibid., ll. 1819–20.

27 Bk v, l. 688.

28 I do not forget the *Satyricon* and *Tristan and Iseult*, but both these have only survived in fragments.

29 *The Parlement of Foules*, l. 291.

30 Ibid., l. 548 seq.

31 Ibid., l. 117.

32 Ibid., l. 582 seq.

33 Ibid., l. 566 seq.

34 Ibid., l. 595.

35 Ibid., ll. 601–2.

36 This would presuppose that *Palamon* depends on the *Anelida*, not *Anelida* on *Palamon*.

37 I am indebted for this suggestion to Professor C. S. Lewis.

38 *The Knightes Tale*, l. 271 seq.

39 E.g. ll. 1951–2.

40 l. 1339 seq.

41 ll. 195–6.

42 *The Legend of Good Women*, B. Text l. 420.

43 ll. 76–8.

44 Cp. the *Knightes Tale*, the *Franklin's Tale*, the *Clerk's Tale* for the first three and the *Monk's Tale* for fortune's wheel.

45 Sir Thopas, probably a parody on a bourgeois group of East Anglian romances stressing their ignorance of fashion (e.g. ll. 20 and 29). I was indebted for this suggestion to Professor Tolkien.

VIII

pp. 74–82   John Gower

1 *Kingis Quair* (ed. A. Lawson, 1910), p. 101, v. 197, ll. 1–2.

2 John Stow, *Survey of London* (ed. C. L. Kingsford, 1908), p. 57 seq.

3 The will is cited in J. H. Fisher, *John Gower* (1965), p. 66.

4 *The complete works of John Gower*, ed. G. C. Macaulay, 2 vols. *The French Works* (1899), p. 335 seq.

5 *Mirour de l'Omme* in G. C. Macaulay, op. cit., p. 3, l. 27337 seq.

6 *Confessio Amantis*, I, l. 2726 seq.

7 E.g. Balades 9, 30, 44.

8 E.g. from Deschamps in Balade 44 and possibly from Granson and Machaut in Balade 43.

⁹ *Confessio Amantis*, Prologue, l. 39.

¹⁰ Ibid., l. 70.

¹¹ Ibid., Bk VIII, l. 2987.

¹² Ibid., Bk VIII, l. 2462 seq.

¹³ 1390 is recorded in a Latin note beside l. 331 of the Prologue.

¹⁴ Duchy of Lancaster Miscellanea, Bundle X, no. 43, printed in J. H. Fisher, *John Gower* (1965), pp. 341–2.

¹⁵ Huntingdon El. 2. 6 A 17 (33).

¹⁶ Cf. C. S. Lewis, *The Allegory of Love* (ed. 1936), p. 201.

¹⁷ Bk V, ll. 5532–3.

¹⁸ Ed. G. C. Macaulay, *French Poems of John Gower* (1899), p. 379 seq.

¹⁹ *Mirour*, l. 25369 seq.

²⁰ E.g. *Mirour*, l. 25465.

²¹ *Mirour*, l. 18781.

²² Notably in the character sketches of Friar and Monk.

²³ l. 18825 seq.

²⁴ l. 26482 seq. Yet there is an obvious reference to Lady Perrers which suggests that the *Mirour* may have been begun as early as 1376; cf. l.22807 seq.

²⁵ Cf. J. H. Fisher, *John Gower* (1965), p. 150.

²⁶ *Vox Clamantis*, Bk VI, l. 497.

²⁷ *Confessio Amantis*, Bk VII, l. 2329.

²⁸ Yet there is one odd gaffe: he distinguishes Tullius from 'Cithero'; *Confessio Amantis*, IV, l. 2648.

²⁹ l. 26930.

³⁰ *Mirour*, l. 26919 seq.

³¹ Cf. *Vox Clamantis*, VII, l. 637 seq.

³² Passus 18, l. 90 seq.

³³ *Vox Clamantis*, II, l. 1267 seq.

³⁴ *In Praise of Peace*, ll. 102 and 105.

³⁵ *Vision of Piers Plowman*, C Text, XVIII, l. 90 seq.

IX

pp. 83–90   'Piers Plowman'

¹ *Testament of Love*, I, 5, 117; I, 7, 61; III, 7, 10. *Piers Plowman* C Text, VII, 24; XVIII, 41; XIX, 4.

² It is also possible, though unlikely, that the C Reviser had read the *Testament of Love*.

³ This includes some fragments.

⁴ There are fourteen manuscripts of the *Vision of Piers Plowman* at Oxford. I have only worked superficially among them but I might record my impression that while all three versions are at some distance from their original the C Version is the farthest.

5 Cf. Nevill Coghill, 'The Pardon of Piers Plowman', *Proceedings of the British Academy*, vol. 31, and E. T. Donaldson, *Piers Plowman; The C Text and Its Poet* (1949).
6 E.g., C II, 5, C VII, 2, C XI, 71.
7 E.g., Notes in Trinity College Dublin MS. D.4.1. and Ashburnham MS. 130 (Huntington Library MS. HM 128).
8 Trinity College MS. D.4.1. This does not exclude the possibility that he was a bastard.
9 C.VI, 45 seq. Throughout the citations have been modernized, and in many cases I have used the modernization by Mr Christopher Dawson, first printed in *The English Way* (Sheed and Ward, 1933).
10 *Piers Plowman, The A Version*, ed. George Kane (1960).
11 E.g., C II, 177, C IX, 9, C XII, 294.
12 Perhaps primarily because of its attack upon the Friars and upon ecclesiastical abuses.
13 *Pierce the Ploughman's Crede, The Compleint of the Plowman, Jacke Upland* and *Jacke Upland's Rejoinder*.
14 B V, 322.
15 Cf. M. W. Bloomfield, *Piers Plowman as a Fourteenth-Century Apocalypse* (1961), Ch. 1.
16 'Constans et perpetua voluntas ius suum unicuique tribuens,' Aquinas, *Summa Theologica,* Secunda secundae, question 58, article 1. He cites as source Digest 1.
17 C XIV, 153.
18 Cf. B III, 125 seq.
19 C XXII, 436–7.
20 B I, 177 seq.
21 B XIII, 60.
22 B X, 51.
23 Cf. A XI, 53 seq.
24 B X, 69.
25 B X, 460.
26 B XV, 12.
27 B XVIII, 22–3.
28 C XXI, 406 seq.
29 B XI, 192 seq.

X

pp. 92–97 *Provincial Art*

1 Morieux, Hales, Kerderston, Clifford and Howard.
2 Cf. the cycle in Sporle Church near Swaffham in Norfolk which again has been dated 1390–1400. E. W. Tristram, *English Wall Painting in the Fourteenth Century* (1955), pp. 249–50.
3 Op. cit., p. 192.

Notes

XI

Social Ideals and the Social Structure

1 E.g. C Text I, 95; IV, 207, 378, 381, 388; VI, 75; XXII, 468, 474, 478.
2 E.g. C Text XVI, 2; XVIII, 216.
3 F. 168 seq.
4 Cf. Maurice Keen, *The Outlaws of Medieval Legend* (1961).
5 Balliol MS. 354; Ashmole MS. 61.
6 Cambridge University Library MS. 4407 (19).
7 MS. Galba E. 1 f. 49 seq. (ed. Hall 1915).
8 This contrast is already stressed in *Waldef*, a thirteenth-century household romance of the Bigods, in the lines that begin, 'ne sui pas fille de burgois' ('I am not a burgher's daughter'), l. 1310 seq.
9 Ashmole MS. 61, f. 7 seq.
10 Cambridge University Library MS. KK I. 5.
11 British Museum Add. MS. 24202, f. 29 seq.
12 This could be illustrated by an analysis of Sloane MS. 2593 in the British Museum; it is a minstrels' repertory book compiled in the West Midlands in the early fifteenth century, and the social details suggest a literate burgess public. It includes the most beautiful of all religious lyrics, 'I sing of a maiden that is makeless'; poems on the imminence of death; and a vivid description of a jeering wife in the lyric *Prenegard*. The classic examples of a strong-minded burgess woman are the Wife of Bath in fiction and Margerie Kempe in fact.
13 E.g. the evidence of Sir Robert Latom in the case of *Scrope-v-Grosvenor* (ed. 1879, vol. 1, p. 111).
14 For its size in its formative period, cf. N. Denholm Young, 'Feudal Society in the Thirteenth Century', *History* (1944).
15 For the composition and political significance of this section, cf. K. B. McFarlane, 'Parliament and Bastard Feudalism', R. *Hist. Soc. Transactions* (1944), p. 53 seq.

XII

The Influence of the Magnates

1 It is anachronistic to contrast the House of Lords and the Commons at this period; a great magnate would have his followers both among lesser peers and the knights of the shires.
2 The Dallingridge and De La Ware estates were both valued at a hundred pounds a year in 1412. Cf. the tables published by K. B. McFarlane in 'Parliament and Bastard Feudalism', R. *Hist. Soc. Trans.*, 1944, p. 74 seq.
3 It may be suggested that very approximately a pound was worth about thirty times its present value.

4 The royal appanage of John of Gaunt with its income of nearly £13,000 a year was of course unique.

5 The results of this had been largely evaded in the last years of Richard II through the creation of family trusts.

6 l. 6223 seq.

7 l. 8181 seq.

8 *Le Livre des Seyntz Medecines*, ed. A. J. Arnould, 1940.

9 Op. cit., p. 239.

10 P. 25.

11 P. 13.

12 P. 47.

13 P. 19.

14 P. 202.

15 P. 77 seq.

16 P. 179.

17 For the books belonging to the Duke and Duchess of Gloucester, cf. M. V. Clarke, *Fourteenth Century Studies* (1937), p. 121.

18 This will is discussed by G. A. Holmes in *The Estates of the Higher Nobility in Fourteenth Century England* (1957), p. 64 seq.

19 It is probable that such great officials would form part of the magnate's council, though not all members of the council would belong to the household. But the composition of a magnate's council is very poorly documented for the last years of Richard II.

20 G. A. Holmes, op. cit., p. 58.

21 *Calendar of Patent Rolls*, 1374–7 (1893), p. 382.

XIII

pp. 115–28   *Chivalry*

1 Worcester College MS. 1, edited by M. K. Pope and E. C. Lodge (1910), cited below as the Chandos Herald.

2 Chandos Herald, ll. 1–43.

3 l. 36 seq.

4 f. 59 v, ll. 4187–8.

5 E.g. f. 45 v, l. 31957 seq.

6 Ibid, f. 32v, l. 2281.

7 Cf. the discussion of the linguistic problems of the text in the Preface of the edition by M. K. Pope and E. C. Lodge (1910).

8 Chandos Herald, l. 1816.

9 l. 2142.

10 l. 2485.

11 There is a facsimile in Early English Text Society, OS. 162.

12 Cf. B.M. MS. Harl. 1879.

13 B.M. MS. Cotton Nero A. X ff 124v 125.

14 Ed. J. R. Tolkien and E. V. Gordon (ed. 1963).

15 Cf. ff. 37, 38, 56, 82r, 90v, 125r, 125v, 126.

16 I am indebted to Professor Francis Wormald for making this suggestion to me when I was working on the MS.

17 It is in the University Library. MS. Camb. Ff. 1. 6.

18 Ibid., f. 80r seq.

19 There is also an imperfect version of *Sir Degrevant* in MS. Lincoln. A.1.17, f. 130r seq., a commonplace book compiled in Yorkshire about 1440.

20 E.g. ll. 315, 1225.

21 *Chevalerie* can also mean an order of knighthood.

22 Chandos Herald, ll. 2729–30.

23 Ibid., ll. 2739–40.

24 Ibid., l. 166.

25 *Amis and Amiloun*, l. 1307 seq.

26 *Rowlande and Otuel*, l. 1809 seq.

27 *William of Palerne*, l. 3852 seq.

28 Cf. M. D. Legge, *Anglo Norman Literature and its Background* (1963), p. 285.

29 Cf. Maurice Keen, *The Laws of War in the Late Middle Ages* (1965).

30 *Gawain and the Grene Knight*, ll. 742–4.

31 *Sir Degrevant*, ll. 21–2.

32 l. 43 seq.

33 E.g. Henry of Bolingbroke.

34 John Gower, *Mirour de l'homme*, l. 23610 seq. for context. Cf. also ll. 23593 seq., ed. G. C. Macaulay (1900), p. 260 seq.

35 *Piers Plowman*, B Text, IV, ll. 37–9.

36 Ibid., I, l. 94 seq. Cf. ibid., C Text, II, l. 90 seq.

37 Preserved by B.M. Add. MS. 23986 and printed in I. Aspin, *Anglo Norman Political Songs* (1953), pp. 16–19.

38 Ibid, verse 4, l. 19 seq.

39 Ibid., v. 17, ll. 41–2.

40 Ibid., l. 39.

41 Preserved in the nineteenth-century BM. MS. Harl. 2253 printed in *Anglo Norman Political Songs* (1953), pp. 28–32.

42 *Mirour de l'Omme*, l. 1397 seq.

43 Chandos Herald, ll. 1871–9, ll. 2927–8.

44 Ibid., ll. 1877–9.

45 *Marchantes Tale*, l. 742.

46 Chandos Herald, ll. 1610–15.

47 Cf. *Sir Cleges*, ll. 13072; *Sir Amadas*, ll. 50–61; *Sir Degrevant*, ll. 81–8; *Sir Isumbras*, ll. 19–24.

48 As late as the thirteenth century this viewpoint is still represented in England by the *Roman de Toute Chevalerie* of Eustace of Kent. This is supported by the English version of the *Romaunt of the Rose*, ll. 1149–86.

49 *Romaunt of the Rose*, ll. 955–7. Cf. l. 1211 seq.

50 Cf. Early English Text Society, E.S. XIII.

51 *Gawain and the Grene Knight*, l. 917.
52 E.g. *Sir Degrevant*, l. 729 seq.
53 Chandos Herald, f. 20r, ll. 1419–20.
54 Ibid., f. 54, l. 3799 seq.
55 Ibid., ll. 2577–8.
56 Prologue to the Canterbury Tales, l. 100.
57 Ibid., ll. 69–70.
58 *Livre des faicts de Jean Bouciquaut*, Pt. 1, cap. 37.
59 MS. Arundel XIV, 'College of Arms', Cf. 'Courtoisie' in C. West, *Anglo Norman Literature* (1938), p. 145.
60 Ibid., f. 237r, 1.
61 *Sir Gawain and the Grene Knight*, ll. 1278–9.
62 E.g. Chandos Herald, f. 22v, ll. 1585–98 and f. 29, ll. 2050–70, for the relationship between the Prince and Princess of Wales.
63 E.g. *Book of the Duchesse*, l. 1285 seq.
64 E.g. Adam of Usk (ed. E. M. Thompson, p. 8).
65 For the conventional union between romantic love and marriage apparently expected by the audience of metrical romances, cf. *Sir Degrevant*, ll. 513–76; *Sir Eglamour*, ll. 145–80, l. 1297 seq.; *Partonope of Blois*, ll. 1220–60, l. 5219 seq. There will be fuller discussion in the next chapter.
66 E.g. *Sir Tarrent of Portyngale*, l. 37 seq., and *Sir Degrevant* passim.
67 *Gawain and the Grene Knight*, l. 1274.
68 Ibid., l. 640.
69 Prologue to the *Canterbury Tales*, ll. 94–6.
70 Ibid., ll. 89–90.
71 *Sir Degrevant*, ll. 37 seq.
72 Cf. *Lyf of Ipomedon*, l. 53 seq.

> Tholomew a clerk he toke
> Who taught the chylde upon the boke
> both to synge and to rede.

73 E.g. *Livre des faicts de Jean Bouciquaut*, Pt. 4, cap. 7.
74 *Histoire de Guillaume le Marechal*, ed. P. Meyer. Paris, 1891.
75 E.g. l. 18708 seq. (op. cit.).
76 l. 18141.
77 l. 18481 seq.
78 ll. 18369–70.
79 l. 607 seq.
80 l. 18532 seq.
81 *Morte D'Arthur*, Bk. XXI, ch. 13.

XIV

pp. 129–36   The Heroine and Marriage

1 Ed. A. Ewert, 2 vols. 1932–3.

2   Caius College Cambridge MS. 107 and Cambridge University Library MS. Ff. II. 38.

3   *Gui de Warewic,* l. 67 seq.

4   E.g. l. 1077 seq.

5   The heroine in *Partonope of Blois* had had a hundred masters; the heroine in *William of Palerne* was 'lettred at the best'; Floredespine knew Latin, chess and the courses of the stars; even Melidor in *Degrevant* had adorned her bed chamber with the statues of philosophers and of Augustine Ambrose, Jerome and Gregory.

6   Downwards from hair to feet.

7   *The Book of the Duchesse,* l. 855 seq. and l. 943 seq.

8   *Les Chansons de Guilhem de Cabestanh,* ed. A. Langfors (1924); cf. I, 2; IV, 3; V, 7.

9   Ed. J. Anglade (1923), XXII, 7; XXX, 1–2.

10 *Book of the Duchesse,* ll. 848–853.

11 Cambridge Gg. IV. 27, *Responcio ad Amicam,* l. 49; printed in *Early English Lyrics* (1921), pp. 18–19. E. K. Chambers and F. Sidgwick.

12 Arundel MS. 14 (College of Arms). For the analysis of this allegory I am indebted to C. West, *Courtoisie in Anglo-Norman literature* (1938), pp. 144–50.

13 The term was first popularized by M. Gaston Paris. It should be described more accurately as '*fyn amour*'.

14 *The Book of the Duchesse,* ll. 1285–6.

15 Early English Text Society (1867), E.S. 1 (3), op. cit., ll. 732 seq.; 874 seq.

16 Ed. A. T. Bodtker (1912).

17 E.E.T.S., E.S. 55.

18 *Frankeleyn's Tale,* ll. 37–8.

19 Op. cit., ll. 21–2.

20 Op. cit., l. 64 seq.

21 Op. cit., ll. 34–5.

22 Op. cit., l. 41.

23 *Knightes Tale,* l. 3103 seq.

XV

pp. *138–45*   *The Conflict of Loyalties*

1   E.g. Chandos Herald, ll. 2266, 4200, 4212, 4236.

2   Corpus Christi, Cambridge, MS. 50; British Museum M.S. Royal 12 C. XII; Carlsruhe Durlac 38. I have done no personal work on these MSS. My knowledge of them is derived from M. D. Legge, *Anglo-Norman Literature and its background* (1963), p. 119.

3   The Auchinleck MS. has also been dated 1330–40.

4   These began in 1387. Cf. E. Perroy: *L'Angleterre et le grand schisme d'Occident,* p. 301 seq.

5   Cf. Thomas Walsingham: *Historia Anglicana*, vol. 2, p. 148.
6   *Summa*, Secunda Secundae, Question 23, article 1.
7   Ibid., Prima Secundae, Question 28, article 1.
8   English version, Fragment B, ll. 5203–4 (ed. W. W. Skeat, p. 53).
9   For a possible Latin source, cf. Ambrose, *De Ociis*, III, 22, but the idea could also be derived from the ceremonies of blood brotherhood.
10 *Amis and Amiloun*, ll. 151–2.
11 Cf. Gervase Mathew, 'The Ideals of Friendship', *Patterns of Love and Courtesy*, ed. J. Lawlor. 1966.
12 Edited by T. Wright in *Specimens of Lyric Poetry* (1842), pp. 18–22.
13 *Amis and Amiloun*, ll. 91–2.
14 *Parlement of Foules*, l. 582 seq.
15 *Troilus and Criseyde*, Bk. I, l. 810 seq.
16 Egerton MS. 2862.
17 Against this, note how Lanval refuses the wife of his lord: 'I have long served the King; I will not now break faith' (Marie de France, *Lanval*, v. 271).
18 *Knightes Tale*, l. 270 seq.
19 Ibid., l. 306.
20 This is of course an echo from Mr. G. Lapsley.
21 Cf. T. F. T. Plucknett, *The Legislation of Edward I* (1941), pp. 102–8.
22 For the indenture companies and their consequences, cf. A. E. Prince in *Historical Essays in Honour of James Tait* (1933), pp. 283–98, and N. B. Lewis 'The Organization of Indentured Retinues in Fourteenth Century England,' *Transactions of the Royal Historical Society* (1945).
23 Op. cit. (1941), p. 110.

XVI

pp. 147–59   *The King's Policies*

1   It is recorded that Richard would wear his uncle's collar of SS as a compliment to him and would hold him by his arm; and he had built apartments for him at the court at Eltham. Cf. Chapter 3.
2   Cf. e.g., the career of Sir Henry Green or the patronage afforded to Geoffrey Chaucer or John Gower.
3   Thomas Walsingham, *Historia Anglicana* (1863–4), vol. 2, p. 196.
4   St John's College MS. 209, f. 57.
5   T. F. Tout, *Chapters in Medieval Administrative History* (1920–33), vol. 3, p. 473.
6   Cf. the verses in Stowe MS. 393, f. 99v.
7   For a detached consideration of this expedition, cf. Edmund Curtis, *Richard II in Ireland 1394–1395* (1928) and *History of Medieval Ireland* (1938), p. 265 seq.
8   Cf. *Annales Ricardi*, p. 174 seq. and *Fasciculi Zizaniorum*, p. 360.

9 Cf. Anthony Steel, *Richard II*, p. 211.
10 Possibly coined because a Lollard was supposed to 'lullen' in a sing-song voice.
11 T. Wright, *Political Poems* (Rolls series, 1859–61), vol. 2, p. 244; the attribution to Hoccleve is only probable.
12 Cf. Roger Dymoke, *Liber contra duodecim errores et hereses Lollardorum*. Cambridge, Trinity Hall, MS. 17.
13 Though there is an attempt to associate this with Wycliffe's teaching in his *Trialogus*.
14 *Annales Ricardi*, p. 183.
15 For a different interpretation of this curious episode cf. Anthony Steel, *Richard II* (1941), pp. 223–6.
16 For the official version cf. *Traison et Mort*, ed. Williams (1846), p. 119 seq.
17 It may be noted that St John the Baptist was shown in the Wilton Diptych as a special patron of the King.
18 In *Political Poems*, ed. T. Wright (1859–61), vol. 1, p. 381.
19 Anthony Steel, *The Receipt of the Exchequer* (1954), pp. 80–1.
20 *Calendar of Patent Rolls*, 1396–9.
21 E.g. ibid., pp. 332, 333, 382, 383, 407, 412, 495, 535.
22 T. F. Tout, *Chapters in Medieval Administrative History* (1920–33), vol. 4, p. 208.
23 Ibid., vol. 4, p. 473.
24 Ibid., p. 475.
25 M. V. Clarke, *Fourteenth Century Studies* (1937), p. 277.
26 Cf. the Commissions of the Peace of the 27th of July, 1397, *Calendar of Patent Rolls*, 1396–9, pp. 227–40.
27 T. F. Tout, op. cit., vol. 4, p. 43.
28 M. V. Clarke, *Fourteenth Century Studies* (1937), p. 105.
29 G. A. Holmes, *The Estates of the Higher Nobility in Fourteenth Century England* (1957), p. 5.
30 It is an argument in favour of his good health during 1398 that he was appointed to two great offices, first on the 11th of March, then on the 18th of August. But these were honours and the work would have been by deputies.
31 Adam of Usk, *Chronicon* (ed. 1904), p. 24. Mowbray died at Venice during 1399.
32 In the case of Thomas Bagehot this was unjustifiable.
33 *Annales Ricardi*, pp. 248–9.
34 It will be noted that I have followed Miss Clarke and Professor Galbraith in accepting a conflation of *Dieulacres Chronicle* with Creton and with the *Traison et Mort*. Cf. 'The Deposition of Richard II', by M. V. Clarke and V. H. Galbraith, published in Miss Clarke's *Fourteenth Century Studies* (1937), p. 53 seq.

XVII

The Revolution

1 Cf. James Campbell, 'England, Scotland and the Hundred years War in the Fourteenth Century', in *Europe in the Late Middle Ages* (1965), ed. J. Hale, p. 215.

2 Cf. G. A. Holmes, *The Estates of the Higher Nobility in Fourteenth Century England* (1900), p. 80.

3 *Calendar of Patent Rolls*, 1396–9, p. 213.

4 Note the apparent identity of dialect with that of the Hales Manuscript written in south-west Lancashire about 1410. Cf. *Sir Gawain and the Green Knight*, ed. J. R. R. Tolkien & E. V. Gordon (1963), p. xxii seq.

XVIII

Henry the Fourth

1 Cf. T. F. Tout, *Chapters in Medieval Administrative History* (1920–33), vol. 4, p. 62 seq.

2 *Annales Ricardi*, p. 252.

3 Ibid., pp. 252–4.

4 It was reported that his mother had died of grief when his lands were confiscated after he had killed Ralph Stafford in 1385.

5 R.3.20. I have not worked on this manuscript and my authority is only the citation in J. E. Wells, *Manual of the Writings in Middle English* (1916), pp. 635–6.

6 Ibid., p. 635.

7 *Calendar of Fine Rolls*, vol. XI, p. 293. He had already been granted Reigate Castle and many of the Fitzalan manors.

8 Royal grants to the Duke of Exeter are recorded in the *Calendar of Patent Rolls* 1396–9, pp. 97, 216, 231, 233, 238, 240, 266, 280, 360, 404, 421, 453, 461, 467, 472, 483, 488, 514, 526, 537.

9 *Calendar of Patent Rolls*, 1396–9, p. 215.

10 Ibid., p. 217.

11 In all Thomas Holland received twenty-five grants from Richard II. Cf. *Calendar of Patent Rolls*, 1396–9, pp. 140, 144, 150, 151, 200, 215, 280, 315, 316, 332, 336, 339, 344, 374, 410, 416, 429, 456, 461, 472, 480, 483, 488, 500, 563.

12 Henry had mustered troops for Richard about August the 28th, had been appointed Trier of Petitions on September the 17th, had attacked the Earl of Arundel during his trial and had been created Duke of Hereford on September the 29th. Ralph Neville had acted as Constable during the trial and had been created Earl of Westmorland on September the 29th.

13 *Calendar of Close Rolls* 1399–1402, p. 110.

14 It does not seem defensible to write of the house of Lancaster as a new dynasty; the Mortimers would have been a new dynasty had they succeeded to the throne.

15 Anthony Steel, *Receipts of the Exchequer, 1377–1485* (1954), p. 147.

16 Ibid., pp. 139, 145.

o

Notes on the Plates

Frontis: Richard II.

Detail from the Wilton Diptych in the National Gallery, London.

This is a detail from the front of the left panel of the diptych. It is in tempera, on a gesso coating applied to oak. It is suggested in the text that the diptych is the product of a court workshop, probably in London; and that it was painted by several masters possibly about 1395 in order to commemorate the coronation at Westminster on the 16th of July, 1377. But it is characteristic of the eclecticism of international court art that there are clear echoes from Siena in the left-hand panel just as there seem to be echoes from Paris in the panel to the right. The patterning and the sense of textile and the background and the arm of St John the Baptist are all reminiscent of the Sienese *Trecento*. There is nothing Sienese in the face and hands of the King. In this detail the hand of St John the Baptist, Richard's special patron, is resting on the King's shoulder in protection. The King is wearing a broomscod collar and broomscods encircle his personal badge, the white hart. It is possible that the broomscods are a play upon the name Plantagenet, though that was not used as a surname until the fifteenth century. It has also been suggested that Richard assumed them as the badge of the Kings of France. His robes are also embroidered with the imperial eagles, probably in reference to his claim to be the 'entire emperor of his realm', though there may be a reference to his father-in-law, the Emperor Charles IV. The badges, with the heraldry painted on the reverse of the panel, seem to make it impossible that the diptych was commissioned before Richard was aged twenty-eight. The fact that he is shown as a young adolescent, like the presence of eleven angels in the opposite panel, could refer to his coronation in his eleventh year.

[*Reproduced by courtesy of the Trustees, the National Gallery, London*]

1   The entry of Charles of Luxembourg into Paris.
     Bibliothèque Nationale MS. Français 2813, f. 470v.   *f.p. 4*

2   A banquet at the Court in Paris   *f.p. 5*
     Biblio. Nat. MS. Franç. 2813, f. 473v.

These two plates were chosen since they seem to reflect the new international court culture as it was being formed in Valois Paris in the year of Richard's accession. In Plate 1 Richard's father-in-law, the Emperor Charles IV, is shown entering Paris in 1377 with his son Wenceslaus of Luxembourg, who had been crowned King of the Romans on July 6, 1376. Charles V of France rides between them. It is very characteristic of the period that there should be

[199]

a reminiscence of the journey of the Three Kings to the Epiphany. In Plate 2 the Emperors King Charles and King Wenceslaus are seated at a banquet in Paris. It has been chosen as a most vivid representation of the dramatic performances provided as entertainment during a meal at court; this was the forerunner of the court masque.

3   The white hart from the Wilton Diptych.   *f.p. 20*
      National Gallery, London.

The white hart on the reverse of the left panel of the diptych represents Richard's personal cognizance first distributed at the Smithfield tournament in October 1390. It is a masterpiece of the court art of Richard II, perhaps its greatest masterpiece. It is clearly by a different hand from the paintings on the front of the panels and does not suggest the same workshop. In the text it is proposed, very tentatively, that it may be the work of John Siferwas. But that is only because it seems unlikely that there were two contemporary artists associated with the court who shared the same mastery of line and the same power of conveying intrinsic animal life.

[*Reproduced by courtesy of the Trustees, the National Gallery, London*]

4   The Court of Heaven.   *f.p. 21*
      Detail from the Wilton Diptych, National Gallery, London.

This is from the right-hand panel of the diptych. The four angels suggest some of its many *courtois* elements: they are the squires of the Mother of God, but they are also King Richard's squires, since they are wearing his livery of the white hart on long blue gowns of the Virgin's colour. They are slender, pale-skinned and yellow-haired and share with the young king on the left panel that curiously epicene quality of adolescence which was so prized in the international court culture and praised by Christine de Pisan. One has an arm on the other's neck in sign of the virtue of friendship.

But the illustration was also chosen because when it is compared to the frontispiece it provides an occasion to discuss a recent theory of Miss Margaret Rickert. This is not referred to in the text since it seemed too unnecessarily complex. Miss Rickert suggests in her *Painting in Britain* (1965), that the two panels of the diptych were painted at different periods and that the left panel was originally part of a quite different composition, possibly a triptych. She emphasizes that Sienese antecedents are apparent in the left panel but not in that on the right. Granted the eclectic character of late fourteenth-century international court art this would be natural since the subjects of the two panels are different. A procession of three saints would suggest a convention ultimately derived from the wing of some Sienese triptych; a representation of the Court of Heaven might reflect a court scene from Burgundian illumination with a dull green foreground sprinkled with flowers. She stresses the different colour schemes of the two panels yet it could be urged that taken together they form a single harmony, and that the right panel depicts the light of the Court of Heaven. But she is obviously correct in noting that the hands of the angels cannot have been painted by the same artist as those of King Richard and St John the Baptist. This would be normal if the Wilton Diptych was the product of a single court workshop rather than of one master.

[*Reproduced by courtesy of the Trustees, the National Gallery, London*]

5   Richard II in Westminster Abbey.   *f.p. 36*

This panel portrait of Richard now in the south side of the nave of Westminster Abbey is 7 ft by 3 ft 7 in. It has been suggested by Professor Borenius and Dr Tristram that it was painted in 1390 when the King was twenty-three; this is unprovable but not unlikely. Clearly it is the work of a court master. The face is modelled softly by shading from dark to white and is balanced by the heavy mass of hair; the elaborate curving pattern of the soft red cloak is emphasized by its ermine lining. The crowned R's on the long inner tunic are placed rhythmically among the lozenge-shaped embroideries. The panel has been attributed to André Beauneveu, who is known to have been in Richard's employment; but there is nothing to suggest that the master was French, nor for that matter that he was English. I have suggested the possibility that the master came from the Rhineland, but there are resemblances between his style and that of the Dubečeker altar piece at Prague and it is also possible that he was a Bohemian court painter who had come with Anne of Luxembourg. There may have been a companion portrait of the queen. For Bohemian parallels to the Westminster portrait of Richard, cf. A. Strange *Deutsche Malerei der Gotik*, vol. II (Berlin 1936), plates 69, 70, 71.

[*Reproduced by courtesy of the Dean and Chapter of Westminster*]

6   The Great Hall at Westminster.   *f.p. 37*

The Great Hall of Richard's palace at Westminster was built between January the 21st, 1393, and 1400. John Godmeston was Clerk of the Works, Hugh Herland was the King's Carpenter, Henry Yevele was the Master Mason with John Swallow and Richard Washbourne working under him. It is 240 ft long by 70 ft in span. Its chief technical innovation lay in the hammer beams and arch rib of Hugh Herland's vaulting.

[*Crown copyright reserved*]

7   The Studley Royal Bowl.   *f.p. 52*
     Victoria and Albert Museum, London.

It is agreed that the Studley bowl dates from the end of the fourteenth century and is English silver-ware but nothing is known of its provenance. For forty years it was used as an alms dish at Studley Royal Church near Ripon. But this does not necessarily suggest a northern origin; a bronze jug from London marked with the white hart badge has been found at Kumasi in Ghana. It is at least possible that it is court ware and from a London workshop. It is a silver gilt covered drinking-bowl engraved with gothic foliage, with letters from the alphabet and with contractions of letters. Clearly it was for secular use and it is of consummate elegance.

[*Reproduced by courtesy of the Trustees, the Victoria and Albert Museum, London*]

8   The Rokewode Mazer.   *f.p. 53*
     Victoria and Albert Museum, London.

The Rokewode Mazer has been chosen to represent another kind of drinking vessel sufficiently prized to be given personal names—'Benedictus', 'Caritas', or 'Benison'; 'Beaulchier' or 'Crumpledud'—but probably not used in the confines of the court though common among the well-to-do. A mazer is a drinking cup of maple wood mounted in silver and usually with an inscription. The Rokewode Mazer is inscribed with the poem.

> Hold your tunge and sey the best
> And let your negbore sitte in rest
> Hoe so lustythe god to plese
> Let his neygbore lyve in ese.

Mr Charles Oman ascribes it to the late fourteenth century in *English Domestic Silver* (1965), p. 22.

[*Reproduced by courtesy of the Trustees, the Victoria and Albert Museum, London*]

9   The Annunciation from the 'Beaufort Book of Hours'.   *f.p. 60*
     British Museum Roy. MS.2.A. XVIII, f. 23v.

This is perhaps the most perfect surviving example of the art of the court illuminators. It is $8\frac{1}{2}$ in. by $5\frac{1}{4}$ in. It has been attributed to Herman Scheere and it was held that the kneeling man and woman were John Beaufort, Marquess of Dorset, and Elisabeth Holland, whom he married in 1399. This was Dr Evans' hypothesis, but it must be noted that it has been challenged by Miss Margaret Rickert in an article in the *Burlington Magazine* for 1962 (CIV, 'The so-called Beaufort Hours and York Psalter.') She maintains that the 'Beaufort' Book of Hours was made for Margaret de Beauchamp, and that the Annunciation scene originally belonged to a psalter which is now at Rennes and which can be dated before 1415. She also holds that though the style is closely related to that of Herman Scheere it is not identical with it. She would date it close to 1400 and would relate it to panels of the Dijon School completed in 1399. (Cf. M. Rickert, *Painting in Britain* (1965), p. 157.)

On either hypothesis the use of the mottoes '*Omnia levia sunt amanti: si quis amat non laborat*' seems to show that the Annunciation scene was painted in Herman Scheere's atelier.

[*Reproduced by courtesy of the Trustees, the British Museum, London*]

10   John, Lord Lovell and John Siferwas.   *pp. 60/1*
      British Museum Harl. MS. 7026, f. 4v.

The painting of the Dominican John Siferwas presenting his lectionary to John, Lord Lovell of Tichmersh, is $11\frac{3}{4}$ in. high by $7\frac{1}{4}$ in. wide. It has a double interest as the self-portrait of a painter and the portrait of a magnate of the second rank. John, 5th Lord Lovell of Tichmersh, built Wardour Castle in Wiltshire in 1393 and died in 1408. He commissioned the lectionary as a gift for Salisbury Cathedral, perhaps about 1400.

But the painting also illustrates the essential traits of Siferwas. He was consciously a master of line and here he relies primarily on line for his modelling. He was probably also a panel painter, and here as in his Crucifixion scene in the Sherborne Missal he uses the page as if it was a panel. He has his own technique for emphasizing the contours of the face by painting heavy white lids over slightly protruding eyes. He had an interest in portraiture and in the details of dress. He used the most expensive pigments: in the Lovell Lectionary the finest gold is combined with the finest ultramarine. He had no sense of background and his human figures, unlike his other animals, are dead.

[*Reproduced by courtesy of the Trustees, the British Museum, London*]

11   Birds in an artist's sketchbook.   *pp. 60/1*
      Magdalene College, Cambridge, Pepysian MS. 1916, f. 13a.

12   Conversation pieces from an artist's sketchbook.   *f.p.61*
      Magdalene College, Cambridge, Pepysian MS. 1916, f.4a.

Pepysian MS. 1916 is the sketchbook of an artist's workshop in the late fourteenth and early fifteenth centuries which would seem to have served both secular and ecclesiastical patrons. The drawings could be used as a basis for either panel painting, wall painting or manuscript illumination. They are in at least four hands; only one is that of a master. It is suggested in the text that this may be the sketchbook of John Siferwas' atelier since some of its birds are identical with those on the margin of his Sherborne Missal.

[*Reproduced by courtesy of the Master and Fellows of Magdalene College, Cambridge*]

13   Thomas Hoccleve and Henry Prince of Wales.   *f.p. 76*
      British Museum Arundel MS. 38, frontispiece.

Thomas Hoccleve is shown presenting his poem the *De Regimine Principum* to Henry of Monmouth Prince of Wales. The miniature is $5\frac{1}{2}$ in. by 4 in. and must have been painted before 1413, when Henry succeeded to the crown. It is clear that it is intended as an individualized portrait of Hoccleve in his dull pink gown with its high collar, with his thick black hair and highly-coloured face, the long nose and his bitterly drooping lips. The young prince is more stylized. There is an emphasis on his rank; his long blue houpelande with its sleeves touching the ground is lined with ermine and its folds are shaded with gilt; his girdle like his coronet is gold. Yet even this is individualized by Henry's pale skin and light brown hair and straight thin lips.

The work of the Hoccleve Master seems easily identifiable through his zest for minute portraiture, strong painting and bright colours. It seems

likely that he was trained in Herman Scheere's workshop and collaborated with him on the illumination of BM. Add MS. 1699B, painting the heads on folio 7. He was employed to illustrate the *Confessio Amantis* of John Gower in BM. Eg. MS. 1991, where his miniature of Gower making his confession is directly derived from that by Scheere in Bodley MS. 294, f. 9 (*see* Plate 14). Philip Repington commissioned him to illuminate the *Compendium super Bibliam* which he presented to Lincoln Cathedral in 1422 and which has been preserved as in BM. Roy. MS. 8 G. 111. The London Charterhouse commissioned him to paint a scene of St Augustine preaching, and the manuscript is now at Cambridge at Gonville and Caius (MS. 433). One of the Scheere mottoes is in its background followed by the letters BEKTLE; it is possible therefore that the Hoccleve Master had some such name as Beckley. He survived to be employed on the Bedford Book of Hours.
[*Reproduced by courtesy of the Trustees, the British Museum, London*]

14   The Lover making his confession.   *pp. 76/7*
     From the *Confessio Amantis* of John Gower, Bodley MS. 294, f. 9.
The scene in which John Gower, the *amans*, makes his confession to the priest, Genius, was illustrated repeatedly by fashionable artists: Bodley MS. 902, f. 8, is in the style of Siferwas but is most probably by the Johannes who painted Venice in Bodley MS. 264 (*see* Plate 16); British Museum MS. Egerton 1991, f. 7v is probably by the Hoccleve master; both Bodley MS. 693, f. 8v and Corpus Christi College, Oxford, MS. 67, f. 9v are by painters of talent. Miss Gereth Spriggs has suggested very convincingly that the illustration in Bodley 294, f. 9 was painted by Herman Scheere. The colour scheme seems characteristic of his work. The Lover wears a deep rose houpelande in contrast with the white robes and dark hood of the priest. The background is gold scrollwork upon a dark crimson wall. The floor of the room in which he is making his confession is covered with green tiles; the moulded frame of the miniature is tinted orange and lined with green. The miniature gives the illusion of a wall-painting and suggests the 'box-space perspective' of Giotto. The contrast between the dark eyes and the pale skin of the priest repeats the colour rhythm of his hood and gown.
     This illustration must not be taken as a portrait of John Gower; it is one of three distinct conventions for the representation of the lover. But it seemed an admirable example of the sensitive art of Herman Scheere.
[*Reproduced by courtesy of the Bodleian Library, Oxford*]

15   Chaucer reading *Troilus and Criseyde*   *pp. 76/7*
     Corpus Christi College, Cambridge, MS. 61, f. 1,v.
This has been chosen to illustrate the relationship between the court and the new literary movement. It is $12\frac{1}{2}$ in. by $8\frac{1}{2}$ in. and represents Chaucer reading *Troilus* to the 'yonge fresshe folkes' of the court within a palace garden. The border of intertwined leaves and flowers is another court allusion. The conception that courtiers may be divided into followers of the flower and

of the leaf seems to be as old as John Gower, and is elaborated in the fifteenth-century court poem *The Flower and the Leaf*: those at court who are virgins or true lovers and good knights belong to the company of Diana, queen of the Leaf; the idle who only delight 'to hunt and hawke and play in medes' follow Flora, queen of the Flower. Perhaps the implication of the border is that the audience consists of both groups, but it is of course a stylized audience. An attempt has been made to identify individual courtiers by Miss Margaret Galway in her article 'The Troilus Frontispiece', in the *Modern Language Review*, XLIV, April 1949, but this seems excessively ingenious and so too is the suggestion that the castle is Windsor. The scene is merely a court at a royal palace.

The painting is early fifteenth century. There is no reason to doubt that it is English, but because it is sophisticated and elegant court art it is also international and influenced by Paris modes. Particularly in its background details there are parallels with *Les Tres Riches Heures du Duc de Berry*, but resemblances have been found as far south as the wall-paintings in the Torre del Aquila at Trent.

[*Reproduced by courtesy of the Master and Fellows, Corpus Christi College, Cambridge*]

16   Venice.   *f.p. 77*
      From *Li Livre du Grant Caam*, Bodleian Library, Oxford, MS. 264, f. 218.

This has been chosen to suggest late fourteenth-century contacts between England and Italy, for it is certainly an English painting but seems based on personal memories of Venice, with its canals and gondolas, the Doge's palace and San Marco and San Giorgio Maggiore, and the winged lion on the column. It is $9\frac{1}{4}$ in. by $12\frac{1}{2}$ in., and forms the frontispiece of *Li Livre du Grant Caam*, which is based on the travels of Marco Polo and has been dated about 1400. It is known that the painter was called John: the signature '*Johannes me fecit*' is written across the cloak of the Great Khan in a later illumination in the same manuscript and in the same hand. His style is so characteristic that it is possible to trace his development. Perhaps he came from East Anglia—his elaborate dresses and gross faces and thick figures suggest some affiliation with the Norwich School—perhaps he visited Venice in the train of Thomas Mowbray in 1398. It seems clear that he was trained in the workshop of John Siferwas and retained his technique for rendering eyes and lids. The first work that could be identified as his is the Crucifixion scene of 1397–8 in the Lapworth missal, now in Corpus Christi College, Oxford. It is likely that he was employed by Siferwas to paint the Ascension scene of the Lovell Lectionary some time before 1408 and he illustrated the *Confessio Amantis* in Bodley MS. 902. He seems to have worked on the Sarum Book of Hours now in Trinity College, Cambridge, and to have been the chief illuminator for *The Hours of Elisabeth the quene* which is now in the British Museum and which may be dated from between 1412 and 1420. He cared for harsh and at times crude colours; he overcrowded his details; he experimented in the vivid expression of strong emotion. His chief quality was his virility.

[*Reproduced by courtesy of the Bodleian Library, Oxford*]

17   The Tree of Jesse.   *f.p. 84*
     Alabaster in the Victoria and Albert Museum, London.

18   The Deposition from the Cross.   *f.p. 85*
     An ivory in the Victoria and Albert Museum, London.

These two plates have been chosen to represent the work of the English alabasterers and ivory carvers at the end of the fourteenth and the beginning of the fifteenth century. Neither of them are court art but both are the work of accomplished craftsmen; it would not be unreasonable to suppose that they were commissioned by some lesser magnate or rich ecclesiastic.

   The alabaster Tree of Jesse is 1 ft. 9 in. high and 11⅛ in. wide. King David rises from his father Jesse and higher in the branches his descendant the Virgin holds the Child Christ in her lap while He is playing with a bird. Above her there are two worshipping angels and she is flanked by the Magdalen holding the ointment jar. There are carefully controlled rhythms that can be traced even in the folds of the draperies. It may be dated tentatively as about 1400.

   The ivory Deposition is perhaps a few years earlier and has some archaic echoes. St Joseph of Arimathea is lifting Christ's body from the cross; behind him the Virgin is kissing Christ's wounded hand. On the left St John the Evangelist leans forward pressing his head towards Christ's breast; beyond him the knight Longinus is still watching. Iconographically it might be suggested that the knight and the woman plucking the nail from Christ's feet were intended to represent the donors. Some of the effects of perspective were intended and were obtained since the carving was in depth.

   Both the alabaster and the ivory would have been painted.

[*Reproduced by courtesy of the Trustees, the Victoria and Albert Museum, London*]

19   Bodiam Castle, Sussex.   *f.p. 100*

Bodiam in Sussex was built for Sir Edward Dallingridge in 1386. It has been chosen to represent the castles built under Richard II, and is characteristic of its period in the delight in geometric precision and in the new zest for privacy: its solar, great chamber, lower lords' hall and lords' kitchen are quite distinct from the retainers' kitchen and the retainers' hall. It is characteristic too of a new class of castle builders. The Dallingridges were typical of these greater landowners who controlled so much of the administration and representation of their counties; Sir Edward Dallingridge was knight of the Shire for Sussex in 1379, 1380, 1381, 1382 and 1384, 1385, 1386 and 1388. His son Sir John was knight of the Shire for Sussex in 1402, 1404, 1406 and 1407. In 1412 their Sussex lands were assessed as worth £100 a year. It is unlikely that such a family would have built a castle earlier; perhaps they only did so then because Sir Edward Dallingridge had close associations with the Court, where he was one of Richard's councillors. Fifty-two licences to build new castles were granted during Richard's reign, normally to be homes for the 'great men of the shires' or lesser magnates—like the quadrangle at Lumley in Durham completed by Ralph Lord Lumley in 1392, or the hexagon at Wardour in Wiltshire built by John Lord Lovell in 1393. It should be noted that this grouping of castle builders usually had a rather larger income than the Dallingridges; thus the Lovell estates brought in £275 a year in 1412.

[*Reproduced by courtesy of the National Trust and A. F. Kersting*]

20   Tiles from a kiln at Bawsey, Norfolk.   *f.p. 101*
       British Museum.

These tiles from the kiln at Bawsey near Kings Lynn have been chosen to represent late fourteenth-century English ceramics. They would seem to be floor tiles rather than wall tiles, though the technique used would be suitable for both. They depend for their decorative value on colour and relief—a design in relief or counter relief was stamped on the surface of the clay and the tile was then covered by a lead glaze; a dark green, a bright green or a clear yellow were the colours most used at Bawsey; a gold brown was very common at other kilns. The average size is about 4½ in. square. The public for which the tilewrights worked was partly ecclesiastical—the kiln provided the pavement of the Chapter House at Castle Acre and at least one tile for the tomb of a Vicar of Snettisham—but the heraldry suggests that they may also have had a domestic use among the magnates and local landowners. The arms of Thorpe and Patten have been identified as well as those of Beauchamp, Warrenne and probably Neville. The Bawsey kiln has been discussed by Miss Elizabeth Eames in the *Antiquaries Journal* for 1955, pp. 162–81.

[*Reproduced by courtesy of the Trustees, the British Museum*]

21   The 'Black Prince'.   *f.p. 116*
       From the effigy in Canterbury Cathedral.

The bronze effigy of Edward of Woodstock, the 'Black Prince', has been chosen to suggest the ideals of knighthood in which Richard would have been brought up. Edward died in 1376 and this is the monument placed by his widow on his grave at Canterbury. It is realist in the detailed treatment of the armour. It is idealized as a portrait; emphasis is placed on three traits then admired in a man's beauty; straight brows, wide shoulders and a narrow waist. The prince is shown as above all calm and '*mesuré*', a courtois quality that it is very unlikely that he possessed. The chief beauty of the effigy lies in its proportions and in the intricate rhythm of the lilies and leopards that were the prince's coat of arms.

[*Reproduced by courtesy of the Trustees, the National Portrait Gallery, London*]

22 Knights jousting. *f.p. 117*
   Wood-carving on a chest in the Victoria and Albert Museum, London.
This carving on an oak chest is 3 ft. 2½ in. long and 1 ft. 3¼ in. high. It is said
to have come from Rufford in Nottinghamshire and it has been tentatively
attributed to a York workshop. It has been dated to the late fourteenth
century, but the armour of the tilting knights suggests that it is not much
later than about 1370. It can be paralleled by the carving on an oak chest
now in the vestry of York Minster, where two knights rescue two women
from their dragons.
[*Reproduced by courtesy of the Trustees, the Victoria and Albert Museum, London*]

23 A heroine. *f.p. 132*
   From the tapestry 'La Dame à la Licorne', Musée de Cluny, Paris.
This detail from the early sixteenth-century French tapestry of 'La Dame à
la Licorne' has been chosen to illustrate the essentially conservative character
of the medieval heroine. There were two variants of the ideal of the twelfth-
century hero: the adventurous adolescent and the accomplished warrior.
Both survived until the sixteenth century, but especially during the fourteenth
century they had gained clusters of fresh nuances primarily owing to the
formalization of the ideals of chivalry.
   There were three variants of the villain in twelfth-century fiction:
Ganelon the Betrayer, the Felon King and the Evil Steward. By the fifteenth
century the cast has been multiplied by being subdivided: thus the Tale
Bearer descends from Ganelon and both the Wicked Sheriff and the Lecher-
ous Priest derive from the Evil Steward.
   But there seems to be only one heroine in a *roman courtois*. The twelfth-
century Latin rhetorical convention, the *Descriptio Puellae*, formalized the
details of her beauty and her character traits were repeated in sanctioned
French epithets. Perhaps it became fashionable to conform to both. In the
fourteenth century she has at times a more active rôle and seeks adventures
as well as endures them, and there seems a new stress on the mutual dependence between her and her lover. But the continuity is so marked that shortly
after 1500 a French tapestry worker can portay a heroine who might have
been the thirteenth-century Felice of Warwick: tall, slender, white skinned,
with clear eyes; completely self controlled, a little didactic.
[*Reproduced by courtesy of the Musée de Cluny, Paris: Photographie Giraudon*]

24 A Virgin at Winchester. *f.p. 133*
   From a window in Thurbern's Chantry in the Chapel
   of Winchester College, Hampshire.
This has been chosen to represent the finest of the stained glass of the
reign of Richard II. It can be dated with exactness to 1393 and was the work
of Thomas Glazier of Oxford. It was commissioned by William of Wykeham
as the centre to the Jesse Tree in the east window of the chapel at Winchester
College. It was removed in the early nineteenth century but was brought

back in 1951 and is now in a window of the west wall of the college chapel, in Thurbern's Chantry.

The influence of Thomas Glazier seems central to the new development of English stained glass. He was employed before 1386 on the glass in the ante-chapel of New College. In 1393 his prestige was so high that his portrait and signature were recorded in the Jesse Window at Winchester. He returned to work on the side windows at Winchester in 1421–2. He was original in the firm delicate modelling of his figure work, in his architectural detail and in his iconography. He had marked influence on John Thornton of Coventry, who was probably his pupil. The technical climax of his school seems to be the great east window in York Minster, 78 ft. high by 32 ft. wide which was glazed by John Thornton between 1405 and 1408.

The serenely wondering humanism of the Virgin, and the Child clutching the bird, are reminiscent of the North Italian international court art of Thomas Glazier's contemporary Stefano da Zevio.

[*Reproduced by courtesy of the Warden and Fellows of Winchester College, Hampshire. Photograph by Dennis King*]

25	Richard's army in Ireland being revictualled. British Museum Harl. MS. 1319, f. 7b.	*f.p. 148*
26	Archbishop Arundel inciting the people against Richard. British Museum Harl. MS. 1319, f. 12.	*f.p. 148*
27	Richard returns with a favouring wind. British Museum Harl. MS. 1319, f. 18b.	*f.p. 149*
28	Northumberland cozens Richard at Conway Castle. British Museum Harl. MS. 1319, f. 50.	*f.p. 149*
29	Henry of Bolingbroke brings Richard back to London. British Museum Harl. MS. 1319, f. 53b.	*f.p. 164*
30	The vacant throne. British Museum Harl. MS. 1319, f. 57.	*f.p. 164*

Harleian MS. 1319 in the British Museum contains the *Histoire du Roy Richard* written in French verse by Jean Creton, a 'valet' of Charles VI of France who had joined Richard's court in 1398, had accompanied him to Ireland in June 1399 and who had the Earl of Salisbury as his patron. It is early fifteenth-century and was in the possession of Charles of Anjou, Count of Maine. Unlike the other nine MSS. of Creton it has some pretensions to be a manuscript de luxe. It has sixteen miniatures which convey vividly Creton's strong prejudices in Richard's favour. They are crowded with realist detail and there are attempts at portraiture; a typical size is 4¼ in. by 4½ in. The six plates chosen stress the points that Creton emphasized.

The difficulties of Richard's campaign in Ireland against Art MacMurrough are illustrated in the first plate, where his starving troops are revictualled by ships from Dublin. Meanwhile Henry of Bolingbroke and Archbishop Arundel have landed in England and the second plate shows Archbishop Arundel attempting to rouse the people against Richard by reading from a forged Papal Bull. In the third Richard sails back from Waterford to Milford with a favouring wind. In the next Richard is at Conway Castle and the Earl of Northumberland is kneeling before him cozening him into surrender. In the next Henry of Bolingbroke is leading Richard into London. And finally there is Richard's deposition with the Earls of Westmorland and Northumberland standing by his empty throne, and Henry of Bolingbroke waiting behind.

[*Reproduced by courtesy of the Trustees, the British Museum*]

31   Henry IV.   *f.p. 165*
       From the effigy in Canterbury Cathedral.

The alabaster effigy of Henry IV was set up at Canterbury in about 1405. It may have come from the London workshop of Thomas Colyn, Thomas Holewell and Thomas Popehove who were employed by his wife in 1408. In contrast to the effigy of his uncle the Black Prince it seems a completely individualized and rather convincing portrait.

[*Reproduced by courtesy of the Trustees, the National Portrait Gallery, London*]

Bibliography

I HISTORY

The Primary Sources

ADAM OF USK, *Chronicon*, ed. E. Maunde Thompson. London, 1904.

Ancient Kalendars and Inventories of the Treasury of the Exchequer, ed. F. Palgrave, vol. III. London, 1836.

Annales Ricardi II et Henrici IV, ed. H. T. Riley, Rolls Series. London, 1874.

Calendar of the Close Rolls. London, 1892.

Calendar of the Fine Rolls. London, 1911.

Calendar of the Patent Rolls. London, 1893.

JEAN CRETON, *French Metrical History of the Deposition of Richard II*, ed. J. Webb, Royal Society of Antiquaries. London, 1819.

Diplomatic Correspondence of Richard II, ed. E. Perroy, Camden 3rd Series, XLVIII. London, 1933.

Eulogium Historiarum, ed. F. S. Haydon, 3 vols., Rolls Series. London, 1858–63.

THE MONK OF EVESHAM, *Historia Vitae et Regni Ricardi II*, ed. T. Hearne. Oxford, 1729.

Fasciculi Zizaniorum, ed. W. W. Shirley, Rolls Series. London, 1858.

JEAN FROISSART, *Chroniques*, ed. Kervyn de Lettenhove. Brussels, 1863.

Issues of the Exchequer, extracted and translated by F. Devon. London, 1837.

Political Poems, ed. T. Wright, 2 vols., Rolls Series. London, 1859–61.

Historical Poems, ed. R. H. Robbins. Columbia, 1959.

[211]

The Scrope and Grosvenor Controversy, ed. H. Nicholas. London, 1832.

Traison et Mort, ed. B. Williams, English Historical Society. London, 1846.

THOMAS WALSINGHAM, *Chronicon Anglie*, ed. E. Maunde Thompson, Rolls Series. London, 1874.

—*Historia Anglicana*, ed. H. T. Riley, 2 vols., Rolls Series. London, 1863–4.

Secondary Sources

M. ASTON, *Thomas Arundel*. Oxford, 1967.

R. CAGGESE, *Roberto d'Angio*, 2 vols. Florence, 1922, 1931.

M. V. CLARKE, *Fourteenth Century Studies*. Oxford, 1937.

H. M. COLVIN (ed.), *The History of the King's Works*, vol. II. London, 1963.

A. COVILLE, *Gontier et Pierre Col*. Paris, 1934.

E. CURTIS, *Richard II in Ireland 1394–5*. Oxford, 1927.

J. G. EDWARDS, 'The Parliamentary Committee of 1398', *English Historical Review*, XL, pp. 321–33.

V. H. GALBRAITH, 'A new life of Richard II', *History*, 1947.

G. A. HOLMES, *The Estates of the Higher Nobility in Fourteenth Century England*. Cambridge, 1957.

MAURICE KEEN, *The Outlaws of Medieval Legend*. London, 1961.

—*The Laws of War in the Late Middle Ages*, London, 1965.

G. LAPSLEY, 'The Parliamentary Title of Henry IV', *English Historical Review*, XLIX, pp. 432–49, pp. 577–606.

—'Richard II's Last Parliament,' *English Historical Review*, LIII, pp. 53–78.

E. G. LEONARD, *Les Angevins de Naples*. Paris, 1954.

N. B. LEWIS, 'Simon Burley and Baldwin Raddington,' *English Historical Review*, LII, pp. 662–9.

K. B. McFARLANE, 'Parliament and Bastard Feudalism', *Transactions of the Royal Historical Society*, 1944, Fourth Series, Vol. 26, pp. 53–79.

Bibliography

M. McKisack, *The Fourteenth Century, 1307–1399*. Oxford, 1959.

J. N. Myres, 'The Campaign of Radcot Bridge', *English Historical Review*, XLII, pp. 20–33.

W. A. Pantin, *The English Church in the Fourteenth Century*. Cambridge, 1955.

E. Perroy, *L'Angleterre et le grand Schisme d'occident*. Paris, 1933.

M. J. Pinet, *Christine de Pisan*. Paris, 1927.

H. G. Richardson, 'Heresy and the Lay Power under Richard II,' *English Historical Review*, LI, pp. 1–28.

A. Steel, 'English Government Finance, 1377–1413', *English Historical Review*, LI, pp. 29–51.

—*Richard II*. Cambridge, 1941; rev. ed. 1952.

—*The Receipt of the Exchequer*. Cambridge, 1954.

M. Thibault, *Isabeau de Bavière*. Paris, 1903.

T. F. Tout, *Chapters in Medieval Administrative History*, 6 vols. Manchester, 1920–33.

—*Collected Papers*, 3 vols. Manchester, 1932.

II ENGLISH PAINTING

Joan Evans, *English Art, 1307–1461*. Oxford, 1949.

—'The Wilton Diptych Reconsidered', *Archaeological Journal*, CV, 1950.

John Harvey, 'The Wilton Diptych, a Re-examination', *Archaeologia*, XCVIII, 1961.

J. A. Herbert, *The Sherborne Missal,* Roxburgh Club. Oxford, 1920.

M. R. James, *An English Mediaeval Sketch Book No. 1916 in the Pepysian Library, Magdalene College, Cambridge*, Walpole Society, XIII, 1924–5.

Charles Kuhn, 'Herman Scheere and English Illumination of the Early Fifteenth Century,' *Art Bulletin*, XXII, 1940.

Margaret Rickert, *The Reconstructed Carmelite Missal*. London, 1952.

—'The So-Called Beaufort Hours and York Psalter,' *Burlington Magazine*, CIV, 1962.

P

Margaret Rickert, *Painting in Britain, The Middle Ages*, Pelican History of Art. Penguin, 1954.

G. Schmidt, 'Two Unknown English Horae from the Fifteenth Century,' *Burlington Magazine*, CIII, 1961.

G. M. Spriggs, 'Unnoticed Bodleian Manuscripts Illuminated by Herman Scheere and his School', *Bodleian Library Record*, Vol. 7, n.4, December 1964.

E. W. Tristram, *'English Wall Painting of the Fourteenth Century'*, London, 1955.

Christopher Woodforde, 'English Stained Glass and Glass-painters in the Fourteenth Century', *Proceedings of the British Academy*, XXV, 1939.

—*The Stained Glass of New College Oxford*. London, 1951.

Francis Wormald, 'The Wilton Diptych,' *Journal of the Warburg and Courtauld Institutes*, XVII, 1954.

III ENGLISH POETRY

The following may be cited:

Printed Primary Sources

The following list includes most of the texts of the English and Anglo-French verses referred to in this study. *The Testament of Love* has been included for convenience. E.E.T.S. represents the Early English Texts Society; O.S., Original Series; E.S., Extra Series; C.F.M.A., Classiques français du Moyen Age.

Amys and Amiloun, ed. M. Leach, 1937, E.E.T.S., O.S., 203.

John Audelay, *Poems*, 1931, E.E.T.S., O.S., 184.

The Chandos Herald, ed. M. K. Pope and E. C. Lodge. Oxford, 1902.

Geoffrey Chaucer, ed. W. W. Skeat. Oxford, 1894.

—*The Text of the Canterbury Tales*, ed. J. M. Manley, E. Rickert, M. Dean, H. McIntosh. Chicago, 1946.

—*Chaucer Life Records*, ed. M. Crow and C. C. Olson. Oxford, 1966.

Sir Thomas Clanvowe, 'The Cuckoo and the Nightingale', ed. W. W. Skeat, *Chaucerian and other Pieces*. Oxford, 1897.

Bibliography

Degrevant, ed. L. F. Casson, 1949, E.E.T.S., O.S., 221.

Floriant and Florete, ed. Francisque Michel. Roxburgh Club, 1873.

Floris and Blancheflour, ed. A. B. Taylor. Oxford, 1929.

Firumbras (and *Otuel and Roland*), ed. M. I. O'Sullivan, 1935, E.E.T.S., O.S., 198.

Sir Gawain and the Green Knight, ed. J. R. R. Tolkien and E. V. Gordon. Oxford, 1936.

JOHN GOWER, ed. G. C. Macaulay, Oxford. *French Poems,* 1899, *English Poems,* 1900, *Latin Poems,* 1902.

Gui de Warewic, ed. A. Ewert, 2 vols., C.F.M.A., 1932, 1933.

Guy of Warwick, Ed. J. Zupitza, 1883, 1887, 1891, E.E.T.S., E.S. 42, 49, 54.

THOMAS HOCCLEVE, *The Minor Poems in the Philips MS.*, ed. F. Furnival, E.E.T.S., E.S., 61, 1892. Cf. *The Minor Poems in the Ashburnham MS.*, ed. I. Gollancz, 1925.

—*De Regimine Principum*, ed. T. Wright, Roxburgh Club, 1860. Cf. E.E.T.S., E.S., 173, 1925.

Ipomedon, ed. E. Kolbing and E. Korschurtz. Breslau, 1889.

JOHN LYDGATE, *The Fall of Princes*, ed. H. Bergen, E.E.T.S., E.S., 121–4, 1912.

—*The Assembly of Gods (Reason and Sensuality)*, ed. O. L. Triggs, 1896. E.E.T.S., E.S. 69.

—*The Minor Poems*, ed. H. M. MacCraken, 1911, 1934, E.E.T.S., E.S. 107, O.S., 192.

—*The Troy Book*, ed. H. Bergen, 1935, E.E.T.S., E.S., 126.

—*The Life of Our Lady*, ed. J. R. Lauritis, Pittsburgh, 1961.

Religious Lyrics of the Fourteenth Century, ed. Carleton Brown and G. V. Smithers. Oxford, 1956.

Secular Lyrics of the Fourteenth and Fifteenth Centuries, ed. R. H. Robbins. Oxford, 1955.

LAURENCE MINOT, ed. E. Hall. Oxford, 1915.

Mum and the Soothsegger (Richard the Redeless), ed. M. Day and R. Steele, 1936, E.E.T.S., O.S., 199.

Sir Orfeo, ed. A. J. Bliss. Oxford, 1954.

The Parlement of Thre Ages, ed. M. Y. Offord, 1959, E.E.T.S., 246.

Partonope of Blois, ed. A. T. Bodtker, 1912, E.E.T.S., E.S., 109.

Pearl, ed. E. V. Gordon. Oxford, 1953.

The Vision of Piers Plowman, ed. W. W. Skeat. Oxford, 1886.

—*The A. Version*, ed. G. Kane. Athlone, London, 1960.

Purity (Clannesse), ed. R. J. Menner. Yale, 1920.

THOMAS USK, *The Testament of Love*, ed. W. W. Skeat in *Chaucerian and Other Pieces*, pp. 1–145. Oxford, 1897.

William of Palerne, ed. W. W. Skeat, 1867, E.E.T.S., E.S., 1.

Secondary Sources

H. S. BENNETT, *Chaucer and the Fifteenth Century*. Oxford, 1947.

J. A. W. BENNETT, *The Parlement of Foules*. Oxford, 1957.

M. W. BLOOMFIELD, *Piers Plowman as a Fourteenth Century Apocalypse*. Rutgers, 1961.

D. S. BREWER, *Chaucer in his Time*. Nelson, London, 1963.

—*Chaucer and the Chaucerians*. Nelson, London, 1966.

J. A. BURROW, *A Reading of Sir Gawain and the Green Knight*. Routledge and Kegan Paul, London, 1965.

NEVILL COGHILL, *The Poet Chaucer*. Oxford, 1949.

E. T. DONALDSON, *Piers Plowman, The C. Text and its Poet*. Yale, 1949.

W. G. DODD, *Courtly Love in Chaucer and Gower*. Peter Smith, Gloucester, Mass., 1959.

PETER DRONKE, *Medieval Latin and the Rise of the European Love Lyric*. Oxford, 1965.

J. H. FISHER, *John Gower*. Methuen, London, 1965.

ANGUS FLETCHER, *Allegory, the Theory of a Symbolic Mode*. Cornell, 1964.

E. P. HAMMOND, *English Verse between Chaucer and Surrey*. New York, 1965.

K. F. HOLZKNECHT, *Literary Patronage in the Middle Ages*. Philadelphia, 1963.

Bibliography

GEORGE KANE, *Piers Plowman; The Evidence for Authorship*. Athlone Press, London, 1965.

P. M. KEAN, *The Pearl: An Interpretation*. Routledge and Kegan Paul, 1967.

THOMAS A. KIRBY, *Chaucer's Troilus*. Gloucester, Mass., 1959.

JOHN LAWLOR, *Piers Plowman*. Edward Arnold, London, 1962.

C. S. LEWIS, *The Allegory of Love*. Oxford, 1936.

THOMAS PARRY, *A History of Welsh Literature*. Oxford, 1955.

ALAIN RENOIR, *The Poetry of John Lydgate*. Routledge and Kegan Paul, 1967.

ELISABETH SALTER, *Piers Plowman, an Introduction*. Blackwell, Oxford, 1962.

W. F. SCHIRMER, *John Lydgate*. Methuen, London, 1961.

JOHN SPEIRS, *Medieval English Poetry*. Faber, London, 1957.

J. E. WELLS, *A Manual of the Writings in Middle English*. New Haven, 1951.

C. B. WEST, *Courtoisie in Anglo-Norman Literature*. Blackwell, Oxford, 1938.

IV MANUSCRIPT SOURCES

Most of the manuscripts consulted are in Oxford; they include Ashmole MSS. 40, 59, 61, 91; Bodley MSS. 48, 264, 294, 581, 591, 638, 687, 851, 902; Digby MSS. 64, 86, 102, 145, 171; Douce MSS. 104, 141, 302, 322, 381; MS. Canon Liturg. 116; MS. Eng. Poet. e.1; MS. Lat, Liturg. f. 2; Laud MSS. 108, 174; Rawlinson MS. 1218; MS. Selden, B.26; and also Balliol College MSS. 329, 354; Corpus Christi College MS. 67; St John's College MSS. 94, 209; Worcester College MSS. 1, 253.

Only three manuscripts were used in Cambridge University Library: MSS. Ff. 1, 6; Gg IV, 27; Kk 1, 5. Thanks are due to the Librarian of Magdalene College for permission to work on Pepysian MS. 1916. The only manuscript in the British Museum Library to have been worked on in any detail is Cotton Nero AX though others have been examined for the purpose of comparing techniques in illumination.

Index

Index

Lydgate, John (*c.* 1370–*c.* 1451), 56, 62, 65, 74, 179 *n.* 3; a court poet, 58–9, 176; and new literary movement, 59–60; links with city, 60; 'aureat' vocabulary, 60, 78; *Aesop*, 58; *Ballet of an Ale Seller*, 60; *Fall of Princes*, 60, 61; *Life of Our Lady*, 58; *London Lickpenny*, 60; *Reason and Sensuality*, 59; *Temple of Glas*, 59; *Troy Booke*, 58

Lytlington, Abbot, 40

magnates, 104, 169; hostility to court party, 19, 20, 109–10; dress, 27, 28; loans from, 53; influence on culture, 53, 54, 105, 107–8; family and social content, 106–7; households, 107, 110–11, 109 *n.* 19; household romances, 108; scattered lands, 111–12; membership, 112; indentured companies, 144; use of livery, 147; R. II and, 150–1, 153, 171

Mallory, Sir Thomas (*fl.* 1470), 128, 142

March, Countess of, 63

March, Edward Mortimer, Earl of (1391–1425), 175

Margaret of Brotherton, 18

Marie de France, *Lai de Fresne*, 133

marriage, ideals of burgher class, 104; court concept of, 124; association with romantic love, 124, 127, 133–7; alteration in ideal, 135–6

Martini, Simone (*c.* 1284–1344), 2, 3

Maudelyn, Richard, royal clerk, 152, 175

Medford, Richard, Clerk of King's Chapel, 18; Bishop of Salisbury, 45, 184 *n.* 18

Minot, Laurence (?1300–?1352), 103–4, 179 *n.* 2

minstrels, 30, 100–1, 117

Mohun, Lady de, 28, 34

monarchy, and court life, 1, 3, 9, 11, 15, 21, 39, 52; patronage of art, 38; magnates and, 112; knightly ideal and, 122; loyalty to, 144–5, 152; Henry IV and, 175

Montfort, Simon de, Earl of Leicester (?1208–65), and knighthood, 120, 121, 145

Mowbray, Thomas, *see* Norfolk

Mum Soothsegger (*Richard the Redeless*), 25, 84, 179 *n.* 2, 181 *n.* 24

Murimuth, Adam (?1275–1347), 14

Naples (court culture), 1–3, 6, 9, 30; and Boccaccio, 4; influence in Italy, 8

Neckham, Alexander (1157–1217), 80

Nicholas de Clamanges, 10, 180 *n.* 14

Norbury, John, 159, 160

Norfolk, Thomas Mowbray, Duke of (?1366–99), 32, 33, 180 *n.* 19, 181 *n.* 5; and R. II, 18, 20, 143, 146, 153; in exile, 156; death, 195 *n.* 31

Northumberland, Sir Henry Percy, Earl of (1342–1408), 81; and Bolingbroke's return, 159, 161; his revolt, 175

Nottingham, Thomas Mowbray, Earl of (1386–1405), 175

Octovian, 102

Orleans, Charles Duke of (1391–1465), 10, 17, 59

Orleans, Philippe Duke of (1674–1723), 8

outrageous, quality of being, 22, 181 *n.* 9

Ovid (B.C. 43–A.D. 17), 134–5

Paris (Valois) Court, 4, 8–9, 10, 11, 16, 58, 65, 75, 82, 151, 168, 199; Orators and Secretaries, 10–11; influence on Court of R. II, 21, 58, 104; presence of women, 29; poems on Marguerite theme, 54–5; and Henry IV, 173; cult of Augustine, 179 *n.* 6

Parlement of Thre Ages, 27, 53, 179 *n.* 2, 182 *n.* 37

Parliament, and R. II, 147, 150, 151, 154, 168; and Henry IV, 175–6

Partonope of Blois, 135, 193 *n.* 5

Patience, 116

Pearl, 53, 116, 179 *n.* 3

Index

H

$\left(\underset{\displaystyle \approx 2 \cdot 10}{} \right)$ $\dfrac{13_{\!\times}}{\underset{\displaystyle =1 \cdot 05}{}}$